"I started my clinical psychology training in
qualified in 1992, and this book was still not
now written. Excellent. And what is this boo   ... essential,
comprehensive, enlightening, challenging and progressive look at the profession I
have loved for thirty years. This isn't just a book for budding/in training/practicing
clinical psychologists about what we do but, more importantly, it's about what we
could do and together we can, must and will do. It's about individual and community, inclusion and collaboration, politics and power, adversity and social justice,
the personal and the professional. This book doesn't tell, it asks. It is descriptive
rather than prescriptive. It offers thinking spaces and reflective activities. I read
this book and felt energised and invigorated because it challenged me to look at
what I think I know and what I know I do, and ask myself what next, what more?
Thirty years melted away and I now feel fresh and eager to rethink, revisit, revise
and review. If this book does that for a 52 year old still loving the privilege of
working within mental health services but somewhat jaded and frustrated by the
ongoing lack of parity with physical health services, the cuts and the unacceptable
waiting lists, the impact of adversity (I could go on) – then this book will also
invigorate and inspire anyone who cares about mental health: our own and that of
the public, communities and the society we serve."

Professor Tanya Byron, Consultant Clinical Psychologist,
Journalist, Author, Broadcaster, Policy Advisor

"This is the best book I have read about this thing we call clinical psychology.
I was pleasantly surprised to find I really enjoyed reading it! The book wrestles
with the dilemmas of pursuing a clinical psychology career. Because of its questioning and aspiring approach, it is relevant for anyone on this career path but it
is particularly relevant to budding psychologists and those that supervise them.
I love the way the book shares many examples of psychologies in action that
seek to be creative and liberating. The reflecting points and exercises in the book
got me to think more deeply about issues and I intend to use them with my colleagues too. Clinical psychology comes out of a tradition of looking at people as
individuals modelled on white middle-class male values and ignoring people's
social, political and cultural contexts. The book acknowledges this and looks at
how we can keep coming back to the importance of social contexts, to power
issues and to the personal wisdoms that can easily get overlooked. The result is
a fresh take on clinical psychology largely from those who are navigating entering the profession. When I was applying to training courses there was no guide
on how to navigate becoming a clinical psychologist without losing touch with
what motivated me to train in the first place. This book fills that gap. For example,
with reflections on how we can try to make space for vulnerability in training and
supervision and our different selves that make us up; how to create more safety
and meet the people we seek to help with humility and integrity. And how to do
psychology creatively in a more community-oriented way. I appreciate how the
theme of social justice is looked at from many angles and how we might support

others and be supported to speak up and find ways to make a difference. If you know anyone pursuing a career in psychology and you like them and you can afford it, buy them this book!"

Rufus May, Clinical Psychologist

"This book offers a refreshingly nuanced discussion of the process of 'becoming', whilst training as a clinical psychologist – considering the reflexive awareness encouraged through training and how this can shape thinking, doing, and being. More than simply rejecting tired binary narratives, complex intersectional processes are explored and discussed through an engaging and accessible narrative, contemplating what it means to be human, however inconveniently, when also developing as a clinical psychologist in a world loaded with inequalities, biases, assumptions, stereotypes and unrealistic expectations.

With an optimistic perspective and hopeful lens, the book embarks upon a critically open-minded contemplation of issues not so easily contained within 'pseudo-certainties'. Cleverly, the book explores how and why it is so crucial for psychologists to consider wider issues and contexts in relation to preventing distress and promoting wellbeing, as well as actively advocating for equality and inclusion as part of the job. Finally, the book is beautifully written, with a poetic tone to guide you gently but purposefully through the 'turbulent times and testing terrains' associated with living in today's world as a developing clinical psychologist."

Dr Sarah Parry, Clinical Psychologist, Senior Clinical Lecturer, Manchester Metropolitan University. Editor of *Effective Self-Care and Resilience in Clinical Practice Dealing with Stress, Compassion Fatigue, and Burnout* (2017) and *The Handbook of Brief Therapies: A Practical Guide* (2019)

"*Surviving Clinical Psychology* is very much more than a text book or a 'how to' book. It is an impressive handbook which invites the reader to explore the profession of clinical psychology through many different lenses and asks thought-provoking, challenging and timely questions. The breadth of contributors and the many other voices included in the book, through stories and reflective accounts, deliver an engaging, moving and detailed narrative using a novel and effective format. The reader is quickly drawn into a dialogue enabled by an invitation to actively engage with the book's contents. This allows a space for self-exploration whilst also providing many helpful resources and references.

The book's inspiring contributors include people from minoritised groups, those traditionally marginalised from the profession and people who identify as service users including those in a range of psychology roles holding dual identities. There are contributions from trainee clinical psychologists, clinical psychologists at different career stages, aspiring clinical psychologists, those working in other health and social care roles and undergraduate students.

Divided into four sections the book explores 'the context of clinical psychology', 'the personal: the selves as human', 'the professional: the use of self in clinical psychology' and 'the political: selves and politics in practice'. The chapters cover an array of pertinent and stimulating topics including the core practices of the profession, questioning what it means to become a clinical psychologist and navigating how to do this. Chapters consider what it means to be a supervisee, reflections on personal experiences of distress and on experiences of using personal therapy. The significance of personal identities and difference within professional development are explored as are matters relating to psychiatric diagnoses, power in organisations, and critiques of psychological therapy. Key recurrent themes woven throughout the book include power, psychological formulation, reflection, a call to activism, community psychology and the political, social, global and financial context. In its totality the book asks what can clinical psychology become?

Surviving Clinical Psychology is a key resource for clinical psychologists, those aspiring to become clinical psychologists and those who have survived, are currently using and working within the mental health system and social care."

Dr Laura Golding, Programme Director, Doctorate in Clinical Psychology, University of Liverpool and co-author of *How to become a Clinical Psychologist (2019)*

Surviving Clinical Psychology

This vital new book navigates the personal, professional and political selves on the journey to training in clinical psychology. Readers will be able to explore a range of ways to enrich their practice through a focus on identities and differences, relationships and power within organisations, supervisory contexts, therapeutic conventions and community approaches.

This book includes a rich exploration of how we make sense of personal experiences as practitioners, including chapters on self-formulation, personal therapy, and using services. Through critical discussion, practice examples, shared accounts and exercises, individuals are invited to reflect on a range of topical issues in clinical psychology. Voices often marginalised within the profession write side-by-side with those more established in the field, offering a unique perspective on the issues faced in navigating clinical training and the profession more broadly. In coming together, the authors of this book explore what clinical psychology can become.

Surviving Clinical Psychology invites those early on in their careers to link 'the political' to personal and professional development in a way that is creative, critical and values-based and will be of interest to pre-qualified psychologists and researchers, and those mentoring early-career practitioners.

James Randall is a tattooed, vegetarian clinical psychologist working with children and young people within the National Health Service (NHS). He previously represented aspiring psychologists for four years as the co-chair of the Pre-Qualification Group within the British Psychological Society.

Surviving Clinical Psychology

Navigating Personal, Professional and Political Selves on the Journey to Qualification

Edited by James Randall

Routledge
Taylor & Francis Group

LONDON AND NEW YORK

First published 2020
by Routledge
2 Park Square, Milton Park, Abingdon, Oxon OX14 4RN

and by Routledge
52 Vanderbilt Avenue, New York, NY 10017

Routledge is an imprint of the Taylor & Francis Group, an informa business

British Library Cataloguing-in-Publication Data
A catalogue record for this book is available from the British Library

Library of Congress Cataloging-in-Publication Data
A catalog record for this book has been requested

ISBN: 978-1-138-36888-0 (hbk)
ISBN: 978-1-138-36889-7 (pbk)
ISBN: 978-0-429-42896-8 (ebk)

Typeset in Times New Roman
by Apex CoVantage, LLC

MIX
Paper from
responsible sources
FSC™ C013985

Printed in the United Kingdom
by Henry Ling Limited

In loving memory of
Courtney Summer Turner
14/03/1998–09/01/2019

Contents

Contributors

Tanya Beetham is a researcher at the Centre for Child Wellbeing and Protection at the University of Stirling, where she is also completing her doctoral research. She is also a counsellor, psychotherapist and lecturer in psychology. Tanya enjoys yoga, running, travelling and spending time outdoors. Tanya has experience of being a client in therapy and being a service user in eating disorder services.

John Burnham is a family and systemic psychotherapist, trainer, supervisor and writer at Parkview Clinic, Birmingham Women and Children's Hospital since January 1977(!). He still enjoys direct clinical practice with families as well as being continually inspired, refreshed and tolerated by his colleagues and trainees. He is eternally grateful to all those who have complimented, challenged and comforted him throughout his career.

Angela Byrne hails from Ireland. She qualified as a clinical psychologist from University of East London in 1999. She currently works in East London NHS Foundation Trust in a service to improve accessibility and cultural relevance of psychology for communities in Tower Hamlets. She also works for Derman, a Hackney-based charity for Kurdish and Turkish communities.

Ben Campbell is a trainee clinical psychologist with a keen interest in the outdoors, social policy and anything avocado based.

Lauren Canvin is a queer, vegan, trainee clinical psychologist from Bristol, currently studying at the University of Hertfordshire.

Danielle Chadderton is currently working as a peer recovery worker at Sheffield Health and Social Care NHS Foundation Trust, and uses her personal experience of mental health issues to support others who have also been given a diagnosis of 'Borderline Personality Disorder'. Professionally, she hopes to end up wherever she can best support the intention to help others have a life they want to live, and personally, to do the same for herself.

Laura Cole is a trainee clinical psychologist at University of Hertfordshire. She carried out her clinical thesis research alongside young people participating in the design and delivery of mental health services in the UK. She is interested in critical approaches and bringing community psychology ideas and practice into clinical psychology.

Angie Cucchi is a chartered counselling psychologist who works both as an academic at Regent's University London and in a Personality Disorder Service in the NHS. Angie won the British Psychological Society (BPS) Division of Counselling Psychology 2015 Trainee Prize and the 2015 BPS Research Prize.

Farahnaaz Dauhoo is a trainee clinical psychologist at the University of Hertfordshire, working within NHS mental health services across Bedfordshire.

Cormac Duffy is a clinical psychologist passionate about community psychology. He facilitates Cafè Psychologique Liverpool to help people connect and talk about life. He works with the NHS and NeuroTriage, a brain injury service for the homeless. Cormac is a strong believer of what can be achieved when people come together.

Anna Duxbury is a clinical psychologist working systemically with schools across Lancashire for the Lancashire Emotional Health in Schools Service. She also works as a clinical tutor on the Lancaster University Doctorate in Clinical Psychology Programme.

Annabel Head is a London based clinical psychologist. Having a sibling with a learning disability has inspired clinical and research work with adults with learning disabilities, and a passion for hearing voices that are often overlooked, including those of carers and service users.

Marta Isibor works as honorary assistant psychologist in Royal Edinburgh Hospital, as well as mental health mentor and tutor at Queen Margaret University. She researches body-focused repetitive behaviours and in particular dermatillomania, which she has a personal experience of.

Hannah Iveson has always cared deeply about using any form of privilege and opportunity to support others. She has begun a career in psychology/neuropsychology because it both interests her and presents an opportunity to use clinical, research, personal and professional skills to work for marginalised individuals and groups. Psychology is just one tool available for understanding and doing something about the inequalities of the world, and it makes sense to use it. In short, she gives a shit.

Emma Johnson is a social worker and psychological wellbeing practitioner with an interest in relational approaches to psychological distress. She has experience of accessing mental health services and navigating the experience of 'dual identity' this can create. She currently works in an integrated Improving Access to Psychological Therapies (IAPT) service.

Dr Lucy Johnstone, is a consultant clinical psychologist and independent trainer. She is co-editor of *Formulation in Psychology and Psychotherapy*

(Routledge, 2nd edition 2013) among other publications, and lead author of *Good Practice Guidelines on the Use of Psychological Formulation* (DCP, 2011). She was lead author, along with Professor Mary Boyle, for the *The Power Threat Meaning Framework* (BPS, 2018).

Kirsty Killick is a trainee clinical psychologist with experience of providing and using mental health services.

Peter Kinderman is Professor of Clinical Psychology at the University of Liverpool and a practicing NHS Clinical Psychologist. He is a former president of the British Psychological Society, was twice Chair of the Division of Clinical Psychology, and drives a VW campervan, painted in the colours of international socialism.

Rosemary Kingston is a trainee clinical psychologist studying at the University of Hertfordshire. Prior to training, Rosie worked in research roles in the UK and Australia, with her PhD exploring the question of why people can be prone to worry and rumination.

Amy Lyons is a clinical psychologist working in a neurological rehabilitation service in Hertfordshire, UK. She also works in a private practice clinic in London, UK. She has accessed various different sources of therapeutic services for psychological support. She is interested in the training of clinical psychologists and has maintained links with the University of Hertfordshire clinical psychology programme since graduating in 2017.

Elizabeth Malpass is part of the LGBTQ community and is interested in anti-discriminatory practice, particularly in relation to institutional racism in mainstream education. She loves nature and is committed to supporting environmental campaigns, as well as being a long-standing advocate for organisations supporting peace in Palestine. She works as a clinical psychologist with children and young people in a Community Psychology Team in Hackney, specialising in work with children under five.

Stella Mo is a clinical psychologist in training with the University of Hertfordshire. She has research interests in further understanding the experiences of people on the autism spectrum and thinking systemically.

Dr Hannah Morgan, is a clinical psychologist working in the NHS with 'looked after' children and their wider networks. Her role involves providing consultations to social workers and working together with professional and parental systems to promote functioning networks around children and young people. She is interested in research that empowers groups of people who could be considered vulnerable and/or may be otherwise silenced in society.

Sasha Nagra is a trainee clinical psychologist at University of East London (UEL) with special interests in forced migration, human rights injustices, policy level change and decolonising the profession.

Dr Lizette Nolte, is a clinical psychologist and systemic psychotherapist and works as a lecturer at the University of Hertfordshire for Doctorate in Clinical Psychology course. Lizette occupies many different identities, including that of South African, immigrant, mother, daughter, partner, family member of someone experiencing psychological distress, friend, student, teacher and many more. In her work, Lizette draws on narrative therapy, community psychology and systemic approaches. Her research focuses on social inclusion, and recently been particularly related to experiences of homelessness, the care system and disability.

Amy Obradovic is a multi-ethnic, multi-careered late-comer to the field, completing her doctorate in clinical psychology at the time of writing. She has particular professional interests in advocacy, trauma and widening access to the profession, and personal passions for live music and dancing it out.

Dr Sarah Oliver, is a clinical psychologist working within Children and Adolescent Mental Health Services in the NHS. She trained at the University of Hertfordshire and has conducted research on the experiences of young people who grow up with parents experiencing mental distress. She is passionate about community psychology and the accessibility of services for families.

Mary O'Reilly is a mental health activist. Despite the hegemony of crude, craven, coercive, commodified systems, she believes in light, laughter, colour, love, joy and creativity.

Kirstie Pope is an undergraduate student at the University of Northampton studying BSc Psychology. She is keen on continuing her studies to master's level and possibly beyond in the future, with specific interests in developmental and feminist psychology as well as mental health. Kirstie is currently a service user and also a client in private therapy, something which she feels is rarely discussed or acknowledged within the classroom. When not in lectures or writing assignments, Kirstie enjoys reading, spending time with animals and going to the cinema.

Sasha Priddy is a trainee clinical psychologist at the University of Sheffield. Prior to training, Sasha spent three years within the Psychosis and Complex Mental Health faculty as a representative for the Pre-Qualification Group of the Division of Clinical Psychology (DCP). She has primarily worked within adult mental health services, across a range of settings, in which she developed her interest in cognitive analytic therapy.

James Randall is a tattooed, vegetarian clinical psychologist working with children and young people within the NHS. He represented aspiring psychologists for four years as the co-chair of the Pre-Qualification Group within the British Psychological Society. His interests include clinical training, co-production, and community approaches to addressing psychological distress. He has personal experience of accessing a whole range of therapies, but has found creativity, writing, and music to be the greatest of supports.

Molly Rhinehart is a trainee clinical psychologist and mental health service user. Her thesis explores the experiences of clinical psychologists in navigating 'dual identities' as service user and service provider. Molly is also a facilitator of in2gr8mentalhealth, a peer support group for mental health practitioners with experience of mental health difficulties.

Dr Jessica Saffer, is a clinical psychologist working within Children and Adolescent Mental Health Services in the NHS. She trained at the University of Hertfordshire and has conducted research on the impact of changes to UK disability benefits on individuals' wellbeing and identity. She is passionate about the inclusion of people with different needs into their communities, and has challenged many of the organisations in which she has worked to become more accessible.

Dr Jacqui Scott, currently works in an NHS community service in an inner London borough, with adults who carry a diagnosis of a psychotic illness. She trained at the University of Hertfordshire and aims to promote social inclusion, ideas from community psychology, and narrative practices in her work and life as a clinical psychologist.

Neha Bharat Shah is an associate mental health worker currently working in a 'personality disorder' service, with special interests in working with children, young people and families.

Vasiliki Stamatopoulou is a European citizen and third year trainee clinical psychologist at the University of Hertfordshire. She has served as Chair of the Minorities in Clinical Psychology Training group. She is currently completing her doctoral research project on trauma-informed care. Vasiliki works clinically with adults with complex trauma.

Sophie Stark is a trainee clinical psychologist at the University of Hertfordshire. She has particular interests in eating disorders, body positivity and weight stigma and has a passion for jewellery and sewing her own clothing.

Katie Sydney is a final year psychology undergraduate who hopes to become a clinical psychologist one day. The type of practitioner she aspires to be is informed by her own experiences of distress, and her Marxist and feminist politics.

Romena Toki is a trainee clinical psychologist studying at Hertfordshire University. Romena is British Bangladeshi, has interests in community approaches, and prior to training she worked alongside other British Bangladeshis in London to preserve the heritage stories of their local community. In her spare time, Romena and her mother bake and create wedding cakes for friends and family.

Dr Stephen Weatherhead, is a consultant clinical psychologist, working with the Liverpool Clinical Psychology Programme, and NeuroTriage (a brain injury service for the homeless). He is father to two wonderful children and wants to help, even in a tiny way, to make society a slightly better place for them than it is now. He has been a long time campaigner on issues relating to exclusion and oppression. He has probably reached his career peak and seems to give less of a shit these days.

Acknowledgements

Here, I would like to thank all of the authors and contributors to this text. We have embodied the values underlying this book within the process: a coming together that does not shy away from a progressive challenging of each other. This book has been an endeavour of love, and I believe that this shines through each and every page and that is thanks to the collective. I am also very thankful to Emma Johnson, whose artwork is used for this book's dedication page.

In writing and editing this book, I am forever indebted to the people I meet within my work – they have taught me what really matters within clinical practice. In particular, I thank my man D – who despite everything stacked against him, would offer a hand and shoulder to anyone admitted – he was the truest of gents. With a big heart and sense of care for all people, D's life ended far too early – but his legacy, I will always carry and for this, I thank him for the spirit he has lent to these pages.

Crucial to sustaining my efforts here are those in my personal life, who I have sat with through the most horrendous of times. Facing adversities together teaches you what really matters. No one should face this shit, but through offering our hands and hearts in solidarity – perhaps we can do something about it for the next person. With love x.

There are some key individuals who have shaped my thinking over time and who have all played a part in the ideas for this book coming together. Pieter Nel and Lizette Nolte have both been so influential throughout and beyond training – fostering a critical, yet kind approach to clinical psychology rooted in relationships and community. As with all journeys into clinical psychology, early supervisory relationships can be very crucial and I remain thankful to have worked with Helen Donovan and Kim Caldwell, individuals who supported me to develop and learn in those early days. I am thankful to my peers, the wonderful Cohort 14 of the University of Hertfordshire – we really did create something magical. Forever curious, with a pebble in my pocket – and even now I still wonder . . . Who is Lee? I also must thank my friends and colleagues within the DCP Pre-Qualification Group – forever 'broadening the now', whatever that means!

Thank you to my family. My parents Polly and Pete, who have accepted me no matter what and my brother, Richard, who is one of the kindest and most genuine of guys that I know. Maybe this book will unmask what it is I actually do – or maybe confuse the matter even further!

I thank Sasha for everything she has brought to my life. Thank you for being my sounding board – from testing out ideas, making sure I haven't just made words up, and offering honest and thoughtful reflections.

And finally, Kiki – despite the breath, you're a good friend. You didn't really do anything in terms of the book – but thought you deserved a hello. *Hey Kiki, do you love me?*

Foreword

The things that matter

Peter Kinderman

Psychology is fundamentally about the things that really matter; relationships, optimism, a sense of meaning and purpose, personal agency. Even philosophical concepts – fairness, respect, identity, equity, dignity and autonomy – are the subject matter of psychology. My own chosen profession of clinical psychology can sometimes feel as if it is trying to distance itself from this reality. When we copy our medical colleagues in using diagnostic language (which tends to locate problems in the individual; minimising social determinants and political context) and applying technological solutions such as the cognitive behavioural therapy (CBT) in the same way that we prescribe medication, we are risking isolating ourselves from an honest understanding of these issues.

Many years ago, when I was being interviewed for what was then a master's qualification in clinical psychology, I was asked what I thought would be the most efficient use of public money in mental health care. I replied that housing might be the best focus, and was asked why I hadn't applied to be a member of parliament rather than a clinical psychologist.

Thirty years later, I was in New Orleans, discussing a randomised clinical trial of psilocybin (the active ingredient of 'magic mushrooms') as an adjunct to psychological therapy for people who had been depressed for many years. A colleague commented that New Orleans was a perfect site for our trial because the people of that city were particularly plagued by poverty, social inequity, racism and the economic blight following hurricane Katrina. Which raises important questions. What would it mean if some kind of medication or therapy (or combination) could allow us to escape depression in such circumstances? What would differentiate our healthcare from the effects seen when people escape their troubles with alcohol, cannabis, heroin, opioids? And what would it mean psychologically and philosophically? What would it mean if we were able to remain optimistic and productive no matter what life threw at us? What would it mean if we, as professional psychologists, were to collaborate with that project – if we were to help people forget about the struggle for democratic socialism and instead look to mindful cognitive restructuring of negative automatic thoughts? And, therefore, what distinguishes clinical psychology from the 'soma' of Aldous Huxley's *Brave*

New World? These kinds of important and provocative questions are the subject matter of this book.

As the reader of these essays will understand, we learn to make sense of the world because of what happens to us. We grow up influenced by our social circumstances, our peers at school, the sense we make of our position in the world. If we grow up in circumstances of abuse, poverty, racism, discrimination, neoliberal exploitation and the denial of our rights, we will grow up devoid of that sense of meaning and purpose, that sense of agency and optimism that is so vital to psychological wellbeing.

This book highlights how many people now proudly condemn the false 'them and us' distinction between people who use mental health services and professionals. But we all too easily slip into this way of thinking, even as we condemn it. It is not good enough, for me, to say that any one of us could become depressed or anxious. Of course, that is true, but it still implies that there is a distinction to be made between these states of being – perilously close to 'being a user of mental health services right now'. The idea of 'being' or 'not being' a user of mental health services is such a pervasive categorisation that I was once asked by a prominent academic campaigner against this very kind of discriminatory thinking to choose between ticking two boxes – as a clinical psychologist, did I, or did I not, consider myself to be a 'former user of mental health services'? Now, it so happens that I had two years of therapy on the NHS in my early 20s, provided by a lovely (if slightly overly eclectic) psychiatrist. But I do not consider myself to be a 'former user of mental health services' any more than I am a 'former user of music'. To choose that label, for me, would support a way of thinking about the applied psychological science that characterises my work, which implies a distinction between 'normal' and 'abnormal' psychology.

What we do – or what we should do, in my opinion – is apply our knowledge of human psychology to much more than treat so-called mental disorders, but to help people realise their intellectual and emotional potential and to find and fulfil their roles in social, school and working life. As the European Commission commented, psychological wellbeing "contributes to prosperity, solidarity and social justice". In the words of the UN Special Rapporteur Dainius Pūras: "The crisis in mental health should be managed not as a crisis of individual conditions, but as a crisis of social obstacles which hinders individual rights. Mental health policies should address the 'power imbalance' rather than 'chemical imbalance'" (Pūras, 2017).

This book speaks to these issues. There may be some psychologists who find value in the biomedical pseudo-certainties of diagnosis and treatment, and regard depression (for example) as an external entity, a pathology. But this book deals with the ways in which we as human beings are affected by, learn from, combat and survive the various pressures that we face. By doing that, the contributions not only humanise our profession and the people who use our services, but also humanise ourselves.

This book covers a lot of ground; from the personal experience of trainee clinical psychologists and how this is negotiated in supervision, the dual identities of both mental health professional and user of mental health services, and the ways in which our experiences, backgrounds and identities relate to our roles as clinical psychologists. As Annabel Head, Amy Obradovic, Sasha Nagra, and Neha Bharat Shah put it, "clinical psychology is a multifaceted, exciting and dynamic career, which can be both challenging and immensely rewarding". This book takes the psychologists' core skill of formulation, and applies it to the profession itself. It encourages reflection; including reflection on the apparent gap between our collective aspirations towards social justice, and the difficulties of actually achieving change in practice.

Fifty years ago, on 1st September 1967, the Nobel Prize-winning civil rights leader Dr Martin Luther King Jr. delivered a speech entitled "The role of the behavioral scientist in the civil rights movement" to the American Psychological Association (King, 1968). Speaking at the height of the civil rights struggle, King stressed how behavioural scientists could and should support those citizens fighting for their fundamental rights. King's speech is still relevant today – a call to arms.

In 1967, King spoke about links between racism, unemployment and living conditions. Now, more than 50 years later, we can see continuing economic crisis and the impact of policies of austerity, right-wing populism and – most likely as a consequence – Brexit. And these are not just economic or political matters; they are crucial psychological issues too. Quite literally, these are matters of life and death. Between 2008 and 2010, immediately following the most recent economic crisis – not yet the self-inflicted economic wounds of Brexit – there were 1,000 more suicides in England and Wales than would be expected on purely historical trends, and many of those deaths can be attributed to rising unemployment.

As the authors of this book demonstrate, psychologists, whose professional role is the promotion of wellbeing and the prevention of such distress, have a duty to speak out about those social, economic and political circumstances that impact our clients and the general public, and to bring such evidence to politicians and policy makers.

For example, it is clear that unemployment and exploitative employment practices – zero-hours contracts, insecure jobs, the 'gig economy' – are damaging to our wellbeing regardless of our age, gender, level of education, ethnicity or part of the country in which we live. The longer someone remains unemployed, the worse the effect, and people do not adapt to unemployment. Their wellbeing is permanently reduced. In contrast, re-employment – finding a job if you are unemployed – leads to higher wellbeing.

Martin Luther King said: "There are some things in our society, some things in our world, to which we should never be adjusted." Another Nobel Prize winner, Albert Camus (distinctive in that he actively resisted the Nazi occupation of France, editing *Combat*, the clandestine newspaper of the Resistance), wrote in his private notebook for May 1937: "Psychology is action, not thinking about oneself" (Camus, 1963).

Psychology is action. And as Martin Luther King said,

> [T]here are some things in our society, some things in our world, to which we . . . must always be maladjusted if we are to be people of good will. We must never adjust ourselves to racial discrimination and racial segregation. We must never adjust ourselves to religious bigotry. We must never adjust ourselves to economic conditions that take necessities from the many to give luxuries to the few. We must never adjust ourselves to the madness of militarism, and the self-defeating effects of physical violence. . . . There comes a time when one must take a stand that is neither safe, nor politic, nor popular. But one must take it because it is right.
>
> (King, 1968)

When I take a taxi, I try to be mindful of the employment status of the drivers, and the tax policies of the owners. When I buy a sandwich, I try to remember issues of sustainable food production and plastic packaging waste. I do not stop engaging with the world, but I engage as wisely as I can. Similarly, we clinical psychologists might well use our education and skills to engage with the world; to develop and implement the best possible plans to help the citizens of New Orleans (or Toxteth or Kampala or the Isle of Lewis) realise their intellectual and emotional potential and to find and fulfil their roles in social, school and working life. By doing that, we too contribute to prosperity, solidarity and social justice. But we could be more mindful. Mindful that people aren't 'ill' or 'disordered'; we learn to respond, psychologically, to the world. Mindful that political, economic, and social obstacles hinder the realisation of our fundamental human rights. And mindful that there is a fine line between pragmatically engaging with the world as it is and tacitly supporting a corrupt system.

References

Camus, A. (1963). *Carnets, 1935–1942*. London: Hamish Hamilton. Retrieved from https://thepsychologist.bps.org.uk/volume-30/june-2017/psychology-action-not-thinking-about-oneself

King, M. L. (1968). The role of the behavioral scientist in the civil rights movement. *Journal of Social Issues, 24*(1), 1–12. Retrieved from www.apa.org/monitor/features/king-challenge

Pūras, D. (2017). *Report of the Special Rapporteur on the right of everyone to the enjoyment of the highest attainable standard of physical and mental health*. United Nations General Assembly. Retrieved from http://ap.ohchr.org/documents/dpage_e.aspx?si=A/HRC/35/21

The context of clinical psychology

Part I

The context of clinical
psychology

Chapter 1

What clinical psychology can become

An introduction

James Randall

This book is an invitation. Within these pages, the authors welcome you to different stories about training and practice within clinical psychology. We invite you to consider not only what clinical psychology currently offers society, but encourage you to explore what *could be* offered. By recognising the fact that you, as pre-qualified clinicians, are the people who shape our profession and are at the core of its future – we hope to invite you to use these pages to challenge us all; to tell us what clinical psychology *should be* offering to our communities and society as a whole.

Surviving Clinical Psychology holds very seriously the fact that the words on these pages can only go so far, and it is through what you do next that change can be fostered for the people we meet within our work and expand the possibilities of what clinical psychology can do for society. The pages that follow do not hold any 'moulds' for you to squeeze into, and do not detail any professional-sounding, award-winning scripts to impart upon those around us. The pages that follow look to remind you of why personal, professional and political differences are at the heart of clinical psychology's future – but it is this, that can connect us.

Whilst this book may help guide your next steps, it will not necessarily pave the way to any predetermined destinations. It simply offers a reshuffling of priorities; a rethinking of what matters most when we are navigating our ways through pre-qualified roles and clinical training. This book redefines these notions of 'becoming' anything else, other than *you* – a person with a repertoire of experiences that clinical psychology would be lucky to welcome into the fold. This book offers a seat in an overly distracted and often damaging world. From here, you might uncover clinical psychology's greatest swindle that to achieve more, you must *do more*. This only serves to perpetuate the individualising cogs that disentangle you from the web of support and community that is within an arm's reach. This book calls on you to reach out to one another and to support one another – to create a sense of community throughout these turbulent times and testing terrains.

What *Surviving Clinical Psychology* invites you to do differently then, is do *less*, in a way. It raises the question of how much more we can achieve through disengaging with compulsive pulls to compete and instead, build platforms for one another in order to focus on doing what matters most to those who need our support. This book recognises that in order to do this, we must embrace our differences and support one another to survive within imperfect and sometimes, toxic systems. At the heart of this text is an invitation to reconnect with your values, your hopes and your passions, and to realise the potential of what you have to offer to clinical psychology – not necessarily what clinical psychology has to offer you.

Navigating the book: sections and chapters

Surviving Clinical Psychology is divided into four sections to enable you to navigate your way through as usefully as possible. Each section concludes with a shorter, reflective chapter, capturing a range of personal perspectives on the topics addressed throughout.

The context of clinical psychology

This section of the book invites you to consider some of the core practices of clinical psychology, what it means to be a supervisee and considers the ways in which pre-qualified journeys tend to be storied. This section of the book then concludes with a reflective discussion exploring the limits of 'reflective-practice'.

The personal: the selves as human

This section of the book invites you to truly consider the 'personal' in personal and professional development, through a focus on personal experiences of distress, integrating values and principles of social justice into our relationships with others, and experiences of using personal therapy. This section of the book concludes with a chapter by two practitioners with lived experience of distress, reflecting on working within psychiatric settings.

The professional: the use of self in clinical psychology

This section of the book explores the significance of personal identities and differences within professional development, through a focus on diversity and the 'Social GgRRAAAACCEEESSSS', using psychological formulation to make sense of our own experiences, and considering the ways in which we can sustain ourselves throughout the journey, particularly training. This section of the book concludes with a reflective paper exploring the experiences of a teacher and student, considering their own experiences of psychological distress, identity and selfhood.

The political: selves and politics in practice

This section of the book invites you to consider a range of topics in which the personal and professional becomes *the political*. In doing so, we address issues relating to experiences of psychiatric diagnoses, power in organisations, and question ideas around therapy itself. This section concludes with a reflective conversation between trainee clinical psychologists as they navigate the political dilemmas faced within their training and practice.

Navigating the book: boxes

Surviving Clinical Psychology also invites readers to engage with the text and explore their own role in creating clinical psychology's future. In supporting readers to do this, the chapters incorporate three different styles of boxes throughout the book:

Thinking space

These boxes provide a series of questions designed to encourage you to not only extend your thinking, but to consider ways to change and improve your practice. These boxes may for example, include particular material or statements for you to consider in greater depth.

In focus

These boxes provide accounts of lived experience, dialogues and reflections on practice, summaries of services, and examples of innovative initiatives. These *In focus* boxes are also used to bring examples of practice to life, through providing further details about particular concepts or models.

Reflective activity

These boxes provide you with short exercises to support you in developing the ideas from within the text, on the one hand to consolidate the information and questions within the text, but on the other, to actively engage with and challenge the material presented. At times, these activities may invite you to connect with others in order to extend the invitation beyond these pages and to open up dialogues with your peers and broader communities.

The values at the heart of *Surviving Clinical Psychology*

Too many books answer the questions of *what is clinical psychology?* And *How do I become a clinical psychologist?* Whilst these questions are important, and no doubt helpful aids on the journey to qualification, what these texts tend to omit is the much more complex, yet richer question of *what can clinical psychology become?* This latter focus is what lies at the heart of this text and within its pulse – a number of shared values and principles:

Inclusion and collaboration: only us

Surviving Clinical Psychology addresses a range of experiences throughout its chapters and includes many examples of adversity, psychological distress and health difficulties more broadly. In editing this book, it was very important for me to challenge multiple falsehoods of clinical psychology (and the helping professions more broadly). One such notion was the idea that individuals experiencing any form of psychological distress are in some way different to the likes of you and I. When working in an in-patient unit as a health-care assistant, I recall a person asking me: "How on earth do you do this?" I recall their surprise, when my answer was simply, "I just start from the point in which this could be myself or any one of my family in here, and I start from there".

Surviving Clinical Psychology welcomes many authors who just like those who access our support, identify as having their own lived experiences of psychiatric services, mental health difficulties, and/or societal adversities. Key to this is a rejection of the discursive divides of *us and them*, and an opening up of dialogues around what it means to sit on both sides of the proverbial therapy chair – to be practitioner and someone with lived experience of distress. As such, *Surviving Clinical Psychology* resigns 'case studies' to a clinical psychology that has pathology rather than social justice at its core, and invites readers instead, to think about psychological distress as defined by those who have experienced it themselves. After all, "the ultimate power is the power to define. We have that power. Let's define our experiences . . . for ourselves. Let's define the world" (Kinouani, 2017).

Surviving Clinical Psychology thus sets out a new vision for clinical psychology that draws its lessons from the lived experience and accounts of the people themselves. Similarly, then, in writing about pre-qualified practice within clinical psychology, this book acknowledges that we must create contexts for individuals and communities to be heard. This book aims to be one such platform. Within these pages, individuals from minoritised groups and those traditionally marginalised from the profession, share their accounts and highlight their vision for what clinical psychology can become. Writing in collaboration with those from across all stages of their career, the authors within this book have contributed to a larger story of advocacy, mentorship and support in process and practice – through coming together, sharing, collaborating, challenging one another, writing, and consulting far and wide. For "omission is a powerful statement" (Starr & Weiner, 1981) and in some ways, this book offers a counter-statement to the profession – *inclusion is a powerful action.*

Reflective activity: joining the conversation

As this book is about and *for* you, it would be short-sighted to not have you involved in some way, shape or form. As such, we invite you to contribute to the topics discussed in this book. Perhaps you would like to share your reflections about some of the activities included, to add to the debates, or to share your own experiences. Importantly, this is about clinical psychology welcoming your perspective to the fold. This is a clinical psychology that reaches out.

Join the conversation at #SurvivingClinicalPsychology

Social justice and community psychology

This book celebrates what clinical psychology can become with you on its side, acknowledging a need for something to change. This is a profession whose history is rooted in disconnecting individuals from their social context. A profession that has secured status and a powerful standing within the professional market, through predominantly placing the impetus for change on the individual. Clearly, "we're working hard, and working harder isn't working. The sense of a particularly individual incompetence [creeps] in. This is the dirty work of isolation" (Reynolds, 2019, p. 7).

From within the walls of clinical psychology itself, *Surviving Clinical Psychology* tries to disentangle clinical psychology from this purely *self-centred* point of view. The connotations here are purposeful. On the one hand, clinical psychology needs to look beyond the individual and to address the needs of communities. In doing so, the profession has to take very seriously that we are already well aware of the key determinants for psychological distress and poor health (e.g., poverty, homelessness).

Surviving Clinical Psychology then, attempts to invite you to (re)consider your personal and professional development, with the political very much at the forefront throughout. As understandable as it is to aspire for a sanitised and 'clear-cut' science, this book cannot accept a clinical psychology without politics. A clinical psychology without politics at its heart would only be reputable in as far as it is farfetched and unintelligible; dangerously decontextualised from the lived reality of hardship and distress and the potential of such an approach to do harm itself.

Surviving Clinical Psychology opens up a dialogue that invites you to join others already addressing the social and material conditions that lead to poor health and psychological distress. The third-sector, charities, grassroot groups, and service-user organisations, among many others, have been leading the way on much of this work for decades, and it is time we started to seriously listen to them and take action *together*.

In focus: the context and language of survival

In naming this book, I chose to use the language that resonated for those within the pre-qualification community. Through years of consultation and representation, the message was clear: for individuals hoping to one day train as a clinical psychologist, the journey is often experienced as turbulent and something to survive. The message has uncomfortable undertones, particularly in relation to the relative privileges aspiring psychologists are often afforded. Also uncomfortable in light that something so hoped for and aspired for – could also warrant a survival of sorts. This on the one hand, reflects the unclear routes to training and structural uncertainties embedded in a hugely popular, yet under-resourced career path. On the other, unqualified practitioners often find themselves in services overstretched, under-funded and facing financial cuts – fostering and perpetuating the very conditions that increase a demand upon our services in the first instance. And so, pre-qualified practitioners find themselves seriously considering ways in which to survive such detrimental conditions and the negative impact such conditions have on their own mental and physical wellbeing. Secondly, they find themselves considering ways to sustain themselves during difficult times, in order to be able to advocate and support those accessing their services to the best of their ability still. Survival, is of course, one of many ways to conceptualise the ways in which individuals navigate their way through – though this would not be the first book to recognise the significance of such a struggle (see *Irreverence: A Strategy for Therapists' Survival* by Cecchin, Lane, & Ray, 1992).

The language of survival is not uncommon for those who have accessed psychiatric services themselves. Although this book provides a platform for many individuals to give voice to their own experiences of mental health services, accounts of navigating what can seem like toxic systems with damaging cogs turning within, are far too common. Survival for those currently within the psychiatric system is often a very real threat with serious consequences, and it is for us to hold this reality in mind as we shape what clinical psychology can become.

So, this book speaks to a different type of survival in that it goes some way to try and tackle the underlying issues that create such conditions in the first place. It uses a potent language that is embedded within the community already, but in a way that confronts the issues that underlie it. In doing so, this book highlights the ludicrous situation in which practitioners find themselves feeling like they have to survive the very institutions in which they choose to work for. But again, this cannot detract from the very real and serious survival by those who continue to use, or be forced to use, psychiatric services.

Readers unfamiliar with accounts of those who have lived experience of mental health and psychiatric services can expect such accounts throughout *Surviving Clinical Psychology* as authors share their experiences or those of invited contributors. Readers may also benefit from further readings, such as:

- The chapter *The Personal is the Political* (Dillon, 2011)
- The accounts of Eleanor Longden and Peter Bullimore as published in *Asylum Magazine*, available via http://asylummagazine.org/2019/03/asylum-17-1-spring-2010
 - The book *Searching for a Rose Garden* (Russo & Sweeney, 2016)

Creative means to liberation

A clinical psychology that has social justice at its heart can be hopeful, angry, courageous, serious – and so much more. A clinical psychology that is worth pursuing holds onto a passion and humility that is both playful *and* powerful. That is:

> [to] not to be so naïve as to think we can change all the problems [we] face, but at the same time not to fall into the cynical trap that we can do nothing . . . To have the freedom to take action. To somehow be able to survive the devastation and disappointment that sometimes inevitably occurs in the course of dealing with the tragedies of living. To be able to keep going and not lose hope, [to be] able to find the humour in the absurdity of seemingly impossible situations.
>
> (Cecchin et al., 1992, pp. 74–75)

Thinking space

Having read these first initial pages of *Surviving Clinical Psychology*, you may have noticed talk of 'invitations', rather than instruction. In this light, we aim to capture your attention and ask for your *participation*. As you navigate through, in what way can you make your reading of *Surviving Clinical Psychology* most meaningful?

References

Cecchin, G., Lane, G., & Ray, W. A. (1992). *Irreverence: A strategy for therapists' survival*. London: Karnac Books.

Dillon, J. (2011). The personal *is* the political. In M. Rapley, J. Moncrieff, & J. Dillon (Eds.), *De-medicalising misery: Psychiatry, psychology and the human condition*. Basingstoke: Palgrave MacMillan.

Kinouani, G. (2017, November). Epistemic homelessness: "Feeling like a stranger in a familiar land". *Media Diversified*. Retrieved from https://mediadiversified.org/2017/11/24/epistemic-homelessness-feeling-like-a-stranger-in-a-familiar-land/

Reynolds, V. (2019). *Justice-doing at the intersections of power: Community work, therapy and supervision*. Adelaide, Australia: Dulwich Centre Publications.

Russo, J., & Sweeney, A. (2016). *Searching for a Rose Garden: Challenging psychiatry, fostering mad studies*. Monmouth: PCCS Books.

Starr, B. D., & Weiner, M. B. (1981). *Sex and sexuality in the mature years*. London: WH Allen.

Chapter 2

What do clinical psychologists do anyway?

Annabel Head, Amy Obradovic, Sasha Nagra and Neha Bharat Shah

> *There are as many ways to be a clinical psychologist as there are clinical psychologists.*

What it means to be a clinical psychologist is a common question for many people at different stages of their journey into the profession – from pre-undergraduate, to pre-training and even amongst qualified psychologists! We want to begin this chapter by giving a broad picture of what a career in clinical psychology entails, while keeping in mind that there is no prescriptive answer to the question posed by the chapter title. While there is plenty of information out there about *doing* more as a means of preparing for a career as a clinical psychologist, this chapter hopes to allow you to think about the experiences you have already gained, and reflect on how these fit with the career.

What is clinical psychology?

Broadly speaking, clinical psychologists work with people to increase wellbeing and reduce distress. They use evidence-based theory and research to support people (and those in their system) to notice and use their strengths to better understand and/or overcome periods of difficulty (while keeping a critical eye on what constitutes scientific evidence). Ultimately clinical psychology is about *being with* people, using skills to try to listen to them and their experiences (while being mindful that we will never really *know* what it is like for them) and working collaboratively with them to make changes in their lives.

Importantly, this work is done not just at the level of individual client work – what makes clinical psychologists relatively unique is our ability to work at wider levels, including with families, staff teams, across multiple agencies, and at the level of policy. Clinical psychologists work with a wide range of people – including children, families, working-age adults, older adults, people with learning disabilities, people who have been in contact with the criminal justice system in forensic settings, people whose physical health impacts on their psychological wellbeing, and people for whom traditional services structures are inaccessible (e.g., people who are homeless or refugees). Some within the profession use the term 'scientist-practitioner', which is used to explain how we are uniquely placed to develop research, use evidence and combine this with clinical knowledge to strive for the best services possible for those we work with. The term 'reflective-practitioner' is also used to illustrate how we value thinking on our work, and use it reflexively to influence our future practice. This approach is enshrined, for example, in the emphasis given to supervision at all stages of the career (See Chapter 2).

Reflective activity: what are the threads that make up your role?

We have found it helpful to think about clinical psychology as a wide array of general and specific skills, knowledge and tasks, which are like threads – these threads are woven together to make a complex and richly textured tapestry that reflects the variety within the role. The tapestry for each role will be different, both with some common themes across the profession and also made up of different threads specific to the role. A number of threads are common to the work done by clinical psychologists in any field, however diverse they may appear at first – the ability to work with people with empathy and compassion, to hold on to multiple complex ideas at once; to work within complex systems; to use evidence critically and thoughtfully in our work. The role is more than just a skill set however, and some of the more subtle, intangible aspects of the role are hard to put down into words. An example of the threads that make up the role of a trainee or clinical psychologist within a child and adolescent mental health service (CAMHS) can be seen in Figure 2.1.

Whatever context you are currently working in, this is a good activity to map out what your key roles are, and also to shed light on some of the skills you are developing without even realising. Try in your own time, or under supervision.

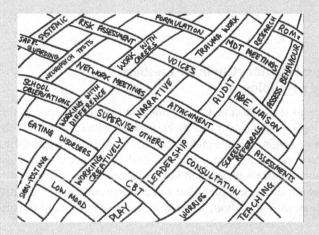

Figure 2.1 The threads that make up a clinical psychologist role working in a CAMHS.

This chapter will begin with some information on the route to becoming a clinical psychologist, and where we work. It is then subdivided into the overall themes that make up some of the core competencies of the profession: assessment, formulation, intervention and evaluation.

How to become a clinical psychologist and where clinical psychologists work

There is a significant amount of information out there already on how to train as a clinical psychologist – more details can be found by using some of the resources listed at the end of this book.

In a very general sense, in the UK you must complete a degree with sufficient psychology modules (as accredited by the BPS), gain some relevant clinical or research work experience, and then complete a doctorate in clinical psychology. What this route looks like in reality can be wonderfully different from person to person! To paraphrase a well-known quote, "when you've met one clinical psychologist, you've met . . . one clinical psychologist".

The NHS is the largest employer of clinical psychologists, who are employed across a huge range of settings. These include inpatient and community mental health services, addiction services, Improving Access to Psychological Therapies services (IAPT – a service model in England, UK), and physical health settings, for example working with people diagnosed with cancer or skin conditions. Try searching for jobs on the NHS website to get a flavour of the wide range of jobs available: www.jobs.nhs.uk.

Outside of the NHS, clinical psychologists may also work for charities (see case study below), social services, forensic services, at policy level (for example at NHS England or the World Health Organisation), at universities training future psychologists, or in private work. See the *In focus* box below for an example.

In focus: HarmonyChoir. Dr Liesbeth Tip, clinical psychologist

The idea to start HarmonyChoir came from my experience as a clinical psychologist (and amateur chorister) speaking with service users about the benefits of singing groups and music therapies. I also heard their stories about how the stigma surrounding mental health made them hesitant to speak about their problems, and how it had an impact on how they lived their lives. It could be difficult for some to join community initiatives. By forming an inclusive choir, I hoped to lower the threshold to participate for individuals with lived experience of mental health difficulties and to make them feel more integrated into society. At the same time, individuals who were not familiar with mental health difficulties would get acquainted with people who had had mental health difficulties, which could lead to change in any existing preconceptions. My skills as a clinical practitioner have been useful for the individual conversations I had with participating choir members, and by leading the choir project and keeping an eye out for participant's wellbeing. I believe my background as a clinical psychologist has helped me be aware of potential group dynamics, to support individuals where necessary, and to create a welcoming and safe atmosphere for participants.

Watch a documentary about the original project at www.harmonychoir.com

Assessment

One of the key skills of a clinical psychologist is to gather information about the person, people or situation they are working with. Sometimes a thorough assessment is a piece of work in itself, which aids understanding of the current context, and identifies where and how the needs can best be met. In other cases, an assessment forms the groundwork for constructing an intervention, which may take many forms. Information from an assessment is brought together through formulation. In reality, the division between assessment, formulation and intervention are somewhat arbitrary, as the processes feed into each other, and run throughout a piece of work rather than being discrete stages of a process.

Many services in the NHS run on a referral-based system, whereby people outside the service can refer individuals in. Even before an assessment begins, it is useful to think about where the referral came from and why; and to ask 'what is the request for?' (Fredman & Rapaport, 2010). Furthermore, does the person know about the referral? It often happens that the request is not from the referred person, who may not actually want our 'help'; but from concerned people around them. This can then pose interesting dilemmas for how to approach the work. As employees of whatever service we work in, we are generally in a relatively powerful position. Does the person really feel able to say "no" to coming to an assessment?

The people we meet with at the assessment are often concerned primarily with the things that are not working; the things that they want an intervention to change. While it is important to gather information about the 'problem', it is also important to listen out for and identify exceptions to these 'problem-saturated' stories (White & Epston, 1990). For example, when are the times that the person has been doing well? What does this tell us about their resources and strengths?

Reflective activity: Kofi's story

Kofi is a 15-year-old with haemophilia who has been referred to psychology services for support around behavioural difficulties. His head teacher describes him as a "very angry young man" who argues with teachers and students and skips lessons. Kofi lives at home with his mother, a Malawian native, and three younger siblings. While he used to be on track for good GCSEs, his grades have slipped significantly in the term. Kofi does not speak much during your initial assessment and you notice that he yawns frequently. Kofi's mother expresses concerns that he will not go on to achieve the grades he needs for an apprenticeship, and you learn that the family are relying on him being able to provide a second income. Kofi's mother currently works two night-time cleaning jobs and is struggling to make ends meet. The family sometimes relies on food banks to help them through the month. Kofi has reportedly been neglecting to administer his desmopressin injections regularly and has stopped seeing his friends at weekends.

There are a number of social and contextual considerations that we may wish to keep in mind when beginning our work with Kofi. Here are some ideas of things we might want to find out a bit more about at the assessment:

Mum works nights: Who is looking after younger siblings? We notice signs that Kofi is tired during the assessment. Is he a carer for his siblings while mum is away at work? Is he consequently tired during the day, and lacking energy to attend/perform at school/with homework? How is this affecting his mood? What does his ability to take responsibility for his siblings tell us about his strengths?

Financial concerns within the system: The family is relying on food banks. Is Kofi sufficiently nourished? How is this affecting his medical condition (haemophilia), and his school performance? Is he able to afford to get to school regularly, and does he have money to go out with friends?

Haemophilia: How does this affect him? As the assessor, are you familiar with this condition or would you want to consult with another professional about this? To what extent is he able to participate in social activities? At weekends, are his friends playing football, or other sports that he is not able to be involved in? Is this increasing levels of social isolation or feelings of difference?

Family factors: Does Kofi see his father? What does he think about becoming an adult man, perhaps based on his own experiences of men in his family? What are the cultural expectations of being 'the man of the house'? Are there expectations that he will stay in the family home, or are the family influenced by Western ideas about moving out? Kofi may be feeling a conflict between the multiple cultures he or may not identify with.

Can you think of anything else that you would be interested in exploring with Kofi and his family? What is the theory behind each of your questions?

As seen above in the example of Kofi, our assessments need to be thoughtful and sensitive to the variety of cultural contexts that our clients exist within; not just in the sense of race and ethnicity, but the person's identity.

Clinical psychologists often use outcome measures in routine clinical practice to measure factors such as wellbeing, functioning, or to measure more specific constructs related to diagnoses. For example, IAPT services use the PHQ-9 (Kroenke, Spitzer, & Williams, 2001) as a measure of low mood and the GAD-7 (Spitzer, Kroenke, Williams, & Löwe, 2006) as a measure of anxiety, and secondary care services may use measures such as the CORE (Evans et al., 2000) to measure wellbeing, functioning, problems and risk. These measures can be used in assessment along with clinical interview, to get an idea of someone's difficulties and strengths. They are also often used throughout treatment and at the end of treatment to assess progress and outcomes, i.e., change (if any).

Outcome measures are mostly self-report questionnaires that are often completed without the clinician present. Many of them are based on problematic assumptions of distress as a 'medical illness' in order to inform diagnoses, without paying appropriate attention to social factors. Some services have clinical cut-offs that service users have to meet in order to be eligible for treatment, or to be seen as 'recovered' and eligible for discharge. Commissioners often require services to collect data on outcome measures in order to provide evidence of effectiveness. Therefore it is important to use these with caution, alongside your own clinical judgement. Idiosyncratic measures like goal-based outcomes can also be helpful to measure change. For further discussion and alternatives see Robinson, Ashworth, Shepherd, and Evans (2006).

Clinical psychologists also have highly specialist training in administering and interpreting neuropsychological tests. These are validated testing materials to assess brain functioning – for example, someone's processing speed, memory or executive functioning (Lezak, Howieson, Loring, & Fischer, 2004). These tests tend to take the form of puzzles or exercises; the person's score is then compared to the expected norms for their age, which helps indicate what areas of cognition they may be struggling with. Neuropsychological assessment is used for two main purposes clinically (Lezak et al., 2004):

- To contribute to giving a diagnosis. For example, assessment may be useful to see whether an older adult's scores on short-term memory tests indicate they have dementia (and speculating what sort of dementia is indicated by their scores); or to ascertain whether someone seems to meet criteria for a diagnosis of learning disability or autism.
- To contribute to someone's care plan. For example, assessment could indicate what brain areas have been affected following a stroke or brain injury; this can then help clinicians to recommend how they can best be supported to overcome the areas they struggle with.

Neuropsychological assessment is always part of a wider formulation about somebody's difficulties. Scores on neuropsychological tests (e.g., an IQ score) should not be used in themselves to give a diagnosis or to make decisions about someone's care.

Formulation

Formulation can be regarded as one of the key skills for clinical psychologists, and underpins all the work we do. This section will briefly describe psychological formulation. We also advise readers to consult the DCP's "Good Practice Guidelines on the use of Psychological Formulation" (BPS, 2011) and the book *Formulation in Psychology and Psychotherapy* by Lucy Johnstone and Rudi Dallos (2014), for further guidance and discussion.

Formulating is a way of making sense of someone's present difficulties and strengths; their life experiences taking into account the context and environment in which they find themselves, and their meaning-making. Theories of psychological distress are continually interwoven with the specific details of the person or situation. As such, psychological formulation is an ongoing process rather than a one-off event (Johnstone & Dallos, 2014), and occurs alongside both assessment and intervention, as new details emerge, and new challenges and opportunities arise. Formulations are never a search for a 'truth', but rather should be assessed according to how useful they are for the person or situation. In fact, one of the key skills of clinical psychologists is our ability to sit with the often-uncomfortable feeling of uncertainty, of accepting the feeling of 'not knowing' rather than trying to say for certain that we 'know' the cause, maintenance and 'solutions' to problems.

One of the joys of being a clinical psychologist is being able to both use model-specific approaches to formulation (e.g., a CBT model for panic), as well to draw on multiple therapeutic models and work integratively to develop formulations.

There are many approaches to this; an accessible initial model is the 5 Ps model, which can be used as a meta-framework for formulating the following (based on Weerasekera, 1995):

- Presenting – what are the 'problem(s)' that have been highlighted as 'needing intervention'?
- Predisposing – what made it more likely that these 'problem(s)' would develop?
- Precipitating – what are the factors that led to seeking 'help' right now?
- Perpetuating – what factors keep the 'problem(s)' going?
- Protective – what are the strengths and resources available to them?

These factors should all be thought about at both the individual level, and at the levels of wider systems, including family, other social support, culture, social and economic factors.

A psychological theory which can be woven into formulation is attachment theory. Attachment is suggested to be "a deep and enduring emotional bond that connects one person to another across time and space" (Ainsworth, 1973; Bowlby, 1969). Attachment theory suggests that our early experiences with our primary caregivers, typically our parents, can shape how we make sense of our emotions, how we relate to others to get our needs met, and to our sense of security with others and with ourselves. Individuals often come into therapy when there is a situation or difficulty in their life they are unable to work through alone. The therapist provides an initial form of security, comfort and safety, which is similar to the function of a child's first attachment with their caregiver. Someone's early experiences of attachment relationships is therefore proposed to impact on how they make sense of their relationship with the therapist or team, and may influence the behaviours they use.

Trauma can also play a significant role in how someone responds to various forms of therapy. Trauma can be defined as "an event, series of events, or set of circumstances that is experienced by an individual as physically or emotionally harmful or threatening" (SAMHSA, 2012, p. 2). Quite often individuals with histories of trauma seek therapy for difficulties in their present lives but are unaware of the impact that trauma has had, either because they may not see the connections or they (perhaps unconsciously) avoid it all together. It is generally not just the trauma, but how it is interpreted that defines it as a traumatic event. In fact, it has been argued that some form of perceived trauma is at the core of all stories that lead to engagement with mental health services (Sweeney, Clement, Filson, & Kennedy, 2016). It is important to be trauma aware, because, like attachment, someone's experience of trauma can influence their engagement with services, how they interact with staff and with other clients. Many teams are now developing trauma-informed models of practice (Sweeney et al., 2016).

In focus: attachment theory in practice. Neha Shah, associate mental health worker

I currently work within a personality disorder service. Individuals who have been given a psychiatric diagnosis of a 'personality disorder' have often experienced challenging and disruptive early attachment relationships. Sally was a 25 year old woman who had experienced neglect growing up and was abused by her parents; something she later re-experienced with a partner. As an adult, she struggled with regulating her emotions, particularly around anger. Underlying this, she also struggled with poor self-esteem and feelings of worthlessness.

I used supervision to reflect on a difficulty that came up in a session, whereby Sally became upset because I had told her I would not be able to make some phone calls to social services on her behalf – she explained it made her feel I did not care about her. I felt torn between wanting to cancel an appointment on her behalf, and a nagging sense of reluctance about whether I should. My supervisor and I used an attachment lens to wonder if my urge of wanting to do something for her could reflect a relational pattern that had developed from childhood in order to get her needs met.

I discussed this in the next session with Sally. We decided to carry out role-plays, discuss strategies she could use if she found herself becoming agitated and angry, and to think through the pros/cons of making the phone call herself. Following this session, she managed to cancel the appointment herself, and reported she was proud of her achievement.

Psychological formulation can be seen as complementary to, or an alternative to, psychiatric diagnosis. There is ongoing debate within clinical psychology, psychiatry, service-user groups, and the public about the usefulness and validity of psychiatric diagnoses (e.g., Kinderman, Read, Moncrieff, & Bentall, 2013).

In practice, psychological formulations often seem to be focused on the problems a person or group bring to the work. To turn it on its head, can you do a formulation of their strengths instead? Focusing on someone's values (i.e., what is important to them) can help us to understand the person and systems behind the diagnosis or 'problem'. For example, it may highlight that someone has used incredible resilience or perseverance to get through the difficulties they have faced in their lives, sometimes not just surviving but thriving. Likewise, at a service level, could we understand 'disengagement' or 'treatment resistance' as empowering attempts to regain control? Could this inform us of systems, structures and pathways that fail to meet these particular needs?

Interventions

There is a wealth of information available already about the interventions and approaches that clinical psychologists might use to foster psychological understanding and change; it is not within the scope of this chapter to do justice to them all. However, brief introductions to some of the main therapeutic models used by clinical psychologists are given here, acknowledging that this misses both the rich content of those included and omits many useful theories and approaches entirely. Following this, other approaches including indirect working and group therapy are discussed.

Psychodynamic – The cornerstone of all therapies that have developed since, psychodynamic theory has developed into various strands and is therefore difficult to summarise as 'one thing'. However, overall theory states that presenting difficulties are the manifestation of underlying intrapsychic processes and the 'squashing down' of psychological distress that is otherwise too painful to process consciously (known as 'defences'). Therapy aims to bring some of these unconscious processes into consciousness, so they can therefore be better understood, and the client can better tolerate some of the painful feelings that they would otherwise be suppressing. Therapy has a focus on the relationship between client and therapist, and examining this interpersonal process illuminates some of the client's typical reactions to interpersonal difficulties. For further discussion, see *Introduction to the Practice of Psychoanalytic Psychotherapy* (Lemma, 2015).

Systemic and family psychotherapy – Systemic psychotherapies focus on relationships between people, systems and processes. Systemic therapy is less interested on working on 'the problem' directly, but rather on how people in the system relate to the problem. What are the meaning-making and beliefs about it, and how do these influence people and their actions within the system? By acknowledging that there is no one 'correct' way of seeing things, systemic work hopes to facilitate change in systems through exploration of current, historical and possible ways of relating; identifying potential solutions thereafter. Issues of power, difference and diversity are built into all stages of formulation (often called 'hypothesising') and intervention. Intervention approaches traditionally took a more structural approach, with therapists not only convening families, but directing individuals to swap roles and experiment with their positions. Later schools of systemic practice developed 'circular questioning', which aims to elaborate and explore different perspectives and relationships between people and concepts. For further discussion, see *An Introduction to Family Therapy: Systemic Theory and Practice* (Dallos & Draper, 2010).

Narrative therapy – Narrative therapy is a therapy originating from social constructionist schools of thinking, predominantly from third-wave systemic practice. Based on ideas developed by Michael White (e.g., White & Epston, 1990), this therapy suggests that people who present to services often have a 'narrow' story, which tends to be focused solely on the problems they experience (a 'problem-saturated' story). Narrative theory states that people actually have a huge array of stories available beyond this 'single story', and a core component of the approach is for individuals to collaborate in acknowledging and celebrating alternative accounts. A key technique is *externalisation*, an approach that looks to disentangle individuals from problem stories in order to shed light on and value the multi-faceted perspective of human experience. These principles are often applied in unique and creative ways, often within communities and with oppressed groups. For example, the Tree of Life intervention has often been used to support those seeking asylum (Hughes, 2014). For further discussion, see The Dulwich Centre website for a range of resources and information: www.dulwichcentre.com.au

Cognitive Behavioural Therapy (CBT) – CBT is one of the core therapeutic modalities used by the profession, and is a required competency of all clinical psychologists. CBT theory suggests that it is not an event per se that affects how we respond, but rather our interpretation of it. CBT focuses on how thoughts, feelings and bodily reactions all interact and influence how we behave. Therapy aims to illuminate and question the usefulness of some of our automatic thought processes. It also encourages clients to work as scientific explorers and test out their predictions about potential outcomes by planning and completing a series of behavioural experiments. A range of 'third-wave' CBT therapies have also been developed, which include acceptance and commitment therapy, compassion focused therapy, dialectical behavioural therapy and mindfulness-based cognitive therapy, all of which explore how individuals relate to their thinking and emotional states. For further discussion, see *An Introduction to Cognitive Behaviour Therapy: Skills and Applications* (Kennerley, Kirk, & Westbrook, 2016).

Cognitive Analytic Therapy (CAT) – CAT is an integration of analytic and cognitive approaches, and was developed by Anthony Ryle in the 1980s. A basic tenet of CAT is that we all tend to fall into patterns of interaction with other people, 'reciprocal roles', which we have learnt from our early experiences. An example of a reciprocal role would be when we experience other people as 'rejecting' and as a result, feel rejected (an 'other-to-self reciprocal role'). Individuals also identify 'self-to-self reciprocal roles', such as experiencing your own thoughts as attacking – feeling attacked and criticised as a result. The therapist and client work creatively together, with a core focus on the emerging therapeutic relationship – collaborating to 'map out' patterns of psychological distress. The therapy aims to identify when these patterns leave us getting 'trapped' into the same ruts over and over, and through a process of reformulation – highlight opportunities to try different ways of being with others. CAT invites individuals to 'revise' their approach through behavioural experiments and new ways of relating to self and others – ultimately, becoming their own best therapist over time. For further discussion, see *Introducing Cognitive Analytic Therapy: Principles and Practice* (Ryle & Kerr, 2003).

Indirect approaches – Another important skill that clinical psychologists have is working indirectly, i.e., not directly with the person who has been referred. This may involve supporting significant others to look after themselves, as much as those they support (e.g., relatives of people living with dementia, foster carers). Also clinical psychologists have an important role in sharing and disseminating knowledge and skills to others to empower, maximise wellbeing, and improve systems. Indirect work may therefore involve training others, or meeting with staff teams to develop formulations about people they find they are struggling to understand, and offering ideas about intervention strategies that others will put in place (sometimes referred to as consultation). To read more, see *Collaborative Consultation in Mental Health: Guidelines for the New Consultant* (Fredman, Papadopoulou, & Worwood, 2018).

Group therapies – group therapies can look very different from one another, largely based on the theoretical underpinning and models that drive their application. Some groups are semi-structured or manualised (e.g., psycho-educational groups, sex offender treatment programmes), whereas others may be analytical (e.g., psychoanalytic groups, therapeutic communities). The latter tend to have a focus on interpersonal processes and group dynamics, rather than content. Understanding how one relates to others in a therapy group aims to highlight one's relational style in all groups (e.g., the family, friendship groups or workplace), such as what roles one tends to take, or one's relationship to power or being challenged. Group therapies can vary in length significantly, with psychoanalytic groups tending to run for much longer than a typically more structured group. Groups can run as stand-alone treatments or alongside individual sessions. They can help service users to realise that they are not alone in their experiences, helping people feel more connected with others. Additionally, if service users are experts in their own experience, a group of service users can be seen as a room full of experts, equipping each other with a broader range of insight and/or skills than individual therapy with a practitioner. Being able to provide as well as receive support also allows more opportunities to enable growth and model therapeutic change. For further discussion see *The Theory and Practice of Group Psychotherapy* (Yalom & Leszcz, 2005).

Evaluation

A core part of a clinical psychologist's skill set is the ability to conduct research in clinical populations and at service levels. These skills are also invaluable in understanding, evaluating and using research from the evidence-base.

Doing research

It is not within the scope of this chapter to fully explore the many methods used to gather and analyse data. However, in brief clinical psychologists may use the following approaches:

* Quantitative: using numerical methods, perhaps to measure a change over time. For example, inviting clients to rate their levels of anxiety on self-report measure both before and after an intervention group, to measure whether this has reduced over time.
* Qualitative: gathering and analysing verbal or other data (e.g., photos) to gain more in-depth understanding of a phenomena (usually from smaller numbers of participants). For example, running a focus group with members of an anxiety intervention group, questioning them about what they felt were the most useful elements of the group.
* Mixed: a combination of qualitative and quantitative methods. This approach can sometimes involve 'triangulating' (i.e., bringing together) various methods of investigation. For example, a project exploring the role of diagnosis in practices could involve self-report questionnaires or psychometrics, focus groups, and observational methods – bringing a range of layers to the analyses of a particular topic area.

Further information on research methods in clinical psychologist can be found in *Research Methods in Clinical Psychology* (Barker, Pistrang, & Elliott, 2016).

Reflective activity: research ideas

Research ideas can come from anywhere! Can you think of any questions you have had about where you work? How would you go about finding this out? Are there any ideas that you think you could talk to your team/supervisor about, and take a lead on? Even if they are just vague questions for now, jot them down, and see if you can flesh them out in supervision.

Mary's story

Mary worked as a support worker for a charity that supports adults to start engaging more with the community, for example going along to the local coffee shop and supporting people to apply for benefits. Over time, she noticed that some people were re-referred while others did not seem to come back. She spoke to her supervisor, and they decided to use the information they already had on file to work out how many people were re-referred to the service over a six month period.

When they looked at the demographic data, they realised that those who got re-referred were more likely to live alone than the people who only attended for one intervention. Mary and her supervisor therefore decided that the team should also focus on supporting the service users to make links in their local community—such as joining a reading group—as being less socially isolated seemed to be associated with fewer re-referrals.

As noted above, the interplay between research and clinical practice allows for us to amend and develop services based on research outcomes; research is therefore a key role for clinical psychologists. Mary's ponderings about why she kept seeing the same faces over and over again led to some research, which led to ideas about how to improve the service. Senior psychologists can use these research skills to shape services, present evidence to commissioners about current practice and influence what and how services are designed, run and evaluated at the highest levels.

However, you do not have to be in a senior psychologist, or even in a 'psychologist' role to think creatively or critically about aspects of a service (when we say critically, we mean questioningly, with an open mind to alternative ways of doing things, rather than being disapproving!). Things going wrong and learning from our mistakes are key aspects of learning and development. When apparent failings are embraced reflectively, we engage in an important skill for leaders at all levels (Skinner, 2011).

Evidence-based practice – a tripartite concept

The term 'evidence-based practice' entered the field of psychology at the turn of the century, having been formally introduced to the medical sciences in the early 1990s (Guyatt et al., 1992; Sackett & Rosenberg, 1995). Yet despite having been firmly established as a concept within psychology for almost 30 years, there is still misunderstanding about what evidence-based practice means in the context of our day-to-day clinical duties.

The confusion can be at least partially alleviated if we step back and challenge our understanding of what constitutes 'evidence'. It is tempting to think of 'evidence-based practice' as a clinical commitment to using the best available scientific research at all costs. Research, after all, provides the evidence base upon which our profession is founded. While this is true in part, evidence-based practice acknowledges a broader definition of 'evidence' than is commonly considered, and recognises clinical expertise (i.e., the practitioner's experience and judgment) and the client's preferences as two further forms of evidence that sit alongside research to inform best practice (Sackett, Rosenberg, Gray, Haynes, & Richardson, 1996).

To understand why we should take this three-strand approach to evaluating the evidence on which our practice is based, we might consider the types of interventions that receive most funding for research. For the best available research, we can look to the National Institute for Health and Clinical Excellence (NICE) guidelines – a set of recommendations based on meta-analyses of existing research on specific clinical interventions. We might question, however, which types of therapeutic interventions lend themselves more readily to the kinds of research valued within clinical professions (and which do not), and which therapies are more or less easy to base in evidence? Does this mean that other types of intervention lack efficacy? Or simply that bias in regards to what 'research' looks like, means that some studies get funded (and therefore incorporated into the evidence-base), while others do not? It is in the gaps between these questions that our clinical expertise, and the client's preferences as an expert in their own experience, can provide valuable second and third strands of evidence to inform the clinical direction of our work (Sackett et al., 1996). We are duty-bound to keep a critical eye on research, especially when it is used to make important decisions, such as what therapies are offered in services (Nel, 2012).

Working at other levels

The previous sections highlight some of the clinical and research tasks that make up the role of clinical psychologists. It is also important to acknowledge the other aspects of the role, which may take up even more of one's time as one progresses up the career ladder. For example, psychologists employed at the highest bands in the NHS tend to hold much smaller caseloads, usually working in highly specialist ways (for example, with people who present with very complex needs); or may have no direct clinical contact time with service users at all. Instead they may take on more senior roles, including:

• Management responsibilities, which may involve dealing with issues such as annual leave for the whole team, or being involved in recruitment;
• Clinical supervision of other staff;
• Training and teaching, both to colleagues within and out of the psychology profession;
• Conducting and supervising research;
• Developing services – using psychological skills and knowledge to develop services that promote psychological wellbeing at all levels. This involves building relationships across agencies, such as working with commissioner to advocate for psychological approaches within services, by convening and coordinating different groups and meetings. This aims to develop clinical pathways, and ensure greater efficiency in organisations.

In focus: **Manchester Resilience Hub. Dr Alan Barrett & Dr Clare Jones, consultant clinical psychologists**

Clinical psychologists in Manchester immediately realised that there would be role for psychology in supporting those affected, following a mass fatality terrorist incident in the local area. They therefore developed a service in the wake of the bombing incident, which was led by psychologists and with psychological theory underpinning all of the work. They promoted the validating message that people's distress following such incidents was normal and to be expected, given the trauma they had been through. The service provided and has continued to provide evidence-based interventions to those who have requested this beyond the immediacy of the situation – recognising the long-term impact of traumatic events. They offer regular follow-ups to people under their service and remain open to not only those affected by the bombing, but also to those who have experienced similar traumatic incidents. Information from people who use the service is being gathered to help shape how it operates. The Hub can now serve as a service model if other such services are needed to be set up in the aftermath of a large-scale traumatic event. The responsiveness and effectiveness in developing the Manchester Resilience Hub has set an international precedence and it is increasingly clear, that the work of these clinicians continues to have a global reach.

As clinical psychologists, we can also use our training to influence broader issues that span beyond healthcare. This might include helping other professions to work in more psychologically-informed ways; consulting on public policy, or proactively promoting wellbeing by interrogating perceptions of mental health and the forces that affect it. Community psychology and systemic theory suggest that problematic behaviours and distress are embedded within the social systems that surround them. To effect change in these stressors, it is often necessary, therefore, to change the system.

Doing clinical psychology or being a clinical psychologist?

Clinical psychology is a multifaceted, exciting and dynamic career, which can be both challenging and immensely rewarding. We hope this chapter has been useful in beginning to share some of the scope of the role of a clinical psychologist. There are many aspects of the job that involve a truly personal take on things, and we cannot help but be affected by it. How much is this a job or an identity?

Acknowledgements

With thanks to Dr Liesbeth Tip, Dr Alan Barrett and Dr Clare Jones.

References

Ainsworth, M. D. S. (1973). The development of infant-mother attachment. In B. Carwell & H. Ricciuti (Eds.), *Review of child development research* (Vol. 3, pp. 1–94). Chicago: University of Chicago Press.

Barker, C., Pistrang, N., & Elliott, R. (2016). *Research methods in clinical psychology: An introduction for students and practitioners* (3rd ed.). Chichester, UK: John Wiley & Sons.

Bowlby, J. (1969). Attachment. In *Attachment and loss: Vol 1. Loss*. New York: Basic Books.

British Psychological Society. (2011). *Good practice guidelines on the use of psychological formulation*. Leicester, UK: BPS.

Dallos, R., & Draper, R. (2010). *An introduction to family therapy: Systemic theory and practice*. Maidenhead: Open University Press.

Evans, C., Mellor-Clark, J., Margison, F., Barkham, M., Audin, K., Connell, J. & McGrath, G. (2000). Clinical outcomes in routine evaluation: The CORE-OM. *Journal of Mental Health, 9*, 247–255.

Fredman, G., Papadopoulou, A., & Worwood, E. (2018). *Collaborative consultation in mental health: Guidelines for the new consultant*. Abingdon, UK: Routledge.

Fredman, G., & Rapaport, P. (2010). How do we begin? Working with older people and their significant systems. In G. Fredman, E. Anderson, & J. Stott (Eds.), *Being with older people: A systemic approach* (pp. 31–59). London, UK: Karnac Books.

Guyatt, G., Cairns, J., Churchhill, D., Cook, D., Haynes, B., Hirsch, J., . . . Tugwell, P. (1992). Evidence-based medicine: A new approach to teaching the practice of medicine. *Journal of the American Medical Association, 268*, 2420–2425.

Hughes, G. (2014). Finding a voice through "The Tree of Life": A strength-based approach to mental health for refugee children and families in schools. *Clinical Child Psychology and Psychiatry, 19*(1), 139–153.

Johnstone, L., & Dallos, R. (2014). *Formulation in psychology and psychotherapy* (2nd ed.). Abingdon, UK: Routledge.

Kennerley, H., Kirk, J., & Westbrook, D. (2016). *An introduction to cognitive behaviour therapy: Skills and applications*. Thousand Oaks, CA: Sage Publications.

Kinderman, P., Read, J., Moncrieff, J., & Bentall, R. P. (2013). Drop the language of disorder. *Evidence Based Mental Health, 16*(1), 2–3.

Kroenke, K., Spitzer, R. L., & Williams, J. B. (2001). The PHQ-9: Validity of a brief depression severity measure. *Journal of General Internal Medicine, 16*(9), 606–613.

Lemma, A. (2015). *Introduction to the practice of psychoanalytic psychotherapy* (2nd ed.). Hoboken, NJ: John Wiley & Sons.

Lezak, M. D., Howieson, D. B., Loring, D. W., & Fischer, J. S. (2004). *Neuropsychological assessment*. Oxford: Oxford University Press.

Nel, P. W. (2012). The trouble with clinical psychology. *Clinical Psychology Forum, 235*(7), 18–22.

Robinson, S. I., Ashworth, M., Shepherd, M., & Evans, C. (2006). In their own words: A narrative-based classification of clients' problems on an idiographic outcome measure for talking therapy in primary care. *Primary Care Mental Health, 4*(3), 165–173.

Ryle, A., & Kerr, I. B. (2003). *Introducing cognitive analytic therapy: Principles and practice*. Hoboken, NJ: John Wiley & Sons.

Sackett, D. L., & Rosenberg, W. M. (1995). On the need for evidence-based medicine. *Journal of Public Health, 17*, 330–334.

Sackett, D. L., Rosenberg, W. M., Gray, J. A., Haynes, R. B., & Richardson, W. S. (1996). Evidence based medicine: What it is and what it isn't. *British Medical Journal, 312*(7023), 71–72.

Skinner, P. (2011). Leadership is our business. *Clinical Psychology Forum, 225*(9), 11–14.

Spitzer, R. L., Kroenke, K., Williams, J. B., & Löwe, B. (2006). A brief measure for assessing generalized anxiety disorder: The GAD-7. *Archives of Internal Medicine, 166*(10), 1092–1097.

Substance Abuse and Mental Health Services Administration. (2012). *Trauma and justice strategic initiative: SAMHSA's working definition of trauma and guidance for trauma-informed approach*. Rockville, MD: Substance Abuse and Mental Health Services Administration.

Sweeney, A., Clement, S., Filson, B., & Kennedy, A. (2016). Trauma-informed mental healthcare in the UK: What is it and how can we further its development. *Mental Health Review Journal, 21*(3), 174–192.

Weerasekera, P. (1995). *Multiperspective case formulation: A step towards treatment integration*. Florida, USA: Krieger.

White, M., & Epston, D. (1990). *Narrative means to therapeutic ends*. London, UK: W W Norton & Company.

Yalom, I. D., & Leszcz, M. (2005). *The theory and practice of group psychotherapy* (5th ed.). New York: Basic Books.

Chapter 3

Making the most of your supervision

Reflecting on selves in context

James Randall, Angie Cucchi and Vasiliki Stamatopoulou

This chapter invites you to consider your emerging identity as a supervisee. For supervision to become as useful, safe, and as progressive as possible, we recognise the need for a shift away from *having* supervision towards *engaging* with supervision. Too often can early experiences define supervision under more mechanistic and procedural terms – as if an hour to check-list through 'cases' and activities; too often experienced as an interface for accountability and 'correcting' practice. We wish to welcome a curiosity and a personal commitment to experiment with supervision. In doing so, we take very seriously the confines of supervisory practice and the need for a 'scrutiny' of sorts – as supervision offers a fundamental safeguard for the people we hope to support within our practice (at all stages of our careers). With safety as paramount within the supervisory context – taken with the sensitivity and seriousness it deserves – we also wish to remind ourselves that supervision is something to be worked on; an unfolding, developmental and imperfect offering. Here, we simply wonder what opportunities can arise when we take this fact for what it is: we play a significant part in shaping our supervision. In this chapter then, supervision is explored in principle and practice, and as fundamentally an emerging, dynamic and evolving process. Namely, at the heart of supervision is a relationship and as for any relationship, we can hope to contribute in ways that foster, nurture and enrich our personal and professional development.

Navigating the terrains of clinical practice can be challenging at any stage of our career. In principle, the supervisory relationship offers a containing space that grants uncertainty and confusion a space to be voiced; searches and forages for lessons learned from mistakes and misfortunes; and names and celebrates the developments and successes of the supervisee. Through the questioning and guidance of a more experienced, qualified colleague, the aspiring psychologist can navigate their way through unfamiliar terrains – emerging from the challenges with a greater sense of competency, courage, and curiosity. In practice, it can also be the space in which relationships are tested, challenges are faced, and problems surface. In this chapter then, we explore the role of being a supervisee in context and the ways in which individuals may experiment with personal and professional risks that are fruitful for learning and in vein of making the most of supervision.

To begin this chapter, we wish to start with a collection of experiences from those who have been supervised – on the joys, challenges and surprises of being supervised.

In focus: experiences of supervision

"For me, supervision had always been about case discussion, at a relatively fast pace using a strategic and structured format (thank you IAPT training). At times I would nervously search for the 'right answer' or what I think my supervisor may want to hear. Little did I know that supervision encompassed so much more than this. One particular day comes to mind, which challenged these ideas and 'activities' of supervision.

On the day in question, I had experienced a real tough session with a client. During discussion, I informed/asked my supervisor if it was okay to swear and before he got the chance to reply I verbally vomited my thoughts riddled with a couple of expletives. Immediately, I was filled with dread. I mentally beat myself up, and questioned why the fuck I just swore! To my surprise he responded *"Don't worry, you don't swear enough!"*

This moment changed my relationship with supervision forever, it permitted me to be myself and be more comfortable with that. So now, I walk into supervision sessions with more confidence and the ability to go with whatever happens in the room, so if I feel the need to throw in the odd 'shit', then I do. I will always be thankful to the supervisor who showed me that it's okay to be the person alongside the professional".

Candice Williams

"It can take a long time for trusting conversations to take root, and to understand and feel comfortable with each other's style. The best supervisors I have experienced have struck a good balance between necessary didacticism with strong modelling, allowing space for ruptures, wrong-turns and 'unconscious incompetence'. The worst have tried to brush aside power imbalances to be chummy, overbearing, and, on one occasion, to ask me to babysit their kids!"

Jenny Doe

"It felt like we figured out where the boundaries of experience were together, through experimenting and pushing my skill set little by little. There was an honesty about things: I was great at *doing things* and doing *many things*, but I was less confident in rethinking what I could have done differently – which probably reflected something about my working-class roots, a striving to succeed (or please, perhaps?), and a family script about 'demonstrating' understanding through tangible and 'real' results . . . Not this 'reflective' waffle that I grew to (hopefully) master through investing in completely deconstructing my perspectives on things. How I did this, was to open myself up as much as possible: inviting my supervisor into sessions, speaking up in meetings, recording sessions, 'psychologising' myself in every way I could . . . But ultimately, this wasn't an individual endeavour, as I would always take this back to my supervisor and try to invite them to challenge me on things. Some days it was easier than others, and on occasion, I no doubt avoided doing so. My development was certainly not a 'once or twice' activity. It continued throughout my assistant work, and continues to this day".

James Randall

"My supervisor's open, transparent and accepting stance gave me permission to take emotional risks and expose my own areas of professional vulnerability whilst realising my own interpersonal resources. They created a secure base for exploration and a safe haven in which I could seek reassurance without feeling judged. This freed me from the pressure of 'premature certainty' and enabled me to explore and tolerate the ambiguity of the pathway towards becoming a psychologist. My supervisor's attitude also paved the way for a reflexive context in which the personal and the professional identities could merge. Above all, the supervisors that I remember most dearly, are the ones who taught me to be kind and compassionate towards myself and encouraged me to embrace and learn from my mistakes".

Angie Cucchin

What is supervision?

Supervision is an integral part of the role of psychologists in both academic and practice settings (Goodyear & Guzzardo, 2000). Psychologists at pre-training and in-training stages are often asked to assess their reasons for wanting to become a psychologist, to review their current and perceived strengths and skills, how their past experiences have influenced and shaped them, and to identify training needs and goals. In order to complete this kind of self-assessment we need to be able to reflect on our past and present experiences – with a view to shaping the way forward. You may also have a particular relationship to supervision already and so it may be worth pausing for a moment and considering the way in which others have shaped your experience of what supervision is (see the *Thinking space* box below).

Thinking space

Think of a time in which you have felt like a supervisor has really helped you to make the most of your practice and learning – perhaps they have lent some wise words during a confusing encounter, or been there during a personally difficult time for you. This may not necessarily be a supervisor from a psychology related role. What was it that made the supervisory encounter helpful in a way that it shaped you as a supervisee? Were there particular environmental factors, or things your supervisor said or did, that contributed to the experience?

Now think of a time when you have experienced a supervisor as less helpful, unhelpful, or damaging even – perhaps you were misunderstood, or had not had enough time to talk through a situation. What was it about the supervisory encounter you brought to mind, that you found unhelpful? Were there particular environmental factors, or things your supervisor said or did, that contributed to the experience?

How could you use these experiences to help shape your future supervisory relationships and encounters?

Each and every person's supervisory experience will be different. As such, it is important to hold supervisory encounters with a tentativeness they deserve – there will be some that are experienced as brilliant; some experienced as pretty bad; others, somewhere in between. This is because supervision is fundamentally a process based on the development of relationships (Cushway & Knibbs, 2004; Wheeler, 2004), and so supervision can evolve and take shape over time. Just like the office plant, supervision requires some nourishing over time in order to truly flourish.

Clinical supervision can be defined as "the formal provision, by approved supervisors, of a relationship-based education and training, that is case-focused and which manages, supports, develops and evaluates the work of junior colleagues" (Milne, 2007, p. 440). In this light, you can note that supervision not only fosters and nourishes personal and professional development, but it also has an evaluative component. This is no truer than for clinical psychology trainees, who face a unique dynamic with their supervisors being both mentor (and often ally), but also someone who has to assess and ultimately decide whether the individual's performance on placement meets the required standards (i.e., whether they should pass or fail the placement).

There are a range of books exploring supervision from the perspective of those supervising (e.g., Scaife, 2019; Vetere & Stratton, 2016), but to our knowledge, none that explore supervision from the role of those accessing it. Our core focus here, is not necessarily to tell you all of the dominant ways of understanding or practicing supervision (as this is beyond the scope of this chapter), but instead to highlight a range of factors to consider as we navigate our way through supervisory contexts – learning and developing in the ways that best fit for us at that point in our personal and professional development. Below, we include the thoughts of some current supervisors, reflecting on their engagement with supervisees as a reminder of the range of experiences supervision can capture.

In focus: experiences of supervising

"I've found that within supervision (as in clinical practice) there can be a temptation to deny the self and our own humanity. I've found that when I fail to acknowledge that I take myself into the room, I place greater emphasis on the tools and techniques rather than the relationship. Whilst supervision is not therapy, there is something about creating a space that is safe, secure and predictable. It is in that situation I have received the best supervision, and what I aim for when supervising. For me creating a space where there is the opportunity to hear and explore whatever needs to be said and thought about is essential. Being a supervisor is anxiety provoking in a different way to working clinically. However, I have found that when I allowed my identity and humanity into the room as I do in my clinical practice, rather than allowing the anxiety of 'getting it right' and fixating on 'doing', rather than 'being', was when both myself and my supervisee bloomed".

Dr. Faye Harrison Yuill

"Supervision, to me, is an object which contains contradictory experiences. It has been looked forward to, dreaded, misunderstood, enjoyed and regretted. An apparent cultural necessity that is, curiously, neither enforced nor agreed upon. Sometimes we have taken a risk to be part of the other person's problem and sometimes not. I remember the feeling of being vulnerable with other professionals. The varied responses to our displays of vulnerability. These not just from within supervision.

Supervision simultaneously supervised by other professionals. Who in turn are supervised by other professionals. The manifestation of the written and unwritten rules of culture. In these ways my experience, and memory, of supervising, and being supervised, blend. We are swimming in the same pool".

Dr Andrew Perry

What type of things could I focus on in supervision?

Supervision is a time-limited opportunity to explore your experiences in clinical practice in much greater depth than is usually permitted throughout the working day. As such, it can be useful to think about the 'types' of conversations held in supervision. Recognising that the practitioner is *part of* the system in which they intervene, similar consideration needs to be given to the supervisory relationship. As such, Mason (2010) elaborated on six aspects of supervision:

- *The therapeutic relationship.* Starting supervision with a focus on relationships can often help focus on the multiple invested *selves* and power dynamics of therapeutic interventions. Voicing struggles in relationships, dilemmas faced with families, exploring confusions or intuitions, can help guide a richer understanding of what to do, or indeed not to do, next.
- *The clients and issues they present.* This not only provides a focus for the individuals you assess and work with, but could also involve an invitation to your supervisor – to explore their clients and formulate together (modelling a range of ways of thinking and working).
- *The client's relationship to help.* This area can include exploration of how the person was referred, who made the referral, and why. What implications are there as a result? Who is most or least motivated, and what does this mean for the work? To what degree has this journey to help been empowering or disempowering for the service user, and in what ways?
- *The self of the practitioner.* Introducing aspects of personal experience, exploring assumptions and your own prejudices can feel like dangerous territory early on in your career path. However, such explorations within supervision can enrich your development and your practice over time – and you may well learn a lot not only about yourself but *from* yourself. This can be a sensitive aspect of supervision though, so contracting can be very important (see below). We introduce some tools below, which you may find useful in exploring the role of the self in clinical supervision.
- *The supervisory relationship.* You may wish to explore your own relationship to help; thinking about the ways in which you have traditionally sought advice or support when struggling; the strategies used to seek and avoid assistance from others. Focusing on the supervisory relationship will enable you to counter any practices to avoid facing the inevitable struggles of our profession. As such, it can again be important to explore expectations and usefulness of supervision, and to review this along the way.
- *The self of the supervisor.* You may develop a sense of your supervisor's self over time, and this can direct or influence the focus on your supervision. Curious beginnings could ask about what the supervisor looks for in supervisees, if there are particular shared values that have helped or hindered their work in the past. The important step here, is that such exploration is focused on your own learning and development, and not an inquiry into your supervisor. After all, they may not consider their own selves to be of particular relevance to the work or relationship, as practitioners take different positions on the use of self in clinical psychology.

In managing some of the uncertainties faced in supervision, we wonder what could be gained (or potentially lost) for supervisees to use the above framework or something similar when addressing their personal and professional development in the context of supervision.

What you can expect from supervision

The different ways in which we understand what supervision is or indeed, what it can become, can enable individuals to use their time more effectively and creatively. The hallmark of good supervision is feeling listened to and understood within the realms of safe emotional connections, where supervisors are curious, responsive and available (Vetere & Dallos, 2016).

Supervision can be about learning skills, monitoring risks, exploring ethical issues and reflecting on how the personal and the professional realms integrate. You most certainly deserve to be supported with all of these aspects. In practice, a complex dilemma emerges in which pre-qualified positions need to create opportunities for individuals to influence change in practice, systems and for the people we work with – yet at the same time, need to keep in mind levels of training and competence. Importantly, this also needs to consider the responsibilities detailed within one's job description and related payment scales (e.g., level of pay within the NHS Agenda for Change is matched to role responsibilities). This arguably, safeguards those in early stages in their careers from being used as equivalents/replacements for qualified staff – a form of exploitation within the profession (Woodruff & Wang, 2005). With this in mind, we wish to draw your attention to your rights if employed as an assistant psychologist – as described in the *In focus* box. These guidelines are now over ten years old, and since then, the range of pre-qualified positions has skyrocketed. As such, we hope that services will abide to these guidelines for all pre-qualified, applied psychology positions and commit ourselves to working to support these rights in whatever way, shape or form we can.

In focus: your rights as an employed assistant psychologist

In 2007, the BPS produced a report in collaboration with Unite the Union, entitled *Guidelines for the Employment of Assistant Psychologists*. This document explores a range of issues pertinent to clinical practice and supervision when in pre-qualified roles. Here, we list what you are entitled to as an assistant psychologist (and arguably, in other applied non-qualified psychology positions) – namely your rights.

1   Have **a formal induction** for the working environment, legislation and local organisational policies, supervisory arrangements, and so on. This must include opportunities for you to observe your supervisor's clinical work.

2   **Supervision** from a qualified psychologist (minimum two hours a week that includes at least one hour of informal supervision/contact).
3   To be exposed to **a variety of work** that includes clinical work (i.e., not a purely administrative job). This includes times for supervision, administration, personal study, and opportunities to meet other psychologists.
4   To work within the **boundaries of your competence** (e.g., to not provide specialist or complex therapies) and for any work beyond this, to be structured and supervised according to the supervisor's own competencies.
5   To be provided with a clear and sequenced **contingency plan** for seeking appropriate advice and support regarding clinical practice in an emergency, during supervisor's absence or within the community (e.g., concerns about a service user's safety).
6   **Protected development time** where you have minimum 3.75 hours a week for personal and professional development activities (such as reading or training).
7   To have a forum in which broader career aspirations are discussed and progression supported through agreed **career development plans** (e.g., identifying gaps in experience in order develop in preparation for clinical training applications).

If you find that these do not reflect your experiences, then you are well within your rights to challenge your supervising psychologist, manager and service. Support can, and sometimes should, also be sought from unions like Unite – who have psychologists in positions such as 'union reps' (i.e., advocates), contacting the ACP-UK or BPS directly, and/or speaking with peers – perhaps from the Clin Psy Forum at www.clinpsy.org.uk/forum/

There are many aspects of supervision that will be outside of your immediate control – such as policies and procedures, or supervisor training, interests and power. Much of how you can make the most of supervision then, can be dependent on building as trusting a relationship with your supervisor as possible – a context where you can take risks and learn from mistakes. Key to your personal and professional development throughout your practice – but particularly within supervision – is reflective-practice and a permission to experiment with your thinking and relating to experiences, practices and theory.

What is reflective-practice?

So, what does it mean to *reflect*? To reflect on something is to be able to think about and reconsider aspects of identity, role, practice and context. Colloquially, you could think of reflection as offering 'fresh eyes' to a situation, but it can also entail adorning lenses that draw upon psychological theory, clinical experience and one's personal life. This can be done retrospectively, through what Schon (1983) calls "reflection on action". You might, for example, reflect on action when unsure about what happened in a recent session, wishing to identify how else you could have responded in the encounter. Likewise, reflecting retrospectively might entail you questioning how you could have managed any emotions experienced during the session differently. Over time, you may feel more confident in reflecting in the moment (reflection-in-action; Schon, 1983), with the potential to adapt and change the course of the session for the better. We demonstrate examples of some reflective questions using these definitions in the *In focus* box below.

In focus: questions of reflective-practice

Reflecting on our practices retrospectively (reflection-on-action):

- What thoughts were going through my mind at the time? Could I have done something differently?
- What was most and least helpful in that session?

Reflecting on our practices in the moment (reflection-in-action):

- I wonder why I am feeling this way?
- What does this question mean in context and how am I being invited to respond to this?

Reflecting on our practices in principle (reflection-on-context):

- How does the service context affect my relationship to this person?
- Does gender play a role in my work?

It is important to note that reflections are not necessarily questions and are often statements. In fact, when we ask ourselves questions as we reflect, as if in dialogue with ourselves, it could be argued that we are in fact demonstrating 'self-reflexivity' (Burnham, 1993). What we mean by self-reflexivity is the actual *process of reflecting* on ourselves and 'how to go on', rather than a lesson learned or endpoint – as described by John Burnham:

> Self-reflexivity as a process in which a [supervisee] makes, takes, or grasps an opportunity to observe, listen to, and question the effects of their practice, then use their responses to their observation/listening to decide "how to go on" . . . The practice of self-reflexivity tends to emphasize the "internal" activity of the [supervisee], as they search their own resources.
>
> (Burnham, 2005, p. 3)

Beyond the essential reflective-practices required within the profession, we would argue that there are some additional threads that can embed reflective-practices into the socio-political contexts that surround practice. In the questioning spirit of *Surviving Clinical Psychology*, we treat the critical and the creative as crucial partners in improving the ways in which clinical psychology engages with reflective-practice and society more broadly. These creative and critical threads include:

- Reflecting on evidence and knowledges (epistemological implications, discourses);
- Reflecting on power and identities (personal, professional and political positionings);
- Reflective processes more broadly, such as 'relational-reflexivity' (Burnham, 2005) – the ability to expose your inner 'workings-out' to others, taking some 'relational-risks' (Mason, 2005) by inviting others to participate in the reflective process.

As such, we do not believe reflective-practice to be a neutral or passive act. However, what we do believe it to be, is an essential tool in which we may organise our abilities and interests, activate our values and apply our principles in practice. With these key threads in mind, we now turn to consider supervision more fully and invite you to give a thought to how reflective and reflexive practices can be used in order to make the most of the supervision, in a way that touches on the lives of the people you to wish to help most creatively and helpfully; that is, to play and take play seriously.

Ways to invest in your development within supervision

The supervisory setting can at times feel like a dress-rehearsal; a curious and playful context in which there is a vague script that all participants roughly know of, but occasionally forget their lines. Supervision creates the opportunity to trial out a range of strategies and approaches; a place where the actors are free to check-in about their lines, go back to the script or manual, and contest it and demand a re-write. As such, we encourage our readers to embrace a full range of approaches – some less intimidating than others – in order to invest in their development and creative futures:

- *Role-plays.* You could role-play a whole range of situations; assessments, particular difficult scenarios or questions, ethical dilemmas, intrusions and ruptures, and so on.
- *Practice.* You could trial out particular assessment tools, such as cognitive tasks.
- *Questioning.* You could invest some time exploring the use of particular question types (e.g., future-orientated). You could figure out what type of question seems to fit in particular situations (e.g., can more direct or closed questions have a place in the therapy room and when?).

- *Self-first.* You could complete the screening tools and questionnaires you ask of the people you meet. This creates the opportunity to experience, empathise, and critique from a different perspective. What is it like to complete psychometrics, in what way do they become meaningful for you, in what ways would you like these integrated into future supervision, etc.
- *Reviewing service-user outcomes.* Discussing not only the use of outcome measures with clients (i.e., the process of completing these, engaging people in discussion about what they can mean), discussing outcome measures within supervision can improve your ability to spot worsening situations for service users and pick up on things you may have otherwise missed out (Lambert, 2010). It is important to include outcome measures as a regular and routine focus of supervision, as evidence increasingly suggests improvements for the people we work with as a result – with an increased speed in reaching good outcomes (Lambert, Harmon, Slade, Whipple, & Hawkins, 2005). Supervision also provides a perfect forum for introducing a critical lens to the use or findings of these tools, based on their reliance on particular constructs and having been tested out on broad or specific sample groups. Good practice warrants questions such as these, in order to question our assumptions in using routine outcome measures and psychometric tools.
- *Hearing and seeing others.* You may seek out shadowing opportunities – joining multidisciplinary team (MDT) meetings or ward rounds, with a particular focus on content (i.e., what is said) and process (i.e., how it is said; roles; power dynamics, etc.). You may join your supervisor for particular assessments or sessions. Your supervisor, with their client's consent, may share recordings or video-footage with you, to model practices and invite discussion. Outside of supervision, you could watch a DVD of others in practice. Ultimately, the idea here would be to return to supervision to discuss your observations and experiences, in order to inform and develop your own practices.
- *Hearing and seeing yourself.* Audio and video-recordings make a great resource for personal and professional development, but they can also be anxiety-provoking for some. In capitalising on this great reflective approach, it seems you just have to take the plunge.

  - *Listening to audio-recording.* Could you record your sessions, listen back to particular extracts in supervision and explore: What theory or idea was I using at this point? What could I have done differently? How was this experienced by the person at the time?
  - *Transcribing audio-recordings.* Could you record your sessions and then transcribe 3–5 minutes' worth of material? Create a column and listen through, making notes about what ideas, hypotheses or theories you were using at particular times. Create another column and listen through again, in what way could you explore this situation differently? Were there times where you had multiple ideas in mind but had to choose a particular line of questioning? If so, what led to that decision? What could you have asked differently?

- *Watching back video-recordings.* Could you video record your sessions? You could apply lots of the same ideas as described above, analysing your reasoning and contributions in sessions. Beyond this, how does it feel to see your *therapist self* sit in a room with others, convening something psychological? What do you observe from your body language? How do others respond to your presence? How do you look to invite contributions from others through non-verbal means?

There are clear ethical implications of recording clinical sessions and interactions, so some of the approaches above take some planning in advance with your supervisor and the people you work with. First, discover the local policies and procedures on this and discuss everything with your supervisor. Second, make sure you have the appropriate equipment that is encrypted (never record on your own equipment). Third, ensure there is a procedure in place that is clear about where to store recordings and then when to delete these. When you have an idea about what provisions are in place, and have sought supervision to discuss the practicalities, your hopes from this, and the ethical implications – you will need to discuss this with the people you work with, making sure they are fully informed of your intentions, the uses of such recordings, their storage/destruction, and their rights in terms of refusal and withdrawal with no implications on the service offered. Written consent is always essential and your service should have a consent form and details available, or you and your supervisor can create one together. This is one way of managing expectations of delivering a safe and effective service, one that encourages learning.

In focus: creating supervisory contracts

Where there are expectations of one another in a relationship, it can be useful to draw up a contract that explicitly names these expectations and any associated actions. Contracting structures conversations around expectations and enables differences in approaches to be voiced, and any dilemmas to be faced together. Additionally, it can provide a reference point for future discussions – revisiting and appraising previously agreed expectations or goals as the individual or relationship develops over time. The contracting of supervision does not necessarily need to be arduous, and can focus on particular areas for future development, rather than supervision as a whole, if preferred. Contracting for supervision may include:

- **Practical arrangements:** when, where, how frequently, and for how long should we hold supervision?
- **Expectations:** Who brings what to supervision, who prepares what, and so on.
- **Focus of supervision:** Whether there are clear distinctions in types of supervision, for example, supervision focusing primarily on dilemmas faced or ruptures in clinical work.

- **Focus on dialogue:** Exploring the preferred ways of talking and listening. Instructing your supervisor about your preferred way for them to listen and contribute to your conversations (and identifying their preferred ways of listening and contributing). For example, providing ideas or curiously questioning.
- **Recurring agenda:** It may be that you agree on a standard set of items that need revisiting each week (e.g., outcome measures).
- **Key area for development:** Highlight a particular competency needing to be developed and using supervision to guide this skill in particular.
- **Methods of work:** Agreeing on preferred learning styles and ways in which development can be most nourished, for example using role-plays within supervision.
- **Trouble-shooting – relational:** Agreeing on how relationships with others can be considered throughout supervision.
- **Trouble-shooting – practical:** Agreeing on actions to take, if running late, for example.

The training journey can be exposing, particularly as we are likely to internalise pressures to perform – often expecting much more of ourselves than we would ask of others. These scripts of performance can often have much to do with the contexts in which we find ourselves, our own histories of achievement and help-seeking, and our cultural and familial upbringing. Our own social, familial and cultural histories, and how these experiences connect with our practice, inform who we become as supervisees and our emerging professional identities.

What's in a tree? Integrating the personal and familial into the professional through the use of genograms

Genograms, otherwise thought of as 'family trees', are symbolic representations of someone's family of origin. They can be extremely useful tools within supervision to guide exploration of personal scripts that guide our practices, having been widely used as tools to enhance the self-reflection skills of those in roles of applied psychology (Braverman, 1997; McGoldrick, Gerson, & Shellenberger, 1999). Guidance on creating cultural genograms, for example, can be found elsewhere (Hardy & Laszloffy, 1995; Shellenberger et al., 2007).

In exploring how the personal may influence the professional within supervisory contexts, you may be able to identify blind-spots or topics you've been holding back from addressing. Very little emphasis has been given on the use of genograms in preparing aspiring psychologists for a new supervisory relationship or for even becoming supervisors themselves in the future (Aten & Madson, 2008). It is with this in mind, that we now draw your attention to the following *Reflective activity*, in which we invite you to develop your own supervisory genogram.

Reflective activity: developing your own supervisory genogram (Aten & Madson, 2008)

Throughout our careers, we encounter a number of supervisors, as we transition from one work context to the next. The experience of changing supervisors over time shape us as supervisees.

The supervision genogram is a symbolic representation of these supervisory experiences, relationships and transitions (Aten & Madson, 2008). Its goal is to highlight complex patterns and influences that can promote self-reflection and self-awareness as well as understanding of the supervisory process. It welcomes you to consider the influence and impact of previous supervisory relationships on your current professional role and relationships. The visual representation of these may allow us to better conceptualise our relationships with our supervisors and help us identify themes and connect patterns across our experiences.

How to make a supervision genogram?

- Draw a horizontal line across the page and list your supervisors in chronological order (see Figure 3.1).
- In principle, this exercise uses the same symbols as family genograms to describe aspects related to the supervisor, such as gender (e.g., shape), and the nature of the supervisory relationship (e.g., two solid lines for a close relationship). However, you can use whatever images or symbols are most meaningful to you.
- The dates and service context can also be added as well as the frequency of supervision (e.g., once weekly).

An example of a supervision genogram

'08-'10	'10-'11	'11-'13	'13-'15	'15-'18
CAMHS	Inpatient	CMHT	IAPT	Older adult CMHT
1 x week	1 x week	1 x week	1 x week	1 x week

Once you have drawn out your supervisory genogram, it can then be useful to ask yourself a range of questions about this, like the following (adapted from Aten & Madson, 2008):

- What factors shaped the focus of your supervision experiences?
- What personal/professional characteristics of your supervisors do you admire and want to emulate? Which are you less keen on and do not wish to recreate?
- How were differences in opinion and/or conflicts between you and your supervisor handled?
- How did these particular supervisory experiences add to your developing/emerging sense of yourself as pre-qualified psychologist, health care worker, trainee, or similar?
- How did culture impact your supervisory relationships (e.g., race/ethnicity, gender)?

In completing the supervisory genogram exercise, you may have revealed previously unnoticed links between your experiences – unmasking the reasons why you found one relationship so different from another, or developed a sense of who taught and supported you the most or least over time. What is clear, is that the ways in which we narrate our experiences can change our relationships not only to our supervisors, but with ourselves as supervisees. This means that the ways in which we tell our stories matter, because it plays a key part in shaping who we are or see ourselves becoming. The ways in which we make sense of our supervisory histories then, can impact our present practices and relationships in meaningful ways – influencing the ways in which we use supervision in the future.

Concluding thoughts

Supervision offers an opportunity to make visible aspects of our personal and professional selves, with a view to facilitate development within our careers and to better the lives of those individuals who access our support. We have presented a range of ideas about discovering the ways in which you can make the most of your supervisory relationships – as supervision is not only a crucial part of our professional development, but a place for playfulness to be taken very seriously. Supervision is entrenched in the political – acting as an interface of identities, roles, interests and power. Indeed, we hope you leave this chapter with a willingness to take some personal, professional and political risks, as we steer you towards a supervision that is as challenging, as it is curious and containing.

Acknowledgements

We would like to thank Candice Williams, Jenny Doe, Faye Harrison Yuill and Andrew Perry for their kind contributions to this chapter.

References

Aten, J. D., & Madson, M. B. (2008). The supervision genogram: A tool for preparing supervisors-in-training. *Psychotherapy: Theory, Research, Practice, Training, 45*(1), 111–116.

Braverman, S. (1997). The use of genograms in supervision. *The Complete Systemic Supervisor: Context, Philosophy, and Pragmatics*, 349–362.

British Psychological Society. (2007). *Guidelines for the employment of assistant psychologists*. Leicester: British Psychological Society.

Burnham, J. (1993). Systemic supervision: The evolution of reflexivity in the context of the supervisory relationship. *Human Systems: The Journal of Systemic Consultation and Management, 4*(3&4), 349–381.

Burnham, J. (2005). Relational reflexivity: A tool for socially constructing therapeutic relationships. In *The space between: Experience, context and process in the therapeutic relationship*. London: Karnac.

Cushway, D., & Knibbs, J. (2004). Trainees' and supervisors' perceptions of supervision. *Supervision and Clinical Psychology: Theory, Practice and Perspectives*, 162–185.

Goodyear, R. K., & Guzzardo, C. R. (2000). Psychotherapy supervision and training. In S. D. Brown & R. W. Lent (Eds.), Handbook of counseling psychology (pp. 83–108). Hoboken, NJ, USA: John Wiley & Sons Inc.

Hardy, K. V., & Laszloffy, T. A. (1995). The cultural genogram: Key to training culturally competent family therapists. *Journal of Marital and Family Therapy, 21*(3), 227–237.

Lambert, M. J. (2010). Yes, it is time for clinicians to routinely monitor treatment outcome. In B. L. Duncan, S. D. Miller, B. E. Wampold, & M. A. Hubble (Eds.), The heart and soul of change: Delivering what works in therapy (pp. 239–266). Washington, DC, USA: American Psychological Association.

Lambert, M. J., Harmon, C., Slade, K., Whipple, J. L., & Hawkins, E. J. (2005). Providing feedback to psychotherapists on their patients' progress: Clinical results and practice suggestions. *Journal of clinical psychology, 61*(2), 165–174.

Mason, B. (2005). Relational risk-taking and the therapeutic relationship. In C. Flaskas, A. Perlesz, & B. Mason (Eds.), *The space between: Experience, context and process in the therapeutic relationship* (pp. 157–170). London: Karnac.

Mason, B. (2010). Six aspects of supervision and the training of supervisors. *Journal of Family Therapy, 32*(4), 436–439.

McGoldrick, M., Gerson, R., & Shellenberger, S. (1999). *Genograms: Assessment and intervention*. New York: Norton.

Milne, D. (2007). An empirical definition of clinical supervision. *British Journal of Clinical Psychology, 46*(4), 437–447.

Scaife, J. (2019). *Supervision in clinical practice: A practitioner's guide*. Abingdon, UK: Routledge.

Schon, D. (1983). *The reflective practitioner: How professionals think in action*. New York: Basic Books.

Shellenberger, S., Dent, M. M., Davis-Smith, M., Seale, J. P., Weintraut, R., & Wright, T. (2007). Cultural genogram: A tool for teaching and practice. *Families, Systems, & Health, 25*(4), 367.

Vetere, A., & Dallos, R. (2016). Supervision and attachment narratives: Using an attachment narrative approach in clinical supervision. In *Interacting selves: Systemic solutions for personal and professional development in counselling and psychotherapy*. London: Routledge.

Vetere, A., & Stratton, P. (2016). *Interacting Selves: Systemic solutions for personal and professional development in counselling and psychotherapy*. Oxon: Routledge.

Wheeler, S. (2004). A review of supervisor training in the UK. In *Supervision and clinical psychology* (pp. 30–50). Abingdon, UK: Routledge.

Woodruff, G., & Wang, M. (2005). Assistant psychologists and their supervisors: Role or semantic confusion. *Clinical Psychology, 48*, 33–36.

Chapter 4

Restorying the journey
Enriching practice before training

James Randall, Sarah Oliver, Jacqui Scott,
Amy Lyons, Hannah Morgan, Jessica Saffer
and Lizette Nolte

Routes to clinical training can be diverse, often with unclear and confusing stories about how to succeed and the ways in which you can make the most of your journey to qualification. This chapter attempts to address these uncertain and complex times through considering the challenges faced and the opportunities created when seeking to become a clinical psychologist. In writing this chapter, we predominantly took our inspiration from the ideas of community psychology, emphasising the importance of power, social contexts and prevention (Orford, 2008); narrative therapy, whereby consideration is given to dominant stories that are told about people or phenomena, and the alternative discourses available (White & Epston, 1990); and systemic theory, which looks at the relational and contextual nature of problems (Dallos & Draper, 2015). Using these theories, this chapter will introduce ways in which readers can hold onto hope, and enrich their journey to clinical training through a process of exploration, critical-thinking, reflective-practice and creativity. We hope that this chapter will alleviate fears about there being a correct route into training, and instead help readers to consider their own relationship to their journeys, connect and strengthen one another, and support readers to embrace and learn from the turbulence that can be experienced when pursuing a career in clinical psychology.

Routes to clinical training in brief

Training to become a clinical psychologist takes time and is not necessarily always straight forward. Psychology is an increasingly popular choice for those continuing with education within the UK. For example, 73,390 individuals selected psychological studies at A Levels in 2013–2014 (Ofsted, 2015) and 106,000 began their undergraduate courses in psychology (McGhee, 2015). Many psychology undergraduates go on to explore other directly relevant positions, forensic and educational psychology for example. For those that decide to pursue a career in clinical psychology, there are a range of ways in which individuals can go about this and a number of books offer practical advice and support on this – most notably, Golding and Moss (2019) who revisit and update the work of Alice Knight on *How to Become a Clinical Psychologist* (2005). One key aspect at the undergraduate stage is completing a course accredited by the British Psychological Society (BPS), which provides Graduate Basis for Chartered Membership on completion. Without this, applicants would then need to complete conversion courses in order to meet the criteria for further progression towards doctoral training. As reflected in earlier stages of career progression, clinical psychology remains a popular choice for psychology graduates – with many proceeding to complete their master's in it. In the UK, there are 33 training courses that each have their own unique identities and preferred ways of working (e.g., with noticeable differences in epistemological alignments). To train as a clinical psychologist in the UK, individuals are likely to have practiced in a range of roles; working across public and private sector contexts. There is potential for changes to routes to clinical training in the UK, with continual reviews of funding arrangements for clinical training and new developments for clinical practice, such as clinical associate roles in applied psychology.

Commonly held scripts about the necessity of assistant psychologist posts can sometimes be unhelpful, as they can overshadow other creative and unique routes to clinical training. Take for example, the peer-recovery worker who has lived experience of psychiatric services, or the applicant who has worked for several years in the charitable sector with survivors of trauma. These posts do not fit so readily into any career trajectories or pathways to clinical training, yet produce trainees who can offer meaningful contributions to the training community and wider profession. In 2018, there were 3866 applications for 593 publicly funded training places – reflecting a success rate of just 15% (Clearing House, 2019). This means that there are a significant number of candidates each year who are unable to start their clinical training and are faced with making decisions about their next steps. In this light, individuals will often revisit why it is that they wish to train in clinical psychology, ask themselves what type of clinical psychologist it is that they wish to become, and remind themselves of the underlying values that guide them along the way.

The values we bring

Given the extent of dedication that is often required in training for this career, it can be useful to reflect on the values that guide us in this career path and more broadly, in life. Values can be thought of as "our heart's deepest desires for the way we want to interact with and relate to the world, other people, and ourselves" (Harris, 2008, p. 1). The core philosophical underpinnings of our profession are characterised by four key ethical values: respect, competence, responsibility, and integrity (BPS, 2018). It is likely that we also bring a set of personal values on our journey. Working and living in line with these values is what brings us meaning, enables us to feel committed to our aspirations, and gives us the energy to continue our journey through difficult times. As such, we invite you to consider the values you bring to your work next.

Reflective activity: values exercise

This is an exercise that can take some time and thought.

First, think of some key moments or times in your life: times when you felt particularly happy, proud or satisfied and fulfilled.

Ask yourself the following questions, and write down the key words that come up:

- What was it about that time that made me feel happy/proud/satisfied?
- Who else was around and what did important others notice about what I was (or we were) doing?
- What other things about this time contributed to me feeling this way?
- Why did I think particularly of that time and what made it memorable?

Keep asking yourself the questions until you have a list of at least 15–20 words. You might describe these words as qualities, attributes or even values. The list might include words such as: achievement, social, family, friends, community, success, creative, generous, sharing, justice, culture, worthwhile, growth and so on (if you feel stuck, look online for lists of values, but only after you have thought about it yourself).

Now work through your list, comparing pairs of words: if I had to choose, which one is more important? You can cross off words that you decide are actually less meaningful to you, or arrange your words in order of importance. Ideally, you end up with a list of remaining words, and the topmost on the list are what we may think of as your core values.

Lastly, check these against yourself: do they seem important?

Do they fit with how you see yourself and how you would want to live your life?

Would you feel proud to tell others about them?

What would you like to change (over next few months?) in order to live your life more in line with your values?

What might others (namely, your family, friends, colleagues or clients) notice if you were living and working more in line with these values?

Inspiration for this exercise was taken from Acceptance Commitment Therapy (e.g., Hayes, 2004); for further exercises please consult LeJeune and Luoma (2016), or the Association for Contextual Behavioural Science (https://contextualscience.org/resources_for_clinicians).

Overcoming the obstacles for getting onto training: remaining hopeful whilst facing uncertainty

For those navigating their way towards clinical training, a rich journey lies ahead where challenges will be faced, opportunities discovered and your identity as a psychologist will emerge from the mistakes you live and learn from. There is no doubt that at times, this journey will be uncertain – and here, we consider some of the obstacles faced and reflect on how individuals can enrich their journey through the very act of navigating through those perceived stumbling-blocks.

Often during the pre-qualifying journey, individuals attend events and workshops specifically addressing this period of their development and voice their concerns about the impact of the process. In writing this chapter we felt it is important that the voices of those living these challenges are given the platform to consider these challenges fully. We also consider experiences of representing pre-qualified individuals within clinical psychology's professional body – including James' involvement in editing and overseeing the BPS' *Alternative Handbook for Clinical Training* (2019) – where trainees across all courses were surveyed every year.

Those aspiring for clinical training often have to juggle multiple demands and expectations across clinical, personal and other professional realms. As we will discuss below, the obstacles faced can vary in nature, but it is not uncommon for individuals to experience them all at some point. As you read, you may recognise some of these obstacles and dilemmas in the way you describe your own experiences or how you have felt about your journey so far. In writing this chapter, we are unable to capture *all* perceived challenges along the way, but instead provide a snapshot of common experiences. As part of this process, we made an open invitation to trainees and clinical psychologists to write a letter addressed to you, our reader, about some of these experiences, requesting them to keep in mind their own journeys as they revisit what it is like to apply for clinical training (see the *In focus* box).

In focus: a rewarding, but rocky road – a letter from practising psychologists

Dear Aspiring Clinical Psychologist,

We're so pleased to see you here, pursuing a career in clinical psychology. With your permission, we'd like to share some of our reflections on our experiences, and the things we wish we'd known when we were in your position; not because we have 'the answers', but because we recognise how tough the process can be for some people. We acknowledge that we write this from the privileged position of now being qualified clinical psychologists, and that each person's experience will be different. However, we hope that our words will remind you that you are not alone, and will suggest some ways to help you survive this venture.

Accessing support from those around you is key to enabling you to acknowledge and work through the many potential frustrations, uncertainties and disappointments along the way, but this can be difficult. Friends and family not working in similar fields can struggle to understand the level of competition, and can seem to assume that you'll "get on no problem." Peer relationships can evoke feelings of jealousy and competition, not to mention increasing one another's frenetic anxiety. Your relationship with yourself can become one driven by self-criticism and self-doubt. Despite all this, it is vital to find people and places where you can talk openly about the ups and downs of the process. Try to listen to what you need at this time and seek support from those most likely to meet your needs.

It is unsurprising that when we are striving towards something we are passionate about, but where there is significant competition and pressure, we can develop very high expectations for ourselves. This can lead to a loud 'inner critic,' and opens us up to comparing ourselves to others and perceiving our imperfections as failings or flaws. We acknowledge that the current application process and systems around it are inherently unfair and we would encourage you to view your emotions as normal reactions to an abnormal situation. Try to engage in a compassionate stance towards yourself, and towards any emotions you experience, pleasant or otherwise. Instead of seeking perfection, aim for 'good enough,' and take the time to celebrate your achievements as well as your bravery for persevering with an undertaking that requires you to be so vulnerable. Those feelings of uncertainty, of being 'an imposter', and of desperately wanting that magic wand do not disappear once you become a trainee. They are things we still experience on a regular basis. We have found that being open about these thoughts, through reflection and supervision, have enabled us to accept, tolerate and learn from them. It also enables conversations that allow for connection and compassion as we recognise that other people feel the same way.

We hope that by encouraging more transparent discussions about our own experiences, we can also give voice to the parts of us that may feel 'different' from our peers. There is something of a stereotype of a clinical psychology trainee (white, female, middle-class, mid-20s etc.), which can lead us to feel somehow 'less than' if we do not fit that picture. There are many different movements trying to diversify the profession, to recognise how much we can learn from each other's experiences and perspectives. When we adopt a position of 'us and them,' in whatever context, we instantly create distance and divides. Try to bring curiosity towards any part of yourself or that of others, something that feels different, to value its uniqueness and the learning it offers. Seek out others, share your views, and know that representation matters.

There can be a temptation to view the year(s) on the cycle of applications, interviews and seeming-rejections as simply a series of tick-box exercises to strengthen your application and move closer to training. Whilst there are inevitably aspects of this, try to see the value in those experiences for their own merit. Each of those roles bring opportunities for development, to see different perspectives and build the foundation for your own clinical identity. Don't be afraid to seek out creative, alternative opportunities, as they can all enrich your understanding of what it is to be human. Nurture your dreams and goals, and the things and people that bring you joy. Try not to lose sight of the fact that whilst it can be a rewarding and fulfilling career, it is not the only career. No job is worth sacrificing your own health or wellbeing for. It can be sensible, and even freeing, to consider what your 'Plan B' (and C and D) may be. There is no shame in deciding to pursue an alternative route, or even to take a 'time out' and return to the clinical psychology pathway in the future.

We are conscious that we could write for many pages about the various possibilities and pitfalls on the way to qualifying as a clinical psychologist (as well as afterwards!) but that may ignore the uniqueness of your experience and give temptation to follow our paths, instead of using our reflections to shape your own journey. Finally, it seems important to pause and acknowledge the many layers of pressure and threat that may exist within the systems we are working within, and how this can inflame our own tendencies toward self-criticism. Be kind to yourself, know that you are 'good enough', and try to turn towards the parts of you that may be hurting with warmth and compassion. We wish you all the luck with your endeavours and hope to cross paths and hear your story one day.

Hannah, Paul, Laura, Rowan, Alice, Maria,
Kat, Ché, Julia and Christy

Messy and testing processes

The ways in which the application and/or training processes are designed and implemented can at times lead to particular anxieties at the individual and collective level. For example, uncertainty about future funding for clinical training appears to lead to increasing pressures to *perform* '*more*', accompanied by a competitiveness and emerging sense of urgency in order to succeed quickly and 'stand-out'. These conditions appear, in part, to have perpetuated individualistic scripts that fuel disconnection and hostility in some circles. The contexts in which we find ourselves can lead to these particular conditions, which require some navigation in order to survive. If curious about how to make sense of these processes and the impact on the self, you may wish to consider using psychological theories to formulate these conditions and context. In doing so, we wonder what

opportunities can arise for connection and change from formulating the circumstances clinical psychology as a profession finds itself in. For further exploration
of these areas, curious readers are advised to see Chapters 11 and 15.

At the same time, the conditions faced when applying for clinical training can
lead to despair, disconnection and damaged hopes. As such, ending up feeling
quite fragile, alone or lost at points in your journey is by no means unusual –
but not inevitable. It becomes increasingly important for us to understand the
ways in which people survive and thrive in the process, and to share these stories.
Our hope is to begin to connect people through the shared desire to change these
unhelpful dynamics, and to enrich their journeys.

Fitting the 'mould': the need to be perfect, good-enough or something else

Individuals often wonder whether they fit the 'mould' for the good-enough can-
didate. Even many good-enough candidates may end up not getting places due to
structural limitations, such as the number of available places, or lack of financial
support for self-funding. Scripts about 'fitting the mould' relate in part to broader
worries about the extent to which people can be 'themselves' – questioning what
parts of the self are acceptable to give voice to or not, and when and how to do
so. Likewise, others may worry about concealing aspects of their identity in order
to stand a greater chance of gaining a place. In doing so, scripts about who to be
are created and sustained over time, as we crave a sense of certainty and direction
about what to do and who to be.

Individuals can then, in a way, build on barriers through privileging narratives
and stories about themselves as not being 'good enough'. For many candidates,
striving and performing to the highest level is a well-rewarded, socially sanctioned and desirable way to be. Perfectionism is rife in modern society – and this
is no different for aspiring psychologists. However, this pattern of relentless 'bet-
tering' creates a recipe for self-critique beyond simply learning from one's misfortunes and mishaps. Perfectionism can present itself as an attractive accomplice
and powerful motivator to strive forward as an individual – after all, why would
you not wish to keep on striving to be the best? However, when we consider
the context of clinical training, including the interest and demand that outweighs
training places available each year – no wonder we encounter competitive comparison. The unfortunate combination of perfectionist individualism and competitive processes sets up unhelpful cycles that for many prevents an enriched and
fulfilling journey. As we would note in delivering psychological therapies, these
'vicious cycles' of perfection may help in the short term but they often feed into
the struggle in the long term.

'Giving up or giving in' are certainly understandable ways of avoiding anticipated failures. Resignation from the dream of training can certainly relinquish
you of those heavy and hard-to-shift emotions at the time. Alongside this though,
there can be a sense that the threads you have spent so long weaving into your

anticipated future in psychology are fraying – perhaps tearing, drawing you to a sense of guilt or regret at the idea of giving up – owing yourself the fight to persist. Examples of these pressures to fit 'the mould' can be drawn from the online discussion website called *the Clin Psy Forum* (see www.clinpsy.org.uk/forum), where individuals can post questions and discuss specific issues relating to clinical psychology and training routes. For example, we encountered one post entitled "*I heard someone with . . . didn't get on, so I'll never make it*" (Miriam, 2011). This highlights some of the dangers in drawing conclusions of what it takes to get onto clinical training through comparisons with peers. Many factors contribute to success in the application process; some within your control, others not.

Unrelenting uncertainty and the search for safety

Individuals experience great uncertainty about 'what to do next' in clinical psychology circles. With no clear pathways into clinical training, aspiring trainees can feel lost and overwhelmed by the multitude of possible routes to take. Many ask questions as to whether they *need* certain experiences in order to get onto clinical training (as discussed above). Within these complex conditions, a significant obstacle for aspiring psychologists is the uncertainty of success – facing the possibility that they may never get onto clinical training. Without clear and secure pathways to qualification, aspiring psychologists take a chance in what may seem like a monopoly of one's future.

Although uncertainty often elicits feelings of discomfort, it can sustain curiosity and creativity over time (Mason, 1993, 2019). If we were able to change our relationship with uncertainty earlier in our journeys and to learn to love, or at least tolerate, uncertainty – in what ways would our practice have been different? Would we have been able to resist the pressures of competition with peers more effectively? Perhaps pause for a moment and consider the last time you were *so* certain about something with a client or colleague – what other possibilities were there?

What do we mean when we talk about uncertainty in this way? Barry Mason (1993), a systemic psychotherapist, sets out four positions of (un)certainty:

- *Safe certainty* involves the finding of a solution that removes uncertainty. For example, in the UK this includes having an undergraduate degree that has been accredited by the BPS – without this, you are unable to become a clinical psychologist.
- *Unsafe certainty* involves being very fixed on what the solution to is, without necessarily seeing other possibilities (e.g., "they struggle to see the forest for the trees" [Mason, 2019, p. 4]). We imagine this is a common experience for us all, in and outside of work. Examples of unsafe certainty may include practising in line with the belief that one *must* have work experience as an assistant psychologist to *ever* be a clinical psychologist (N.B. this is not the case).
- *Unsafe uncertainty* involves feeling disempowered, confused and unable to see any solutions in a moment – a likely point of despair. Examples of unsafe

uncertainty may include experiences of hopelessness and rejection following numerous unsuccessful applications on one's 'last shot' submission. We
recognise moments such as this throughout all of our journeys – as supervision and solidarity with others can take significant roles in enabling us to
move into safe grounds. These can be extremely distressing moments, with
self-care being essential in order to sustain and move you to a position where
opportunities can arise.

- *Safe uncertainty* involves allowing situations and solutions to emerge and
evolve. Examples of this may include engaging in supervisor-led invitations
to consider one's personal story in relation to the people you work with, or
volunteering for a 'live' reflective discussion or being part of a panel discussion at a conference. It is through these moments that we have found we can
learn through making mistakes or through experimenting with different ways
of being present in our work.

Whilst practising in line with this notion of safe uncertainty may sustain our
curiosity over time, open up new opportunities and support us in our creative
endeavours, we wish to share some words of caution. When learning to 'tolerate'
uncertainty, we do not wish to become complacent or reluctant to pursue certainty.
If we sat only with uncertainty, we could never learn or progress beyond the present moment or indeed experience some sort of existential crisis as we persist with
our certain ways that the world only seems to invalidate. In this light, the systemic
concept of circularity can really lend towards the nature in which we formulate or
hypothesise our contributions and influences in interactions. We must not 'marry'
our hypotheses (Cecchin, Lane, & Ray, 1992), through embracing uncertainty,
but instead use it as a companion in our journeys. Most certainly, we need to dip
in and out of learning the 'ins and outs' of all aspects of training – but if we can
master the art of feeling less uncomfortable with uncertainty early-on, the road
will not necessarily be less turbulent – but you will feel more confident about
what might lurk around the corner.

The perfect trap: doubts and never being "good enough"

Similar in nature to experiences of perfectionism and desires to fit the mould, is a
growing sense of doubt. Many people go on to describe experiencing an 'imposter
syndrome' and in doing so, emphasise the competencies of others, whilst under-
valuing, critiquing and negating one's own competencies. This sense of being the
'fraud' and waiting for others to discover your relative inabilities is not uncommon
at various stages of career development. Throughout the journey, individuals often
require the support of mentors and supervisors to deconstruct what it means to be
capable and competent, in order to consider what can be realistically achieved at
different points in training. For example, the conscious competence model (Howell, 1982) can be used to consider the extent to which individuals perceive themselves to be competent, or indeed, incompetent. Although incompetence may at

face value seem a rather undesirable characteristic, with effective support from important others, individuals can become more aware of their areas of strength and weakness – opening up the possibility for self-evaluation and changes in practice to become more competent over time.

Side-stepping competition

Exiting patterns of competitive comparison can also lead to helpful ways forward. If you were working with someone with similar struggles to yourself, in what way could you understand their difficulties and how would this shape your ideas of moving forward? In our practice, we can sometimes forget to apply the very same principles we consider useful for others, to ourselves, and so here, we will begin to explore narrative approaches that could be useful to sustain us and enrich our journeys.

Services are often structured to enable particular types of stories to be told; that is, for particular accounts of *distress* or those of a *problem-focus* to be retold (White & Epston, 1990). As an aspiring psychologist, you may have noticed similar practices within the community of aspiring psychologists or the clinical requests placed upon you. In this light, how different would practices be if we were instead to focus on the resources, strengths, resilience and community of individuals? This is the very notion of narrative therapy, a progressive shift from problem-saturated narratives to alternative stories (White & Epston, 1990).

What do we mean by this moving towards alternative stories? This process is different from 'positive data logging' – a cognitive behaviour therapy (CBT) approach to observe and gather exceptions to more problem-focused accounts (e.g., achievements, acts of kindness). Building one's alternative account can involve a similar process that involves moving from a perspective of "what I did poorly at interview" to a position of "what I did well at interview". What then becomes important from a narrative therapy perspective is to find the history of these actions, that is to link them to events in the past that might explain why and how this went well; and to consider implications for the future; for example, if I was to be able to draw on these actions more in the future, what new developments might this lead to. Therefore, narrative theory involves a consideration of how these particular events can be organised across time to represent particular themes (e.g., survival, progress). That is, these different aspects of one's story are not only noted but are integrated into the person's meaning-making, their story, and their sense of self. This process can reflect significant shifts in one's appraisal of the situation, from seeing oneself as a 'fraud' to a more nuanced sense of developing in one's role as a pre-qualified psychologist: competent but still learning.

These different ways of viewing our experiences and indeed, in retelling, our experiences become not only meaningful, but conjure up the drive to act in different ways to sustain this preferred way of understanding ourselves and our story. When we think of different stories about ourselves, it can be difficult to shake off those sticky, problem-focused stories about our achievements, or lack of. In the activity below, we invite you to explore these alternative stories further.

Reflective activity: using narrative questioning to invite your alternative stories

We recommend you meet with a friend to work through this process of exploring your alternative stories together. The other person may wish to listen in a way that notices the threads that can tie your experiences with (e.g., a commitment to put the person's voice first; wanting to create a more just society) or the unvoiced themes that seem to underlie your exclamations (e.g., "You survived every single challenge this process has chucked at you"). Michael White explored similar ideas in his writings on *double-listening* (White, 2003). Below we include some questions to help guide you as interviewer and listener, as influenced by White and Epston, (White & Epston, 1990, 2005) and Carey and Russell (2003):

- Identify a moment in your journey where something changed for you, that you would like to talk about further – talk about this in as much detail as you can.
- What was your intention/why do you think you wanted to do that? Or why do you feel it was important to talk about today?
- Would you say that this reflects particular values or beliefs that you hold?
- What would you say are the hopes and dreams associated with these values?
- What would you say are the principles of living that represent these hopes and dreams?
- What are the commitments you make, or would like to make, in order to pursue this in your life?

If you are taking the role of the listener, perhaps sharing your thoughts can be useful for your friend to shift towards alternative stories. Listen out for those quieter or unvoiced stories of intentions or purposes; values/beliefs; hopes and dreams; principles for living; and commitments (Carey & Russell, 2003).

What follows in this chapter now, are some brief reflections and thoughts on writing applications and interviewing – however, this is by no means exhaustive and we would also recommend you seek the advice of friends and colleagues. For a range of other practical ideas, we recommend the Division of Clinical Psychology (DCP) annual *Alternative Handbook for Clinical Training* (BPS, 2019) for course-specific feedback and ideas from current trainees, and more generally, Golding and Moss' book on *How to Become a Clinical Psychologist* (2019). As you explore these topics, we wonder what possible opportunities could unfold if you were to revisit the above narrative questions in relation to applications and interviews.

Writing applications and facing interviews

Applying for clinical training can be a daunting task, where you face the challenge of summarising your journey so far into a brief personal statement to secure the interest and curiosity of your short-listing audience. Similar can be said of clinical interviews, where individuals are invited to demonstrate how they are well suited for clinical training. Sometimes the application or interview process can appear to demand seemingly paradoxical requests: the modest yet confident self, the reflective yet decisive self, the comprehensive yet concise self, the personal yet professional self. In what ways do you feel you could demonstrate these range of qualities, whilst at the same time manage these conflicting demands? Below, we consider some strategies you may wish to experiment with.

When applying for clinical training:

- **Prepare yourself for writing and do not just jump in.** Revisit values-based tasks and other activities within this book in order to consider: *which course would appreciate my approach most? Where would I feel most at home – in terms of philosophical approach, community values, research interests, and so on?*
- **Consider the ways in which the self can be made visible in your application form.** *How can you stand out in a way that is meaningful and authentic to you and your values?* Rather than a form that is job-focused (e.g., "In my role as a/my experiences as a . . . taught me . . ."), perhaps focus on your values first (e.g., "I learned a lot when faced with the challenges of . . .").
- **Be as clear as you can be during the process and make the short-lister's job as easy as possible.** Share your form with a psychologist, but also with a non-psychology friend – if they have to ask what particular terms or phrases mean, consider simplifying your writing style and using language that is easily accessible to all. Listen to the feedback of others, but do not completely lose yourself in the process.

In approaching clinical interviews, individuals may wish to consider their previous interview experiences. Did you seek feedback? What were your strengths and what were your areas requiring development? We have found that a helpful reminder is to *prepare yourself, not just your answers.* Interviews can be very stressful for anyone and we will never be able to know everything, detail everything we want to, or give that 'perfect' answer, or demonstrate every skill we have picked up along the way. There can be a lot of pressure to succeed at interview and so it is understandable that many attempt to prepare for all possible questions and variations. For your next interview, in what ways would an approach focused more on process over content enable you to give voice to your competencies and make most visible the practitioner you feel you can become? We have indicated some initial thoughts next, but encourage you to meet with peers and further discuss the similarities and differences in your approach.

- What if you prepared the *process* of interviewing: mock interviews with friends, family or supervisors; have 'ghost interviewers' as you speak your answers aloud (perhaps to a Dictaphone or pet). Perhaps listen back to your answers and 'become the interviewer' – what do you feel worked well? What would you liked to have heard more about?
- What if you prepared yourself in terms of *self-care*? Make sure you have time to develop your understanding of your body and own wellbeing; how do you manage physical signs of anxiety – could you use mindfulness techniques? Or narrative ideas, such as the 'club of life', which we describe elsewhere in Chapter 12. Could you use transitional objects to 'carry' your confidence and comfort into interview with you? Are there other psychological theories that could help you make the most of your interview opportunity? Perhaps ask your peers for their ideas on this too?

As we draw this chapter to a close, we wish to draw your attention to another means of enrichment and a possible invitation to restory your journey thus far, or for the road ahead. That invitation is to embrace the creativity that can be accomplished through critical engagement and an irreverence for the conventions of clinical psychology and the profession itself.

How learned rebels, trouble-makers and critical thinkers can enrich the journey

There appears an appetite for a more liberating and democratised clinical psychology within the community of aspiring psychologists – with an emerging energy across practice, research and academia. There is no doubt that these endeavours appear to pull together pre-qualified communities, highlighting what are often shared underlying values – rooted in a desire to change society for the better. These drives for changing the social-materialist conditions, remind us of the importance of critical thinking and collaboration with others. As Pieter Nel wrote, "we urgently need to welcome more learned rebels and trouble-makers onto clinical training" (Nel, 2012, p. 20). We wonder, in what ways could your trouble-making be made visible and available to your peers within clinical psychology – in a way that hopes to address social inequalities, improve collaboration and support, and align with your values. The DCP accreditation guidelines, for example, require courses to support individuals to become critical consumers, interpreters and disseminators more broadly (DCP, 2017). What would it mean to practice in such a manner at your stage of training now? Take this book for example; if you were to revisit its pages with a critical lens, in what way would your consumption and interpretation change? How would the way you talk about its content, and the ways in which you implement its ideas, change for you?

In considering the costs of being a 'trouble-maker' (Nel, 2010, 2012) early on, one may wish to consider some ideas in order to alleviate any associated anxieties:

- Invest in knowing yourself and your own self-development; practicing reflective activities, mindful self-awareness, journaling, values identification, clarification and continual revisiting, so as to make this journey authentically your own and find the 'rebel' within yourself.
- Inform yourself on the topic areas of interest – gathering perspectives across a wide range of sources will help enrich your understanding. Reach-out beyond psychology and read related work from other disciplines, and importantly, read the work of those you tend to disagree with – you may be surprised what you can learn.
- However, do not just read; discuss these with friends, and present these topics at meetings. The more these topics stay in your dialogue, the richer your understanding and the more likely you are to debate, persuade and negotiate on inevitably complex problems when you face challenges along the way.
- Find allies along the way. What this does not mean, is simply associating with people that agree with you. Find people who listen to you, but can also hold you to account, challenge you, and be curious about how you came to your position. These people will be your true allies, enabling and supporting you to reach your best on your journey.
- Consider your perceived position with a tentativeness and fluidity. Perhaps 'trouble-making' is only one aspect of your identity? It is important throughout our development and training that we experiment with shifting our positions over time. Essentially, we may wish to loosen our grasp on comfortable convictions, and see where other less travelled paths can take us.

Indeed, in shaking loose the hold of 'trouble-making', the systemic concept of *irreverence* could come in handy:

> We need frequent consultation and dialogue with colleagues to protect clients from the consequences of our own rigidity, and to help us avoid becoming locked into one right story. Irreverence is a flexible state of mind, which includes being irreverent to reverence for one's own convictions.
>
> (Cecchin et al., 1992, p. 46)

Conclusion

Re-engaging with stories of personal, professional and political experiences shape our ideas about the clinical psychologist we wish to become. Rethinking and talking about our practice using a range of perspectives and tools can help us look at experiences in a new light, at the same time as creating opportunities for us to enrich clinical psychology itself. So we end this chapter with some parting thoughts – which we invite you to remind yourself of from time to time:

- Let the journey be meaningful, not just the point of arrival – whatever the direction it may take.
- Find moments of joy and community/connection – do not let this journey separate you from others, or from what matters to you. Allow it to bring you closer to others.

Acknowledgements

We would like to thank the following people for their kindness in participating in this process and collaborating on the enclosed letter for our readers: Hannah Wilson, Clinical Psychologist, Public & Private sector; Paul Watson, Clinical Psychologist, Adult Psychology Service, NHS Fife; Laura Golding, Programme Director, University of Liverpool and Chair-Elect BPS Group of Trainers in Clinical Psychology; Rowan Tinlin, Trainee Clinical Psychologist, Northumberland, Tyne & Wear NHS Trust & Newcastle University; Alice Kennedy, Clinical Psychologist, Private & Education Sectors; Maria Qureshi, Clinical Lecturer, University of Hertfordshire and Clinical Psychologist LD/AMH; Kat Alcock, Principal Clinical Tutor, Admissions Tutor and DCP BME Mentoring Scheme Lead, UCL DClinPsy; Ché Rosebert, Director – The Association of Clinical Psychologists UK; Julia Faulconbridge, Consultant Clinical Psychologist, DCP Vice – Chair; Christy Laganis, Clinical Psychologist, Care in Mind.

References

British Psychological Society. (2018). *Code of ethics and conduct.* Leicester: British Psychological Society.

British Psychological Society. (2019). *The alternative handbook 2019: Postgraduate training courses in clinical psychology.* Leicester: British Psychological Society.

Carey, M., & Russell, S. (2003). Outsider-witness practices: Some answers to commonly asked questions. *International Journal of Narrative Therapy & Community Work, 2003*(1), 12–29.

Cecchin, G., Lane, G., & Ray, W. A. (1992). *Irreverence: A strategy for therapists' survival.* London: Karnac Books.

Clearing House. (2019). *Numbers.* Retrieved from www.leeds.ac.uk/chpccp/numbers.html

Dallos, R., & Draper, R. (2015). *An introduction to family therapy: Systemic theory and practice* (4th ed.). Maidenhead, Berkshire: Open University Press.

Division of Clinical Psychology. (2017). *Clinical accreditation handbook.* Leicester: British Psychological Society.

Golding, L., & Moss, J. (2019). *How to become a clinical psychologist.* London: Routledge.

Harris, R. (2008). *Values worksheet* (Adapted from Kelly Wilson's Valued Living Questionnaire). Retrieved from www.thehappinesstrap.com/upimages/Values_questionnaire.pdf

Hayes, S. C. (2004). Acceptance and commitment therapy, relational frame theory, and the third wave of behavioral and cognitive therapies. *Behavior Therapy, 35,* 639–665.

Howell, W. S. (1982). *The empathic communicator.* Belmont, CA, USA: Wadsworth Publishing Company.

Knight, A. (2005). *How to become a clinical psychologist: Getting a foot in the door.* London: Routledge.

LeJeune, J. T., & Luoma, J. (2016). *Seven values "greatest hits": Our favourite values exercises from acceptance and commitment therapy.* Retrieved from https://learningact. com/blog/2017/07/16/favorite-values-exercises-to-use-in-therapy/

Mason, B. (1993). Towards positions of safe uncertainty. *Human Systems: The Journal of Systemic Consultation & Management, 4*(1), 189–200.

Mason, B. (2019). Re-visiting safe uncertainty: Six perspectives for clinical practice and the assessment of risk. *Journal of Family Therapy, 0*(0). doi:10.1111/1467-6427.12258

McGhee, P. (2015). What are the most popular degree courses? *BBC News.* Retrieved from www.bbc.co.uk/news/education–32230793

Miriam. (2011, March). "I hear that someone with . . . didn't get on, so I'll never make it". *Clin Psy Forum.* Retrieved from www.clinpsy.org.uk/forum/viewtopic.php?f=32&t=11 644&sid=44780bec9fd81797467d17ab2bff8641

Nel, P. W. (2010). Clinical psychology in the noughties: The good, the bad and the nice. *Clinical Psychology Forum, 214,* 7–11.

Nel, P. W. (2012). The trouble with clinical psychology. *Clinical Psychology Forum, 235,* 18–22.

Ofsted. (2015). *A level subject uptake: Numbers and proportions of girls and boys studying A-level subjects in England.* Retrieved from https://assets.publishing.service.gov. uk/government/uploads/system/uploads/attachment_data/file/426646/A_level_subject_ take-up.pdf

Orford, J. (2008). *Community psychology: Challenges, controversies and emerging consensus.* London: John Wiley & Sons.

White, M. (2003). Narrative practice and community assignments. *International Journal of Narrative Therapy and Community Work, 2,* 10–23.

White, M., & Epston, D. (1990). *Narrative means to therapeutic ends.* New York: W.W. Norton & Company.

White, M., & Epston, D. (2005). Externalizing the problem. In C. Malone, L. Forbat, M. Robb, & J. Seden (Eds.), *Relating experience: Stories from health and social care* (pp. 73–78). New York, USA: Routledge.

Chapter 5

Everyone reflects, but some reflections are more risky than others

Romena Toki and Angela Byrne

This chapter is a conversation between Romena Toki, a third-year trainee clinical psychologist at the University of Hertfordshire and Angela Byrne, a clinical psychologist who qualified from University of East London in 1999 and now works at East London NHS Trust and Derman – a charity for the wellbeing of Kurdish and Turkish communities (www.derman.org.uk).

Reflecting through dialogue

A: I wondered if we should say something about how this chapter came about and why we're doing it in this conversational way. I suppose it relates to this whole idea of reflection.

R: I am cynical about how 'decolonising' psychology is being talked about within the profession but not enough being done. This has sparked off conversations about reflection, like how clinical psychology can have 'token brown people' coming into training and 'just enough brown people' being invited for interviews, but really what they're really looking for is a brown person who has met certain 'Western standards' of what it means to be a psychologist, as opposed to a brown person who has very good knowledge of their community and the complexities that exist.

A: That really chimes with some of the things that I've been thinking about the issue of 'diversity' within our profession and I feel that some of the impulse behind that is about 'looking right'. You used the term 'enough' – having 'enough' people to look right – but actually without even touching on the knowledge base of our profession, not considering if this is of any relevance or interest to communities that aren't represented. What theories are we drawing on? Do we need to diversify those?

What you say about reflection as well, is really important. The idea has been put forward that one reason for the underrepresentation of trainees from black and minority ethnic communities is that candidates don't meet certain standards for 'reflection', with the implication that what needs to happen is that the aspiring trainees need to improve themselves somehow. I feel like this is a really appalling discourse and an example of institutional racism in our profession. Why are we not stopping to say "hold on a minute, what do we mean by reflection? Who decides this? What are we actually talking about?" It brings us back to what we're doing here because we decided to do this because reflecting by means of dialogue is something that seems to feel more comfortable for us.

R: Yeah, reflecting via dialogue is definitely something I feel more comfortable with. It feels more natural; you can judge what someone is thinking before you share too much. I'm very conscious of sharing too much, partly because I know there are so many negative narratives about my culture and religion and family, so when I'm reflecting or sharing these stories, I need to know how it's being received. When you're writing you don't know who's going to see that and where that's going to go and how that's going to be interpreted.

A: It makes me think about the idea of safety in sharing. You mentioned certain discourses that would influence how well you're able to share what you're thinking, right?

R: If I was to think of an example, I mean, Islam is so stigmatised now, the narratives around it are just horrific and it's a very difficult time to practice Islam freely and openly. It's my religion and I feel close to it and I feel protective over it and often, when I'm reflecting, I'd be very cautious of how I present it to others because of how it's misunderstood and misrepresented. I might not feel comfortable talking about it and it's such a fundamental part of my identity, of how I live my life – but it's something that I can't talk about, at all actually.

Invisible whiteness

A: How does that silencing play out in terms of being a trainee clinical psychologist?

R: I suppose when case studies of Muslim families are given out at any level of training or at workshops, assumptions are made of how they may treat their daughters, how they perceive women and when they're building formulations, sometimes people try to present it as a strength, as a protective factor, but really often, it is presented as something that has probably caused the difficulties in the family. It's almost framed as a 'systemic problem'.

A: Yeah, and the bit that's invisible there is whiteness, isn't it? That assumption of secularism and whiteness as a standard or a norm and so therefore, anybody else is seen as somehow deviating from this unspoken but assumed norm.

R: Totally. I think it's interesting because my course is quite diverse, which is lovely and enables us to have really rich discussions. I remember talking to my friend who was on a course where they were all white women and she said, "I feel like we missed out on so many perspectives, we kept having the same conversations from the same perspectives", so I feel happy that I have that opportunity, but I do still find myself defending parts of my culture especially when I hear Western ideas of what it means to be 'healthy' being enforced. I think when you're taught in a very similar way by similar people over and over again, and the way that theories are presented, "this is what works, we know this works", I feel conscious about bringing the perspective that I don't have 'evidence' for apart from my own knowledge that comes from my experience of being part of my community. We have to critique using literature that's already out there that's been done by the same type of people, namely white men, who have done the research, who have published the papers, who have justified why their theory is better than others, like that's what we're using. We can't just bring in our personal experiences into an essay and call it critical thinking. That's been so stripped away from us, from early schooling; that perspective is so undervalued, has been so undervalued.

A: Yeah, and I think that we white people underestimate the freedom that not being in a minority brings, y'know, and I think this is all part of this notion of reflection – the freedom to kind of play with ideas, to make a mistake. Because, let's face it, if you're white and you say something that could be seen as wrong or naïve or whatever, no one's going to say 'that's representative of white people', but if you're the one person in your group or one of a small number of people . . .

R: Absolutely. We're expected to write these reflective essays and every time I try and look for references that support my view, you always see this 'brown person feels pressured' and I never really knew what that honestly meant until you become the minority person in a group and you're honestly thinking about 'if I say this thing. . .' and that's often my thought process before I disclose what my thoughts are in terms of when it comes to sort of 'brown people things'. It's "is this representative of as many brown people as possible? And is this okay for me to say? Will it be offensive to people? Will they get it? Will they ask me too many follow-up questions, 'cos this is just a fleeting thought?" like I feel like I can't have as many of those discussions within clinical psychology.

A: Yeah, and I guess that's what I mean about being playful, like there isn't that same freedom to just think out loud.

R: Yeah, I don't often feel the freedom of thinking out loud. I suppose I can do it with my friends who share experiences similar to mine, but it's difficult to do it in clinical psychology settings, much more difficult.

A different view of reflection

A: It's really making me think, about what a different way of looking at reflection could be? And I suppose one thing we didn't say is that we're sitting in your house, we have food and tea, and it makes me think about some of the conversations I have at work around the things that people find important, and they often are about being in a safe place, sharing food, sharing hospitality and co-constructing something, y'know, the dialogue.

[handwritten margin note: Reflection = priviledge.]

R: And when we're thinking about migrant families, it is a process of surviving for a while when you're trying to understand the culture, you're trying to find your feet here and you're trying to build a home, a career and so on, I feel like it's a very privileged thing to do, to sit there and reflect. That takes time and not all families have that kind of time.

A: That's so true, isn't it? I was also thinking about the idea of reflection and what it actually means, and I was brought back to when we worked together with a Bangladeshi women's group and a woman spoke about how her mum and all the other mums would drop the kids to school and then gather at her mum's house to do their cooking together, and that's when all the problems would be shared and turned over, and solutions found and advice given, and then they would all go at school pickup time and disperse and go to their own houses. And it made me think, isn't that reflection? But it's reflection that happens through dialogue and I was also thinking about another aspect of reflection that we don't ever talk about in our secular world of psychology: the reflection that takes place in a spiritual or religious context.

[handwritten margin note: standards' of reflection bringing author -nicity]

R: We reflect when we pray! It's all about reflecting. When we pray, make our *dua* at the end, that's all about reflecting; it's all about your family and just that dialogue and speaking to God, Allah. And it is, it is, it's just not done in the way that's expected at interviews and when you're training, or when we're writing reflective essays. It's done in a very different way, in a very private way and non-judgmental. Reflective essays tend to be marked within clinical psychology and training courses. That's not 'non-judgmental'.

A: (laughs) How are reflective essays marked? What are the 'standards for reflection'? Marked against what standards, though? What are the indicators for reflection?

R: It's 'reflective enough', like 'who knows' (both laughing), does it relate to clinical practice and so on.

A: So, if you were to say, erm, "I prayed about this issue and another way of thinking was revealed to me", for example. Would that be seen as . . . Would that pass? (both laughing).

R: I can try it (laughs).

A: (Laughs) Or if I said "I had a conversation" rather than "I thought about this"? This is what I mean by "what do we mean by reflection" and whose values are implicit in that and what kind of cultural values are implicit in the idea of reflection. For some people, reflection might be a relational process, like we're doing now.

R: Absolutely. I struggled with writing reflective essays at first now that I think about it, because I felt like it had to be phrased like 'I wonder if I made the right decision because. . .' and 'I'm just curious about . . .', 'I'm just thinking about . . .', like I had to use that language and that framework to reflect and it's something that I wasn't familiar with, because my active reflecting was through dialogue with my family and my friends and now my husband.

So, it's a very psychological language, what we call reflection now; very individualistic.

A: Right. And like it can be measured on a scale? It also brings to mind this idea of who decides that? What would clients say? What would their definition or way of measuring it look like?

Surviving clinical training

A: I suppose a burning question for me is, ostensibly, clinical psychology training is a very privileged position and people involved in it are very privileged in the sense of its high status, well paid, funded training towards a doctoral degree. When you're training, you're earning more than probably most staff and yet, it is experienced as something that needs to be survived. What do you think is going on there?

R: *Everything* is assessed – from your views, the decisions you make clinically, the conversations you have with your supervisor, both at the university and the ones you have at placement. Everything you write about, the way that you reflect and we're 'reflective practitioners', so everything we reflect on, the reflections we have will then be assessed. Everything is so assessed that it just adds a layer of anxiety and stress and feels like a process of survival.

A: Remembering my training days, I think there's a bit of a mixed message, which is like you're part of this cohort of people and you need to bond as a group but at the same time, we're going to assess you in relation to each other and I think there's a sort of covert competition that we often don't talk about – whether it's who gets the best mark or who gets the most prized placement.

R: And finding a thesis supervisor. My friend said it's like the *Hunger Games* (laughs) because everybody wanted the same supervisor, which can make things very tense. I pitched the idea of working with my community and my heritage and I was so anxious about whether or not they'd 'get it' or see the value of it. There wasn't a Bangladeshi tutor (laughs). And that's kind of representative of what real life is going to be like afterwards as well. Like if I want to work with my community, and I have this idea, how am I going to pitch this and who am I going to pitch this to? Who's going to get it?

A: So, basically every time you're making decisions in relation to your ideas, or expressing them or researching them or whatever, you're having to think about 'is this person going to get it'?

R: Absolutely. *Every. Time.*

A: So, you're having to take a risk almost every time?

R: Yeah. Every time. I think especially when it comes to that part of my identity. When it comes to, family, spirituality, culture, choices. It's a risk every single time. I guess one can say that any particular reflection is a risk.

A: Mmm, but some reflections are more risky than others.

R: More risky than others, yeah. If we were to think about Social GRRRAAACCEEESSS and layers of someone's identity that has been oppressed by

GRACE's

society. Every time I have had to reflect in these settings, it is with people who are more powerful than me, who will remain privileged and powerful in society. Why would I want to put myself in a position where I will be thickening an oppressive narrative in front of them? You should put yourself in that position, in front of a group that has been part of the group that has been oppressing you, and that is a minimum expectation.

A: I think it puts the onus on those of us in positions of power. It's really our job to make those situations as safe as possible.

R: And actually, we need a more culturally-relevant idea of what reflection is. If we think about the education system, psychology especially, I have never learnt that that act of conversing with my family or praying are still acts of reflecting. Reflection was a very 'black and white' thing. Being taught 'what' to reflect rather than having the confidence to do it. Well I do it anyway, but doing it in different settings.

A: Or having the way that you reflect recognised and validated? Because everybody reflects.

R: Everybody reflects, everybody reflects, mmm.

A: Do you think that's a good place to stop?

R: (Laughs) Yeah, everybody reflects.

The personal

The selves as human

Part II

The personal

The selves as human

Chapter 6

On being a practitioner and a client

Molly Rhinehart, Emma Johnson and Kirsty Killick

We encounter a range of reactions when people get to know that we are practitioners working in mental health services. They often assume that we must have our emotional and personal lives sorted, and always approach difficult situations calmly and rationally. Whilst it is true that working therapeutically requires resilience and emotional awareness, it is important not to confuse this with being an emotion-proof superhero. We may have had similar experiences to our clients at some point in our lives, or go on to in the future. These experiences can be a catalyst for deciding to pursue this career, referred to in the literature as a 'wounded healer' (Benziman, Kannai, & Ahmad, 2012). Practitioners may hold dual identities as both a provider of mental health support and also a user, or ex-service user, of the same services. Navigating dual identities can be tricky, particularly within a culture that contains a high level of unspoken stigma towards practitioners who have been 'on the other side of the couch'. However, in recent years there have been moments signifying a shift towards a greater level of acceptance and understanding of those who are 'dual-experienced'. The emergence of this shared terminology for referring to service-user-practitioners allows for a move away from a previously invisible position.

We hope that this chapter will encourage you to consider the experience of holding dual identities as service provider and service user, to explore some of the issues to consider when sharing these experiences, and to reflect on some of the strengths and challenges of holding dual identities. We are practitioners working in mental health services who also identify as having experience of mental health difficulties and accessing mental health services. Molly Rhinehart and Kirsty Killick are trainee clinical psychologists; and Emma Johnson is a mental health social worker working as a psychological wellbeing practitioner within an Increasing Access to Psychological Therapies (IAPT) service.

Reflective activity: listening to the experiences of others

We invite you to consider what your initial thoughts/assumptions/feelings might be if a colleague disclosed their experience of mental health difficulties and/or using mental health services. You may wish to pause for a moment, place this book down, and write some of your thoughts down on paper or speak your responses out loud. We would then like you to consider how your life experiences might have contributed to this response.

Furthermore, imagine how you might feel if someone in a position of power to you, for example, a therapist or supervisor, disclosed their experience of mental health difficulties and/or accessing mental health services. Again, consider how your life experiences might have contributed to this response. Did your response to this differ from that to the previous question? If so, reflect why this might be. Later on, we will invite you to consider your own experience of talking about personal mental health difficulties.

Practitioners with lived-experience of using services

Evidence on the mental health of mental health practitioners, including clinical psychologists, is sparse, dated, and predominantly based on small sample sizes (Tay, Alcock, & Scior, 2018). The limited evidence suggests that it is not uncommon for clinical psychologists to experience mental health difficulties (BPS, 2017). In a cross-sectional questionnaire study of 364 UK-based trainee clinical psychologists, 18% reported significant problems with anxiety and 14% reported significant problems with depression (Brooks, Holttum, & Lavender, 2002).

The most recent evidence suggests a substantial portion of clinical psychologists in the UK have experience of mental health difficulties: 63% of qualified clinical psychologists and 67% of trainee clinical psychologists in the UK reported experiencing mental health difficulties in their lives (Grice, Alcock, & Scior, 2018; Tay et al., 2018). When interpreting these figures, it is important to note that a number of factors may influence the incidence of mental distress in mental health practitioners. Individuals with experience of mental health difficulties may be particularly drawn to working in helping professions (Huynh & Rhodes, 2011), resulting in an increased number of dual-experienced mental health practitioners. It is also likely that those participants with experience of mental health difficulties are more likely to participate in research exploring this experience (Grice et al., 2018). The nature of clinical practice and the psychologist's role can also make practitioners vulnerable to experiencing distress. Repeated exposure to trauma narratives, systemic pressures, a stressful training environment, worries about client safety, professional isolation, and poor work-life balance can all contribute to the development of mental health difficulties (APA, 2010).

The British Psychological Society (BPS) Code of Ethics and Conduct states that psychologists should "seek professional consultation or assistance when they become aware of health-related or other personal problems that may impair their own professional competence . . . [and] refrain from practice when their professional competence is seriously impaired" (2009, p. 17). Whilst it can be difficult for individuals generally to seek help for mental health difficulties, studies have suggested that seeking help can generate unique challenges for practitioners working in mental health services.

Good, Khairallah, and Mintz (2009) posit that psychologists can develop dualistic perspectives on wellness and wellbeing, with Tay et al. (2018) suggesting that the culture within mental health services may result in practitioners viewing mental health difficulties as 'weaknesses' and perceiving that they should be 'mentally resilient' and able to cope. This culture can result in an 'us and them' discourse, or "noble us and troubled them" as characterised by Good et al. (2009), which, combined with the profession's helping role, may result in clinicians being reluctant to 'cross-over' and adopt the role of client (Tay et al., 2018).

Being unable to recognise or acknowledge their own difficulties may also hinder practitioners seeking help for mental health difficulties. Good and colleagues (2009) suggest that the usual human processes of denial, shame and reluctance to seek help may be amplified in those whose professional role is to provide help.

There can also be considerable stigma attached to mental health professionals seeking help for difficulties with their mental health. This includes fear of being judged by colleagues, family, friends, and clients, in addition to concerns about confidentiality and help-seeking negatively impacting on career prospects. Tay and colleagues' 2018 survey of qualified clinical psychologists explored participants' external, perceived and self-stigma in addition to attitudes towards, disclosure of, and help-seeking relating to current and past mental health difficulties. Participants' expectations of stigma was found to be a significant factor, with participants more likely to disclose mental health problems to personal contacts rather than work contacts. Some participants reported that shame and perceived negative consequences for themselves and their careers prevented them from disclosing and seeking help for mental health difficulties.

It is also noteworthy that there are polarised debates within clinical psychology that could also contribute to stigma. Psychiatric diagnosis, for example, is a controversial topic (Kinderman, Read, Moncrieff, & Bentall, 2013). It follows that this may impact on practitioners' experiences, for example, practitioners who have received a diagnosis and find it helpful, may feel stigmatised by colleagues who reject the notion of psychiatric diagnosis and vice versa.

Reflective activity: talking about personal experiences of distress

Earlier on, we invited you to consider your response if someone disclosed their experience of mental health difficulties to you. Now we would like you to consider how you might feel or have felt disclosing experience of mental health difficulties and/or using mental health services to your colleagues or supervisor. Why do you think this might be the case? How have your life or work experiences to date contributed to this response?

Disclosing dual identities

As previously discussed, practitioners who are 'dual-experienced' can experience significant stigma. This can influence dual-experienced practitioners' decisions on sharing information about their own mental health difficulties. There are three potential areas of opportunity for practitioners to disclose dual identity: to clients, to the public, or to colleagues and/or supervisors. This section will focus solely on decisions relating to disclosure to colleagues and/or supervisors from the perspective of clinical psychologists at the pre-training and trainee stages of their career. For discussion on the decision to disclose to clients, please see the latter section of this chapter.

There are some accounts of clinical psychologists speaking publicly about their dual identities, such as Emma Harding (2010), Jamie Hacker-Hughes (2016), and Rufus May (2000). Further accounts exist, many of which remain anonymous (for example, Anonymous, 2016). We were unable to find any published, formal accounts of pre-training or trainee clinical psychologists speaking about their experiences of distress, although these experiences are starting to be shared on less formal platforms such as Twitter. Whilst there are high levels of stigma around disclosing dual experience in both training and qualified mental health practitioners, there may be specific factors that are particularly pertinent for individuals at the pre-training and trainee stages of their clinical psychology journey.

Both pre-training and trainee roles inevitably involve a position of disempowerment (Bender, 1996; Harkness, 2013). These power dynamics may be visible, such as being reliant on a supervisor to write a reference for clinical psychology training (Rezin & Tucker, 1998), or they may be subtler, such as many pre-training roles involving low-paid or honorary positions which may include varying levels of, or sometimes the absence of, clinical supervision (Byrne & Twomey, 2011; Taylor, 1999). For dual-experienced individuals, this power imbalance may also echo their own experiences of power inequality when accessing mental health services, where service users frequently have their agency and expertise dismissed (Brosnan, 2013; Carr, 2007). In addition, both pre-training and trainee roles inherently include frequent evaluation, which may contribute to and maintain an experience of reduced power in these roles. This may impact on an individual's decision to disclose difficult experiences, such as mental health difficulties (Ladany, Hill, Corbett, & Nutt, 1996).

In addition, clinical psychology training in the UK is highly competitive, with a success rate of approximately 15% (Clearing House, 2017). The high level of competition implicitly creates a narrative that only the best and strongest can get onto and survive training (O'Shea & Byrne, 2010). This narrative can result in further comparison to or competition with peers during pre-training (Galvin & Smith, 2017) and trainee experiences (Golding, 2018), or alienation and isolation from other trainees (Barkataki, 2010). Trainees may experience 'imposter syndrome' (Jones & Thompson, 2017), a phenomenon where individuals feel the need to project an image of skill and expertise whilst secretly feeling that they are lacking in competence and will be 'found out' (Clance & Imes, 1978). This can perpetuate an environment in which disclosing information that identifies oneself as 'different' from peers, or sharing experiences that could be perceived as a 'weakness' may feel threatening, and therefore inhibit disclosure of experiences such as mental health difficulties.

Whilst there is a growing acknowledgement that trainees may be likely to experience psychological distress, this is only considered in their professional guidelines in the context of the trainee's responsibility to monitor the impact of psychological distress on their fitness to practice, and to disclose any issues that are impairing their ability to practice safely (BPS, 2018; HCPC, 2015). There is little information on how 'impairment' in being fit to practice is conceptualised (Collins, Falender, & Shafranske, 2011), which reflects the broader complexities in conceptualising mental health difficulties under similar lines to physical disabilities and impairments (Spandler, Anderson, & Sapey, 2015). The fear of being found unfit to practice if a disclosure is made may again echo an individual's experiences of fear as a service user, where there is often a threat of professionals 'taking over' (McGruder, 2002) or of being involuntarily detained (Lewis, 2012). For trainees, impairment is even more difficult to easily conceptualise, as by their very nature, trainees are in the process of gaining competency (Schwartz-Mette, 2009). This uncertainty can potentially lead to a situation whereby individuals in pre-training or trainee roles may feel unsafe disclosing experiences of current difficulties, and may feel safer disclosing partial information, or narratives of difficulties that are 'resolved' (Irvine, 2011; Yourman & Farber, 1996).

Although impairment may be difficult to conceptualise, professional guidelines are clear that trainee and qualified psychologists are required to disclose any mental health difficulties that are currently impairing their practice and to seek appropriate support. However, when considering historical difficulties, or difficulties that are currently appropriately managed, the decision to share information is less straightforward, as illustrated by Jason's experiences below.

In focus: Jason's account

"Sometimes I have to read a vignette that could be about me, then listen to my lecturers and colleagues dissect it. No matter how sensitively they do this, it presents a negotiation with the self that is not prepared for by the teaching programme. What position should I operate from? My madness is generally 'out of the closet'. Owning the things that have happened to me has made me more compassionate and better at my profession. I should be able to speak up comfortably.

But then there was the time I met a 'schizophrenia' researcher who said I have a disease, and we should think carefully before letting people like me have children. Or when a previous manager implied

I should come into work as it was "just mental health". Or when my course told us that we were welcome to share our distress with our tutors in private. The implication felt clear: in there, not out here.

If I contribute to a discussion as a professional, I silence my voice as a service user and risk betraying my values and politics. If I share my lived experience, my professionalism is compromised, and I risk ongoing prejudice. The implication that we must be either, not both is pervasive, unaddressed, and exhausting".

Jason, trainee clinical psychologist

As illustrated in Jason's account, reactions to disclosure can vary enormously, leading to uncertainty about how this information will be received. Studies suggest that the clinical training environment may further inhibit conceptualisation of impairment and disclosure of difficulties by viewing competency as a static, 'obtainable' concept rather than a fluctuating process which allows for movement along a spectrum (Zahir, 2018). Clinical psychology in the UK works within a scientist-practitioner framework, a model which promotes objectivity, and which is often viewed as being at odds with self-reflection and self-disclosure (Spence, Fox, Golding, & Daiches, 2014). In addition, the professional culture of clinical psychology is often cited as viewing self-disclosure as being synonymous with impairment, leading many practitioners to only disclose if they feel unable to self-monitor or self-support (Spence et al., 2014).

For individuals in pre-training roles, the value of disclosing this experience during an interview for clinical training is frequently debated. This is a complex, personal decision, and one which many individuals wrestle with. Different training courses place different emphasis on the value and importance of personal experience. Encouragingly, many courses appear to be welcoming of personal experience of mental health difficulties, as described by Camilla below.

In focus: Camilla's account

"Working as a 'peer support worker' with its primary feature being lived experience, I was already 'out' when the time came to apply. I decided I wanted to be as authentic as possible going forward as if a course didn't like my background, I wouldn't be a good fit with them – especially if I needed support whilst on the course.

Following a discussion with a course tutor amongst others at a conference, I subsequently started to compile information for a poster presentation on how courses supported applicants who disclosed. At this point I was generally getting the impression that gone were the days of disclosure being a no-go zone.

So, my first interview arrived. I can't recall exactly what or how I disclosed but I gently dipped my toes in and when I got my feedback it specifically mentioned they valued me talking about my experiences. I ended up as a high reserve and as time was going on, I was feeling more confident about the positives of disclosing.

The next year brought a different interview with an academic and clinical panel. In the first panel I disclosed on one or two questions. I felt that every answer had me disclosing to some degree or other. I came out of the interview and decided that I had shown Camilla off but had been too 'service user-y'! I didn't get feedback as I got a place but reflecting back six months down the line, I am happy with my choice and knowing that disclosing gave me a wealth of expertise that I could draw on, that undoubtedly helped".

Camilla, trainee clinical psychologist

It is also important to note that the decision to not share information is equally valid, or that this decision may change over time.

For trainees, deciding whether to share information with supervisors whilst in training can present additional challenges. Trainee psychologists change placements on a regular basis, meaning that their supervisor changes on a frequent basis, limiting the development of a strong, familiar supervisory relationship (Galvin & Smith, 2017; Jones & Thompson, 2017). In addition, trainees are often assessed by supervisors or course tutors who occupy dual roles as both assessor and clinical supervisor or pastoral support. Having a dual role as assessor and supervisor can lead to 'double power' where the power differential in the supervisory relationship is amplified (Tromski-Klingshirn & Davis, 2007). This may potentially be a barrier for trainees to disclose as they can feel pressured to maintain a positive relationship with their supervisor or feel inhibited due to a fear of negative evaluation (Ladany et al., 1996; Wilson, Davies, & Weatherhead, 2016). There are a wide range of theoretical orientations within clinical psychology, which may contribute to the differing views within the profession about disclosure of mental health difficulties, and which may further impede disclosures if trainees are unsure about how their supervisor is likely to react (Spence et al., 2014). The high levels of stigma within the profession may also preclude supervisors or other colleagues sharing information about their own experiences, thus depriving individuals from both pre-training and trainee roles of the opportunity to witness positive modelling of disclosures.

Much of this section has focused on barriers to sharing experience of mental health difficulties whilst in pre-training or trainee roles; however, there can be aspects that support disclosure, such as appropriate role models, and safe/containing supervision. There can also be benefits to disclosing. As Camilla mentioned, it was important to her to feel authentic in being open about her past experiences, and to train on a course which would welcome this experience. It is well documented that there can be a high emotional cost to concealing a significant part of one's identity (King, Reilly, & Hebl, 2008). Feeling able to share information about experience of mental health difficulties can be cathartic, powerful, and provide opportunities to reduce self-stigma and enable people to engage in positive social action, such as advocating or mentoring those who have experienced similar adversities (Bril-Barniv, Moran, Naaman, Roe, & Karnieli-Miller, 2017; Richards, Holttum, & Springham, 2016). Whilst many studies have highlighted high levels of stigma around practitioners disclosing mental health difficulties (for example, Good et al., 2009; Pope & Tabachnick, 1994), few studies have considered how disclosures are received by colleagues also working in mental health services. In a study exploring colleagues' reactions to a clinician's disclosure of accessing personal therapy, psychologists generally reacted positively and were not hesitant about referring clients to their colleague following the disclosure (Schroeder, Pomerantz, Brown, & Segrist, 2015).

We are hopeful that a shift in clinical psychologists sharing personal accounts of distress appears to be on the horizon. The high frequency of disempowerment and evaluation within individuals in pre-training and trainee roles means that often the responsibility to share experiences and strive for change falls on qualified psychologists and supervisors. Training courses are also well placed to model positive disclosure and self-care practices, rather than focusing on individualising discourses such as 'resilience'. We hope that these changes will pave the way to normalising the fact that practitioners are also human beings, with our own experiences of distress, and that rather than these experiences being stigmatised, the system around us will begin to see dual identities as bringing opportunities for increased compassion and understanding to our roles.

Dual identities

This section aims to explore the way in which dual-experienced practitioners can draw upon their experience to inform and strengthen their professional role. It will examine the ways in which this sense of dual identity informs their clinical practice and offers ways to manage potential pitfalls. Next, we share the reflections of a cognitive-behavioural therapist on the interaction between their identities as a therapist and a service user.

In focus: A Cognitive-Behavioural Therapist's account

"I think as a therapist, having my own difficulties and being in therapy myself has helped me to look beneath the surface more, to not make snap judgements based on a person's initial presentation. It has helped me to recognise that there are people who present to services who may on the surface seem to be fairly 'well' but who are really struggling underneath. Similarly, to this, I think my own experience of therapy has taught me that it takes me a long time to get to the crux of the matter, to start talking about the things that need to be talked about. Having first-hand experience of this has helped me to be more tentative and explorative as a therapist, to know that it takes time, sometimes a lot of time to be able to say (or even know) where the difficulties are. I also think that my own experiences of therapy have given me an awareness of how important the therapeutic relationship can feel for people. Knowing that you might be a really big thing in a person's life for the time you are working with them and beyond is a massive responsibility, and perhaps we sometimes hold that too lightly, particularly in the face of service demands, pressures and targets. So, thinking about how you are, how you respond, how you behave in tiny ways, being very aware of the significance of that relational stuff is really important. I don't think I would appreciate that in quite the same way had I not had that experience of sitting in the 'client' chair myself'

Anonymous, CBT psychotherapist

As illustrated above, mental health practitioners with dual experience may use their own experiences to inform and strengthen their practice in a number of ways:

- Personal experience of mental health difficulties may enhance a practitioner's understanding of what it means to experience intense distress. They may hold a greater appreciation of the effort required to begin to change unwanted behaviour due to their own experiences (Adame, 2011; Oates, 2017). The account above highlights how the experience of help-seeking can give rise to strong feelings of vulnerability and powerlessness. First-hand experience of this can be drawn upon to enhance empathy, strengthen the therapeutic relationship and improve clinical practice.
- The 'insider' awareness provided by dual experience can potentially reduce the power differential inherent within therapeutic relationships. Experience of psychological distress and the process of accessing support for this may offer an awareness of subtle and overt practices which disempower or harm clients (Goldberg, Hadas-Lidor, & Karnieli-Miller, 2015). With this 'felt sense' of awareness, such practices may then be avoided or changed. Practitioners with dual experience can offer a unique perspective in discussions surrounding team dynamics and service developments, although this may feel like a daunting task in view of the stigma existing within services discussed earlier in the chapter.
- Practitioners with dual experience have described how this experience has intensified the empathy they feel for clients, understanding where the person is 'at' on both a cognitive and emotional level. Jamie Hacker-Hughes (2016) spoke about highly valuing "the empathy that comes with one's own

experiences" (p. 810) and the sense of being able to more deeply understand a client's position due to having previously occupied this space. The 'wounded healer' narrative offers a framework for understanding how one's own experience of psychological distress may be used to help others (Gilbert & Stickley, 2012). Practitioners who identify as dual-experienced describe how this offers a unique standpoint that can benefit their practice. Some clients have reported similar experiences, reflecting that "they've been there, they know" (Lewis-Holmes, 2016), although further research is needed in this area to better understand the perspectives of clients on dual experience.

- Richards and colleagues (2016) and Gilbert and Stickley (2012) suggest that professionals who are dual-experienced are able to offer a normalising, compassionate discourse in relation to mental health difficulties and recovery. Dual-experienced individuals who have been able to integrate the two 'poles' of this identity within a normalising narrative are in a position to powerfully contest the 'us and them' dichotomy, and the self-stigma this can engender in staff, service users, and the general public alike (Goldberg et al., 2015; Richards et al., 2016) Similarly, those who openly speak about their dual identities may offer an antidote to broader, societal stigma. Writing in *The Psychologist*, David Pilgrim (2017) comments "professionals speaking out about their own difficulties are . . . exposing that experience to fuller public understanding and reducing the probability of the 'othering' of psychiatric patients" (p. 4).

Whilst many strengths can arise from a position of dual experience, the journey to a comfortable negotiation of these two identities may not be straightforward. One reason for this is the 'us and them' dichotomy referenced throughout the chapter, and in what follows, we share the reflections of a social worker with experience of mental health difficulties.

In focus: a social worker's account

"The attitude of 'us and them' continues to persist. I have heard comments from colleagues such as 'too old', 'manipulative', 'nightmare to work with' when discussing eating disorders. The same colleagues are happy to work with me professionally and I have a good relationship with them. Those two things don't sit together easily, and I wonder whether sharing my own experiences might encourage them to reflect upon that. To me, the best way to challenge 'them and us' is to give the message that when you speak about 'them' you are also speaking about 'me'. People with mental health difficulties are not 'those different people', they are us and they are part of us".

Anonymous, social worker, blogging at
https://progressnotperfection.co.uk

The quote above highlights how the dichotomy within mental health services can feel particularly problematic for workers with lived-experience due to the sense that they do not 'fit' easily within either group (Oakley, 2016). As with Jason's reflections, 'service-user' experience creates a feeling of 'difference' to the professional group, whilst their 'professional' status and training can exclude individuals from broader 'psychiatric survivor' and 'service-user' narratives.

Managing potential pitfalls

Challenges of dual status may include 'fitness to practice' considerations, the way in which personal experience can cloud objectivity, and the ethical implications of self-disclosure. Where a practitioner shares any common life experience with a client, it is important to safeguard against over-identification and ensure that the needs of the client remain at the centre of the work (Gilbert & Stickley, 2012; Oates, 2017). When considering the use of self-disclosure, is vital to consider whose needs are being served by sharing? What is to be shared, how, and what is the purpose of this? What are the long-term implications of sharing for the therapeutic relationship and the client's recovery? These tensions are present within all therapeutic interactions; however, dual experience may add a further layer of consideration. Interestingly, whilst practitioners may be cautious about disclosing dual experience to clients (Bottrill, Pistrang, Barker, & Worrell, 2010), clients generally report experiencing careful self-disclosure on the part of the clinician to be helpful, whilst blanket policies of non-disclosure were experienced as less helpful (Lewis-Holmes, 2016).

Self-care and supervision are vital when we are routinely working with high levels of psychological distress in pressured environments that often do not lend themselves to staff wellbeing and that have the potential to exacerbate existing or historical mental health difficulties.

Possible ways of managing pitfalls and tensions:

- Use of clinical supervision: the provision of a consistent, safe, supervisory space which provides the opportunity to make sense of what is happening for the client both through the use of psychological formulation, and through exploration of any feelings and re-enactments that may occur. Adams (2014) discusses how the supervisory space can allow the clinician to separate out the feelings of the client from their own, which may relate to their own life story and inner processes, and may provide an important space to navigate the interaction between dual identities and clinical work.
- Use of reflective practice: the use of reflection-in-action can assist dual-experienced practitioners in considering how their own experiences may be impacting upon their decisions within clinical practice (Lavender, 2003; Schön, 1987) and also provide a framework to reflect upon the impact dual identities may have upon others and upon the self. Ongoing examination of the reasons for one's choice of profession and any specialism within this can

also be helpful as such awareness may deepen with clinical experience and maturity (Barnett, 2007).

- Professional standards and codes of conduct: Health and Care Professions Council standards (2015), BPS Code of Ethics and Conduct (2018), and APA Code of Conduct (2017) offer frameworks within which all psychologists must conduct themselves. Further guidance examining the particular needs of dual-experienced practitioners could be helpful.
- Choice of working environment: considering working within 'recovery' oriented services, including services that openly value lived experience in staff may be another way to sidestep the 'us and them' narrative traditionally found within statutory services. Some services, for example, third-sector domestic and sexual abuse services, have traditionally welcomed and valued staff with lived experience, situating this within a feminist, 'survivor' narrative (Plumb, 2004).
- Use of a 'Work Wellness Action Plan': this can be developed from the traditional Wellness Recovery Action Plan and designed to support practitioners to maintain 'wellness' at work (Mind, 2013).
- Peer Support: The Honest Open Proud initiative seeks to support staff with lived experience to consider their options around disclosure in a safe and meaningful way (Scior, 2017). www.in2gr8mentalhealth.com is a forum specifically established for mental health practitioners who identify as dual-experienced and seeks to offer a safe environment where mental health practitioners can explore this experience.

Parting thoughts

We hope that this chapter has provided an introduction to the strengths and challenges that can arise from being a dual-experienced practitioner. Clinical psychology is still in its infancy in considering the experience of practitioners who hold dual identities and how to tackle the stigma that is interwoven into the culture of mental health services. Those who are dual-experienced threaten the default position of power often adopted in mental health services and the aforementioned false dichotomy of 'us and them', reminding us that practitioners are humans and vulnerable to distress in the same way as our clients. We are all on the same spectrum. Dual-experienced practitioners invite us into a more flexible, continuum model of psychological health within which we are all situated. They offer an alternative, normalising narrative. They offer hope.

References

Adame, A. (2011). Negotiating discourses: The dialectical identities of survivor-therapists. *The Humanistic Psychologist, 4*, 324–337. https://doi.org/10.1080/08873267.2011.618038

Adams, M. (2014). *The myth of the untroubled therapist: Private life, professional practice*. East Sussex, London: Routledge.

American Psychological Association. (2010, August 31). *Survey findings emphasise the importance of self-care for psychologists*. Retrieved from www.apapracticecentral.org/update/2010/08-31/survey.aspx

American Psychological Association. (2017). *Ethical principles of psychologists and code of conduct*. Retrieved from www.apa.org/ethics/code/

Anonymous. (2016, February 8). Confessions of a depressed psychologist: I'm in a darker place than my patients. *The Telegraph*. Retrieved from www.telegraph.co.uk/health-fitness/body/i-was-an-nhs-psychologist-but-i-suffered-from-depression/

Barkataki, I. (2010). Peer alienation and hostility among clinical psychology trainees and the pre-qualified. *Clinical Psychology Forum, 208*, 30–32.

Barnett, M. (2007). What brings you here? An exploration of the unconscious motivations of those who choose to train and work as psychotherapists and counsellors. *Psychodynamic Practice, 13*(3), 257–274. https://doi.org/10.1080/14753630701455796

Bender, M. (1996). The strange case of the invisible underclass: Clinical psychology training and assistant psychologists. *Clinical Psychology Forum, 87*, 27–31.

Benziman, G., Kannai, R., & Ahmad, A. (2012). The wounded healer as cultural archetype. *Comparative Literature and Culture, 14*(1), 2–9. https://doi.org/10.7771/1481-4374.1927

Bottrill, S., Pistrang, N., Barker, C., & Worrell, M. (2010). The use of therapist self-disclosure: Clinical psychology trainees' experiences. *Psychotherapy Research, 20*(2), 165–180. https://doi.org/10.1080/10503300903170947

Bril-Barniv, S., Moran, G., Naaman, A., Roe, D., & Karnieli-Miller, O. (2017). A qualitative study examining experiences and dilemmas in concealment and disclosure of people living with serious mental illness. *Qualitative Health Research, 27*(4), 573–583. https://doi.org/10.1177/1049732316673581

British Psychological Society. (2009). *Code of ethics and conduct*. Leicester: Author. Retrieved April 10, 2019, from www.bps.org.uk/files/code-ethics-and-conduct-2009pdf

British Psychological Society. (2017). *New Savoy survey shows increasing mental health problems in NHS psychotherapists*. Retrieved from www.bps.org.uk/news-and-policy/new-savoy-survey-shows-increasing-mental-health-problems-nhs-psychotherapists

British Psychological Society. (2018). *Code of ethics and conduct*. Leicester: Author. Retrieved April 10, 2019, from www.bps.org.uk/news-and-policy/bps-code-ethics-and-conduct

Brooks, J., Holttum, S., & Lavender, A. (2002). Personality style, psychological adaptation and expectations of trainee clinical psychologists. *Clinical Psychology & Psychotherapy, 9*(4), 253–270. https://doi.org/10.1002/cpp.318

Brosnan, L. (2013). Power and participation: An examination of the dynamics of mental health service-user involvement in Ireland. *Studies in Social Justice, 6*(1), 45–46. https://doi.org/10.26522/ssj.v6i1.1068

Byrne, M., & Twomey, C. (2011). Volunteering in psychology departments-quid pro quo? *The Irish Psychologist, 38*(2), 75–82. Retrieved from www.lenus.ie/hse/

Carr, S. (2007). Participation, power, conflict, and change: Theorising dynamics of service user participation in the social care system of England Wales. *Critical Social Policy, 27*(2), 266–276. https://doi.org/10.1177/0261018306075717

Clance, P., & Imes, S. (1978). The imposter phenomenon in high achieving women: Dynamics and therapeutic intervention. *Psychotherapy: Theory, Research and Practice, 15*(3), 241–247. https://doi.org/10.1037/h0086006

Clearing House for Postgraduate Courses in Clinical Psychology. (2017). *Numbers*. Retrieved July 5, 2018 from www.leeds.ac.uk/chpccp/numbers.html

Collins, C., Falender, C., & Shafranske, E. (2011). Commentary on Rebecca Schwartz-Mette's 2009 article, "Challenges in addressing graduate student impairment in academic professional psychology programs". *Ethics and Behaviour*, *21*(5), 428–430. https://doi.org/10.1080/10508422.2011.604547

Galvin, J., & Smith, A. (2017). It's like being in a little psychological pressure cooker sometimes! A qualitative study of stress and coping in pre-qualification clinical psychology. *The Journal of Mental Health Training, Education and Practice*, *12*(3), 134–149. https://doi.org/10.1108/JMHTEP-05-2015-0020

Gilbert, P., & Stickley, T. (2012). "Wounded Healers": The role of lived-experience in mental health education and practice. *The Journal of Mental Health Training, Education and Practice*, *7*(1), 33–41. https://doi.org/10.1108/17556221211230570

Goldberg, M., Hadas-Lidor, N., & Karnieli-Miller, O. (2015). From patient to therapatient. *Qualitative Health Research*, *25*(7), 887–898. https://doi.org/10.1177/1049732314553990

Golding, L. (2018). Comrades and competitors. *Clinical Psychology Forum*, *309*, 25–28.

Good, G., Khairallah, T., & Mintz, L. (2009). Wellness and impairment: Moving beyond noble us and troubled them. *Clinical Psychology: Science and Practice*, *16*(1), 21–23. https://doi.org/10.1111/j.1468-2850.2009.01139.x

Grice, T., Alcock, K., & Scior, K. (2018). Mental health disclosure amongst clinical psychologists in training: Perfectionism and pragmatism. *Clinical Psychology and Psychotherapy*. Early view. https://doi.org/10.1002/cpp.2192

Hacker-Hughes, J. (2016, November). Experiencing what clients experience [Letter to the editor]. *The Psychologist*, *29*, 810–915. Retrieved from https://thepsychologist.bps.org.uk/volume-29/november-2016/letters

Harding, E. (2010). A psychologist's progress. In H. Cordle, J. Carson, & P. Richards (Eds.), *Psychosis: Stories of recovery and hope* (pp. 134–143). London, England: Quay Books.

Harkness, F. (2013). He's just not that into you: An open letter to clinical psychology. *The Psychologist*, *26*(5), 314–321. Retrieved from https://thepsychologist.bps.org.uk

Health and Care Professions Council. (2015). *Standards of proficiency: Practitioner psychologists*. London: Author. Retrieved from www.hcpc-uk.co.uk/assets/documents/10002963SOP_Practitioner_psychologists.pdf

Huynh, L., & Rhodes, P. (2011). Why do people choose to become psychologists? A narrative inquiry. *Psychology Teaching Review*, *17*(2), 64–70. Retrieved from https://eric.ed.gov/?

Irvine, A. (2011). Something to declare? The disclosure of common mental health problems at work. *Disability and Society*, *26*(2), 179–192. https://doi.org/10.1080/09687599.2011.544058

Jones, R., & Thompson, D. (2017). Stress and well-being in trainee clinical psychologists: A qualitative analysis. *Medical Research Archives*, *5*(8), 1–19. Retrieved from https://journals.ke-i.org/index.php/mra/index

Kinderman, P., Read, J., Moncrieff, J., & Bentall, R. (2013). Drop the language of disorder. *Evidence Based Mental Health*, *16*(1), 2–3. https://doi.org/10.1136/eb-2012-100987

King, E., Reilly, C., & Hebl, M. (2008). The best of times, the worst of times: Exploring dual perspectives of "coming out" in the workplace. *Group & Organisational Management*, *33*(5), 566–601. https://doi.org/10.1177/1059601108321834

Ladany, N., Hill, C., Corbett, M., & Nutt, E. (1996). Nature, extent, and importance of what psychotherapy trainees do not disclose to their supervisors. *Journal of Counselling Psychology*, *43*(1), 10–24. https://doi.org/10.1037/0022-0167.43.1.10

Lavender, T. (2003). Redressing the balance: The place, history and future of reflective practice in clinical training. *Clinical Psychology-Science and Practice*, *27*, 11–15.

Lewis, L. (2012). "It's people's whole lives": Gender, class, and the emotion work of user involvement in mental health services. *Gender, Work and Organisation, 19*(3), 276–305. https://doi.org/10.1111/j.1468-0432.2009.00504.x

Lewis-Holmes, E. (2016). *"They've been there, they know": How mental health service users think about mental health staff with lived-experience.* (Unpublished doctoral thesis). Royal Holloway, London.

May, R. (2000). Routes to recovery from psychosis: The roots of a clinical psychologist. *Clinical Psychology Forum, 146*, 6–10.

McGruder, J. (2002). Life experience is not a disease or why medicalising madness is counterproductive to recovery. *Occupational Therapy in Mental Health, 17*(3), 59–80. https://doi.org/10.1300/J004v17n03_05

Mind. (2013). *Guide for employees: Wellness action plans.* Retrieved from www.mind.org. uk/media/4229240/mind-guide-for-employees-wellness-action-plans_final.pdf

Oakley, D. (2016). Reflecting on year 1. *Insight: People Panel Newsletter (North Wales Clinical Psychology Programme).* Retrieved from www.nwcpp.bangor.ac.uk/ documents/newsletters/3%20%20Edrychiad-Insight%20Hydref-Autumn%202016%20 (002).pdf

Oates, J. (2017). Editorial: Being a mental health nurse. *Journal of Psychiatric and Mental Health Nursing, 24*(7), 469–470. https://doi.org/10.1111/jpm.12397

O'Shea, G., & Byrne, M. (2010). In pursuit of clinical training. *The Irish Psychologist, 36*(4), 79–81. Retrieved from www.lenus.ie/hse/

Pilgrim, D. (2017, March). Silence, power, evidence, and a debate with no clear answers [Letter to the editor]. *The Psychologist, 30*, 2–5. Retrieved from https://thepsychologist. bps.org.uk

Plumb, S. (2004). The social/trauma model: Mapping the mental health consequences of childhood sexual abuse and similar experiences. In J. Twed (Ed.), *Social perspectives in mental health: Developing social models to understand and work with mental distress.* London, UK: Jessica Kingsley.

Pope, K., & Tabachnick, B. (1994). Therapists as patients: A national survey of psychologists' experiences, problems and beliefs. *Professional Psychology: Research and Practice, 25*(3), 247–258. https://doi.org/10.1037/0735-7028.25.3.247

Rezin, V., & Tucker, C. (1998). The uses and abuses of assistant psychologists: A national survey of caseload and supervision. *Clinical Psychology Forum, 115*, 37–42.

Richards, J., Holttum, S., & Springham, N. (2016). How do "mental health professionals" who are also or have been "mental health service users" construct their identities? *Sage Open, 6*(1), 1–14. https://doi.org/10.1177/2158244015621348

Schön, D. (1987). *Educating the reflective practitioner: Toward a new design for teaching and learning in the professions.* San Francisco, CA: Jossey-Bass.

Schroeder, K., Pomerantz, A., Brown, D., & Segrist, D. (2015). Psychologists' responses to the disclosure of personal therapy by a professional colleague. *Counselling and Psychotherapy Research, 15*, 50–57. https://doi.org/10.1002/capr.12010

Schwartz-Mette, R. (2009). Challenges in addressing graduate student impairment in academic professional psychology programs. *Ethics and Behaviour, 19*(2), 91–102. https:// doi.org/10.1080/10508420902768973

Scior, K. (2017, May). More not less please to challenge the "us them" divide' [Letter to the editor]. *The Psychologist, 30*. Retrieved from https://thepsychologist.bps.org.uk

Spandler, H., Anderson, J., & Sapey, B. (Eds.). (2015). *Madness, distress and the politics of disablement.* Bristol, UK: Policy Press.

Spence, N., Fox, J., Golding, L., & Daiches, A. (2014). Supervisee self-disclosure: A clinical psychology perspective. *Clinical Psychology and Psychotherapy, 21*(2), 178–192. https://doi.org/10.1002/cpp.1829

Tay, S., Alcock, K., & Scior, K. (2018). Mental health problems among clinical psychologists: Stigma and its impact on disclosure and help-seeking. *Journal of Clinical Psychology*. Early view. https://doi.org/10.1002/jclp.22614

Taylor, A. (1999). Supervision experiences of assistant psychologists. *Clinical Psychology Forum, 125*, 26–28.

Tromski-Klingshirn, D., & Davis, T. (2007). Supervisees' perceptions of their clinical supervision: A study of the dual role of clinical and administrative supervisor. *Counsellor Education and Supervision, 46*(4), 294–304. https://doi.org/10.1002/j.1556-6978.2007.tb00033.x

Wilson, H., Davies, J., & Weatherhead, S. (2016). Trainee therapists' experiences of supervision during training: A meta-synthesis. *Clinical Psychology and Psychotherapy, 23*(4), 340–351. https://doi.org/10.1002/cpp.1957

Yourman, D., & Farber, B. (1996). Nondisclosure and distortion in psychotherapy supervision. *Psychotherapy: Theory, Research, Practice, Training, 33*(4), 567–575. https://doi.org/10.1037/0033-3204.33.4.567

Zahir, V. (2018). Do doctoral training programmes actively promote a culture of self-care among clinical and counselling psychology trainees? *British Journal of Guidance and Counselling*, 1–10. https://doi.org/10.1080/03069885.2018.1461195

Chapter 7

Values in practice

Bringing social justice to our lives and work

Jacqui Scott, Laura Cole, Vasiliki Stamatopoulou and Romena Toki

Setting the context

In this chapter we introduce reflective opportunities for considering how we relate to social justice values in personal and professional areas. Throughout we will use words such as 'community' and 'social justice' work, while the approaches we draw on include critical theory (e.g., Kagan, Burton, Duckett, Lawthom, & Siddiquee, 2011); community psychology (e.g. Orford, 2008); and liberation psychology (e.g., Martín-Baró, 1994; Freire, 1970); as well as decolonising practices (e.g., Kessi, 2016), and service-user movements (e.g., Wallcraft, Rose, Reid, & Sweeney, 2003). Such practices have taken place for decades in community groups, in social work, and in many other fields that take interest in the social aspects of mental health. We acknowledge that during much of this time, the profession of clinical psychology had other interests, such as in establishing its worth as an objective science, in developing theories that are largely grounded in individualism, and in bringing about cognitive revolution (Smail, 2005). We therefore do not claim that these ideas are new or unique to psychology, but rather that psychology has much to learn from theories and practices that lie outside of its traditional paradigms.

As clinicians, our everyday interactions raise our awareness towards the lived experiences amongst people we work with, and the impact of social injustices upon these experiences. This leads us to consider: what opportunities for social justice work are available to us in professional and personal areas of our lives?

The chapter is divided into three parts: firstly, we consider personal actions and opportunities for personal involvement in groups and activism; secondly, we move to recognising their relevance in our training institutions, the ground that has the power to open or close doors to our learning; and finally, we consider its relevance in our professional roles and practices.

Social justice in everyday life

In this section, we begin by introducing some ideas for the enactment of values that relate to social justice, through simple personal actions, influences in social and media conversations, social activism, and by influencing policy.

Acts of personal solidarity

Activism need not be all about taking big actions such as demonstrations and boycotts, but includes, in addition, small but pertinent interventions at required moments, and speaking out to social injustices. We include here a conversation that one author had with an old friend, who talks about some of her own experience, and the small actions of others that can make a difference.

In focus: a conversation

Are there any ways that you've been defined by others?

I think being labelled with mental illness was one of the hardest things ever, the first time I was told I had schizophrenia was a nasty shock for me and my family. I've experienced stigma; judgement for being a burden on the state. I feel guilty every day, and I'm conscious of it every day. I feel judged for the colour of my skin and having to claim benefits. It's also tough being in a wheelchair now – I judge myself and I'm sure that others do as well.

In those moments (that you experienced discrimination), was there anything that anyone did or said that was helpful?

It's very helpful when you're not able to stick up for yourself for someone to say it for you, and little things you've said along the way – like *do* fight for yourself and what you're meant to have. I've been crushed for so long mentally, I tend to accept what people tell me, and not feel as upset as I used to get. But it makes it much harder to stand up for yourself when you're in that situation. We know about empowerment, but what I know now is that having someone to stick up for me really helps, and sometimes you just need a friend by your side.

What could someone do or say to help out?

It depends on the situation. I had a situation (of racism) where I felt very uncomfortable, but it's not always fair to expect someone to take on that responsibility. At the same time, it's not good to ignore it either. React on your own life experience and your sensitivity towards what others might be feeling. Even just to say quietly, I heard that and that wasn't okay – are you okay? Just acknowledge what has happened, and say that it's not okay. You always remember the person that was there for you.

Everyday interactions are areas where acts of oppression are routinely expressed, whether overtly or implicitly (Sue et al., 2007). Our learning begins with recognising our own positions, biases, and responses, and allowing ourselves to move beyond neutrality to continually reflect on "whether or not we are enacting our ethic of justice-doing in any moment-to-moment interaction" (Richardson & Reynolds, 2012, p. 6).

Thinking space

Consider a time when you felt unsafe or emotionally vulnerable:

- Was anyone there for you to notice and stand up for you or with you?
- What did that person do that made a difference to you in that situation?
- What would you have liked someone to do/say that wasn't done/said?
- What has your experience taught you about the value of being alongside others?

inspiration for this exercise, and many further questions if you are interested, can be found in Reynolds (2013).

Media activism

Moments of standing alongside others apply not only in social interaction, but online and in all media formats as well. Research, as well as our clinical and personal experience, suggests that social media can be detrimental to mental health, or may offer opportunities for education, connecting people with online communities, and expressions of support (e.g., Pantic, 2014).

Social media can be utilised to start conversations about mental health, share stories and bring information to a range of audiences and communities, who may not be accessing support in more traditional ways, such as through NHS services. We can contribute to such media conversations, and also use such opportunities to disseminate our findings broadly, not just in academic circles. For example, a recent clinical doctoral thesis on the impact of changes to the benefits system on the wellbeing of people with physical health difficulties, was disseminated in many creative ways, as along with being published in an academic journal (Saffer, Nolte, & Duffy, 2018). To reach different audiences and communities, the author presented at a range of conferences, the findings were summarised in an article for *The Conversation* (Saffer, 2018), and a further publication in *Context* (Saffer, 2019). The research was also shared on ResearchGate, on a leading charity website, and was promoted on twitter.

Media training is run regularly by the British Psychological Society (BPS), although there exists a range of views within the profession on the benefits and drawbacks of engagement with the wider media (e.g., BPS, 2018).

Social activism

Psychologists and aspiring psychologists are well-placed within social movements that seek to go beyond individual models of distress and engage with macro-social issues. Psychologists can make a collective impact by working together to engage in such issues, while sharing ideas, and engaging in critical discussion. Examples of such ventures include the community psychology section within the BPS, and Psychologists for Social Change (PSC).

In focus: psychologists for social change

Psychologists for Social Change (PSC) is a growing network of applied psychologists, citizens, academics, therapists and psychology graduates, who share the central aims of mobilising psychologists, breaking down barriers to dissemination, and influencing public and policy debates. PSC members have highlighted the need to collectively publicise the strong psychological evidence base of the impact of austerity and other social inequalities on individuals and communities in spaces where it is less often heard.

We asked assistant psychologist Orla Gormley about why she became involved with PSC:

"I have found that the competitive nature of the pursuit onto the doctorate has led to feelings of pressure, insecurity, or a tendency to become stuck. As such, I have taken time to consciously find the joy in my continued personal and professional development. This inspired me to pursue my passion for social justice. I am mindful of my strong knowledge of the wider determinants of wellbeing, such as economic hardship, unmet civil rights, discrimination, and social marginalisation. With this awareness I believe comes a responsibility to challenge systems or status quo that are damaging or not meeting people's needs, and to encourage change at a societal level, thus preventing impact at an individual level. It is for that reason that I am an active member of PSC in Northern Ireland. Initiatives that I have been involved with locally with PSC include joining a steering group aiming to create trauma-informed communities, campaigning for the right to equal marriage for the LGBTQ community and recently working to support migrants, refugees and asylum seekers. This experience has been invaluable for building confidence both personally and professionally, it has opened up many avenues for further learning, either through building relationships with the psychologists in my area or through attending and even presenting at conferences. If anyone is interested in joining their local group, I would strongly recommend it. Irrespective of what stage of your career you are at, PSC are always welcoming to new members and everyone's opinions and ideas will be warmly received."

Orla Gormley, assistant psychologist

Engagement and participation outside of explicit psychology-affiliated groups can be equally valuable. This could include union membership, membership of support networks or local committees calling for inclusion and participation in online actions, such as petitions or letter-writing.

Political activism

Policy has direct influence for the delivery of services and social welfare. These rely on evidence and consultation with professional groups, with key influences being the Royal College of Psychiatrists and the British Medical Council. As research is heavily weighted towards medicalised perspectives of distress, the voice of psychologists, bringing alternative perspectives and plurality of views to the discussion, is important to be heard.

A published clinical doctoral thesis concerning 'practice to policy' involved interviews with 37 UK clinical psychologists, from a broad spectrum of specialties, who had engaged in social action and policy work. This has resulted in recommendations around the competencies that psychologists can build on for working in this area, such as communicating with wider audiences, partnership-working, and knowledge of policy-making (Browne, 2017; Browne, Zlotowitz, Alcock, & Barker, 2019). We asked the lead author, Nina Browne, about her experience of becoming involved in policy work as an aspiring psychologist.

In focus: involvement in policy

"When I discovered community psychology in Australia over a decade ago, I found a framework for working and thinking that legitimised social action and policy work as a valid role for clinical psychologists. It makes sense to me, but the work itself is never comfortable. It's a continued state of listen, test, learn.

'Practice to Policy' was trying to answer the questions being asked by psychologists wanting to do more to tackle inequalities. Through the research, I journeyed with psychologists into the realms of their careers influencing policy. This was with the intention that as a profession we could learn how to do the same. Many highlighted that it was never too early to start this work, but you needed to find your allies. Much like therapy, this work is all about relationships. The skill is to see where there are opportunities to have a broader impact, and then grab them, even if it feels like a risk. Policy work is all around us, in the everyday. The more we listen the more its impact is evident. You don't need to be a maverick or an activist to move beyond individual practice, it's just about using our skills and knowledge differently. If you're motivated by social change, then it's for you".

Dr Nina Browne, clinical and community psychologist

Prominent examples of speaking out include Dr Lisa Cameron MP, a clinical psychologist, Member of Parliament since 2015, and chair of the all-party group on disability. Cameron delivered a keynote during the pre-qualification group conference in 2016, giving a message that psychologists have the ability to get involved in using research to inform government policy and make an impact. Radio presenter and psychology graduate Claudia Hammond has also been quoted saying, "Policy-makers won't even realise there are psychologists out there doing relevant research . . . Sometimes researchers will say that it's hard making definitive recommendations until more research has been done, but policy decisions are being made right now" (Rhodes, 2016).

We have explored the enactment of social justice values in our everyday interactions, with illustrations of how we can become active on a wide spectrum of capacities. However, as ideological values of neoliberalism underpin the general field of psychology and the society that it functions within, our own profession can serve to create and replicate injustices through its research, theories and practices. These biases are apparent in our training contexts as we struggle to achieve a diverse and population-representative psychology workforce. In the next section we consider experiences and what needs to change.

Social justice in our training

There are many challenges along the journey to qualification, however such barriers can be exacerbated for those holding marginalised identities. The nature of competing for jobs, experience and places on training courses sets up an environment of competition and fear, which can in turn drive the aspiring psychologist to assume individuality rather than cooperation. This unfortunate and complex dilemma is summed up neatly by community activist Anne Bishop:
  "As long as we who are fighting oppression continue to play the game of competition with one another, all forms of oppression will continue to exist"(Bishop, 2002, p. 19).

According to the data published on the Clearing House website (2019), dispro-portionately low percentages of training places seem to be taken by people who identify with minority groups, including sexual orientation and minority ethnic backgrounds; for example, in 2017 just 2% of training places were taken by peo-ple of African, Caribbean or other black background. Efforts have been made by the BPS, Division of Clinical Psychology (DCP), and training courses to address these low numbers. For example, Widening Access schemes aim to increase the ethnic diversity of the profession by offering local mentoring and work experiences to Black, Asian and minority ethnic (BAME) candidates, although despite these efforts, little noticeable change has occurred.

Within training, research has found that those who belong to minority groups are more likely to feel isolated, sidelined and concerned with their legitimacy on the pro-gramme. Daiches and Anderson (2012) found that clinical psychologists with minority sexual orientations experienced the ongoing dilemma throughout training of whether they felt safe enough to disclose. Meanwhile, research looking at the experiences of BAME trainees (e.g., Shah, Wood, Nolte, & Goodbody, 2012; Odusanya, Winter, Nolte, & Shah, 2017), finds that trainees often feel that they carry all the burden of issues related to race and culture, such as avoidance and resistance to discuss issues of race in supervision and in training. In the words of psychologist Guilaine Kinouani,

"As minorities, many of us have learnt to deal with feelings of exclusion and marginalisation alone, possibly because of shame, or fear of exposing one-self, of being silenced, misunderstood and/or rejected".
(Kinouani et al., 2015, p. 25)

This shows there is a need for aspiring psychologists to have the support of others throughout and beyond their journey to qualification.

Supporting others

Providing support towards others requires releasing ourselves of our positions of individuality, through a process of unlearning what we think we know, and learn-ing more about ourselves and others. As professor, media commentator and author Roxanne Gay explains:

We need people to stand up and take on the problems borne of oppression as their own, without remove or distance. We need people to do this even if they cannot fully understand what it's like to be oppressed for their race or ethnicity, gender, sexuality, ability, class, religion, or other marker of identity.
(Gay, 2016)

As aspiring psychologists, we are in a unique position to develop our skills in self-reflection and reflective practice, and we invite you to explore this further in the *Thinking space* below.

Thinking space

What does it mean to be part of a dominant group?

How does this impact your experience of the journey towards becoming a psychologist?

What are the strengths, limitations and resources of being in this position?

How can we take steps to make the voices of our fellow aspiring psychologists heard at work, within teaching, and on placement?

(See McIntosh (1988) for further thoughts on recognising privilege)

In showing support, the actions we take may look different for different people and in the different spaces that these are relevant and useful. For example, through our personal acts of solidarity, we can listen and validate our colleague's experience of receiving a racist or homophobic comment from a supervisor or colleague. We can start a conversation in a training cohort about race or sexuality (for example), so that those who hold minority identities do not feel alone in starting these conversations. We can take a critical stance in recognising how our profession has contributed to and maintained these oppressive systems that now affect our colleagues and classmates. And we can educate ourselves on the histories of oppression that marginalised groups have faced and are still facing.

A step towards highlighting these issues and offering support has been forming the Minorities in Clinical Training Group, which sits under the Executive Committee of the DCP.

In focus: the Minorities in Clinical Training Group

In 2012, aspiring psychologist Guilaine Kinouani, set up this group as she wanted to create a safe space to offer support for people from BAME backgrounds, those who identify as LGBT, and individuals with disabilities or caring responsibilities on their pathway to the profession. Since then, the group has also incorporated support for aspiring psychologists who experience mental health difficulties.

The main aims of the group are to offer a better understanding of marginalised experiences, peer support, and connection with others with similar experiences. The group organises networking meetings, an annual conference, and has published journal articles addressing issues of marginalisation within training.

Vasiliki spoke with a new committee member about their experience of becoming involved in the group:

"I became aware of the minorities group through attending last year's conference. I really enjoyed the variety of perspectives that were presented and decided to become more involved. As an LGBT individual who also has a 'disability', I have experienced considerable difficulties related to these identities as I have pursued a career in clinical psychology. I have experienced discrimination and harassment, and fearing stigma I have at times attempted to conceal my stigmatised identities. When I attended community member meetings, I really valued being able to talk openly with people about these experiences, being able to hear that I was not alone, feeling understood".

Genevieve Wallace, Minorities Group committee member

The training environment, and opportunities it brings, links essentially to the psychologists we become, and the values that are sanctioned in the profession. We move forward to shed light on the implications of social justice aspirations in shaping the work we do in professional practice, including our work as therapists, our roles within services, within communities, and within research.

Social justice in our practice

Working in line with values is what brings energy to our work, as we recognise the differences we can make and experience valuable connections with people and communities who grow through the work that we do together. However, at times when we feel our values risk being compromised, such as through service demands and long waiting lists, this can lead us to feel what Reynolds describes as "spiritual pain" (2011, p. 30); the pain of transgressing our values, leading us to feel burnt-out, incompetent, and other painful feelings.

We also find ourselves connected to a profession that has an unfortunate history of oppressive practices within clinical work, for example, the use of therapy to 'treat' sexuality; as well as the propounding of theory that has influenced societal discourse and effectively legitimised the oppression of certain groups. We may look back on this current time in history and regard certain current practices as oppressive, for example, the medicalising, labelling and individualising of people in distress using categories that give limited weight to social circumstances or experiences of oppression. Furthermore, McClelland (2014) discusses the current trend of neoliberalism in mental health services as indicating "the potential commodification of relationships, and the consequential stripping of ethics and meaning inherent in this version of practice" (McClelland, 2014, p. 127).

We consider, therefore, how to enact values in clinical practice.

Within therapy

Clinical training entails developing competence in more than one therapeutic model, giving psychologists skills to draw on and consider multiple possible perspectives. We argue for our practice not to decontextualise individuals from their social context, and for formulation to give due weight to community and societal-level factors, including issues of power and inequalities. Systemic perspectives, for example, involve recognition that not just the immediate relationships, patterns and context are central, but that these are also in relation to systems of power. In this context we can consider ways of being alongside, rather than 'doing to', as traditional medical (and therapeutic) relationships are often expected to entail.

Within the constraints of our models there are possibilities to make explicit our ethics of standing alongside. This may include hearing, and expressions of support, to the service user perspective on issues of disempowerment, whether through 'label', other elements of experience, diversity or intersectionality. Borrowing from narrative approaches in therapy (White & Epston, 1990), the role is to broaden the single story, to recognise and validate the multiple stories that illustrate the complexity of human experience. Above all, providing people the opportunity to author their own stories, rather than have a story told about them.

We find importance in recognising that any formulation is reductionist, and to acknowledge that formulation does not imply an objective reality. Rather, we can be guided on the use of words that can otherwise contribute further to experiences of disempowerment. Alternative frameworks and tools could be considered, which acknowledge the impact of socio-political issues, for example, societal case formulation (Leonard, 1984; as cited in Burton & Kagan, 2008) or power-mapping (Hagan & Smail, 1997).

In focus: power-mapping

"It may be important in clinical work to take account not only of the amount of power available to individuals, but also of their having to deal with damaging powers bearing down upon them from their proximal worlds".

(Hagan & Smail, 1997, p. 264)

Power-maps can be drawn within therapeutic spaces in order to make explicit the resources available, or lack thereof, to an individual, and to acknowledge that psychological change is constrained by "more powerful, distal factors which neither client not clinician can affect" (ibid, p. 261).

Power-maps include taking account of resources available, as well as subjection to power held by others. These are considered in four main areas: material resources (e.g., employment, education); home and family (e.g., partner, parents); personal resources (e.g., confidence, ability-level); and social (e.g., social connection, support).

Societal case formulation would take this further, to include the person within the state, including the experience of systems such as educational and health, as well as their own historical, cultural context.

While we find it important to name sources of oppression, and learn from our conversations, we also remind ourselves to recognise that if we fail to address the underlying fundamental issues of inequality, interventions can only be partial solutions. Our expectation of this work is not of individual 'empowerment', which can position the oppressed as responsible, and thereby serve to perpetuate oppression. In addition to this important part of the work we do, in the next section we consider how we contribute to shaping our services in ways that align with a social justice approach.

Within services

Too often within our practices and within our services, the systems of power that operate in society, such as the stigmatisation of particular groups, are recreated.

The processes by which people take part in and have opportunities to influence their own healthcare and wider service provision are described using the concepts of participation, co-production, involvement and consultation, each of which are often used interchangeably within services and academic literature. Participatory approaches in the design, development and delivery of mental health services is an integral part of current policy (NHS England, 2016), and these intend to build on people's intrinsic strengths whilst actively involving them in addressing issues that they themselves identify. This active involvement deconstructs power dynamics in service provider/service user relationships, supports social change in the way that services are delivered, and enables learning from and alongside people who access services. For example, Arnstein's ladder of citizen participation (1969) is considered one of the most influential participation models, and rests on the premise that participation depends upon sharing and re-distributing power.

Despite these opportunities, within services we have often witnessed participation falling under tokenistic gestures, such as weak forms of service-user consultation (Beresford, 2002), resulting in limited sustainability and limited impact on decision-making (Tisdall, 2017). Such challenges may be due to the increasing emphasis on a performance culture that limits resources and flexibility (Innes, Macpherson, & McCabe, 2006). This gap is the area in which aspiring psychologists can begin a project, facilitate staff training, or begin a conversation. We were introduced to an example of participatory practice called 'problem-solving booths' by Dr Nina Browne, described in the *In focus* box below.

In focus: problem solving booths

Problem solving booths bring members of the community together to have conversations that they might not usually have. The idea is to switch the traditional roles between who does the "helping" and who are the "helped". With movement between roles, everyone has both the potential to have problems as well as to offer help.

The idea was suggested by a young person recently released from prison who, when asked by clinical psychologist Charlie Howard, about what would help with his feeling stressed, he answered, "a problem-solving booth right here on my street". And thus, a movement began around community-led mental health innovations and a vision of changing the way we all think about help. The Owls Organisation (Owls) tested this idea in collaboration with the general public, organisations and policy-makers. With the ambition to scale, they have now been used as a tool to enable new conversations beyond the UK, such as in Sydney, Bermuda and Zurich.

> "The most interesting thing we learnt from testing problem solving booths was that it wasn't the tool itself that was going to change practice, but the values and ideas that underpinned it. It was fascinating to me that after running training for at least 50 psychologists, they all proposed a slightly different adaptation for how they would use them where they lived or worked. Such as re-designing a care-leavers' service, improving the traditional way of consulting families and carers, or talking to residents on a housing estate. The contexts were different every time, but the core concept remained the same. Everyone was giving a voice to those who weren't traditionally asked for help and the professionals were getting out of their usual 'helper' role. People also had different ways to describe the process, whether it was as empowerment, participation, co-production or community engagement. It didn't matter, it was about authentically giving some power away; the two chairs gave them the permission to do that".
>
> Dr. Nina Browne, clinical and community psychologist,
> Owls: www.owls.org.uk

Within communities

We largely work within a healthcare system in services designed to deliver interventions for specific groups of people or clusters of symptoms. Despite the remit and skill set of psychologists being much broader than individual therapeutic work, our services are often streamlined to provide for those who are most able to access, and to benefit, from services. In consequence, we effectively exclude those with the most complex needs, and people from communities that are the most underserved. It can be challenging to acknowledge working within structures that we feel are colluding with oppressive practices. Psychologists may be in positions to speak out about service inaccessibility, contribute to projects that find creative ways to reach out, and find small windows of opportunity to break down these barriers.

In demonstrating the value of such projects, we may need to look beyond routine outcome measures, and consider a range of creative ways to show the benefit to communities, including the things that people from communities tell us are important. We may need to engage people where they are at instead of expecting them to find our clinical spaces acceptable. We draw inspiration from approaches such as Mac-UK's project INTEGRATE, which means "to go out to where they are and offer a flexible, responsive and holistic service . . . working in communities (sometimes even in the streets)" (Mac-UK, n.d., para. 2). We encourage you to find out about your communities, and to think about its histories: of past projects, of possible identities, and of the possibilities of oppression.

We spoke to Noreen Dera, trainee clinical psychologist, about how she came to co-found BreakingMad, an outreach programme bringing mental health awareness to black communities.

In focus: BreakingMad

Noreen was a senior psychological wellbeing practitioner and lead for BAME service development in a diverse London borough, where it was noticed that some sectors of the community were rarely accessing the Increasing Access to Psychological Therapies (IAPT) service, and in particular, the service was keen to move towards improving access for young black men. Noreen made links with local community resources, with a focus on outreach, building relationships, destigmatising mental health within the black community, and raising awareness about how to access support.

However, she was met with various challenges in taking this work forwards, and her concerns sometimes fell on deaf ears. The service was looking for measurable targets, and service leads questioned the use of resources in developing these community links. At the same time, Noreen felt the service was unresponsive to needs of black people accessing the service, with lack of diversity within the team, a lack of diversity and cultural considerations embedded within the training courses and professional development, and reluctance of staff to talk about issues of race. As the only BAME representative within the team, Noreen was left with the main responsibilities for the project. When issues of race were raised, she describes a deafening silence in the room. Even though the research and service audits unearthed huge disparities in service provision for different cultural groups, one person lacked the power to address and to challenge this systemic injustice.

As a consequence of this experience, Noreen found support outside of services and within her own community. She co-founded BreakingMad in 2017 with two other psychological therapists, Christabel Adebayo and Pamela Akemu. The project aims to challenge the 'madness' narrative around mental health, a common misconception in the black community. The group engages with people in the community and set up 'chill-spaces' to start conversations about topics surrounding mental health, aiming to share information, debunk myths, and spark debate. These conversations are then shared on social media to bring awareness to the wider community, and has achieved wide following on YouTube, Facebook, Instagram (@breakingmadteam), and Twitter (#teambreakingmad).

Within research

As psychologists, we learn about and are expected to draw on an 'evidence base' to inform interventions, and apply skills in research methods to advance 'practice-based evidence'. While drawing on a full range of research approaches can be useful for influencing policy and practice, in this section, we look specifically at research methods that work towards the ethos of a critical community psychology, whose research "goals are to address oppression, encourage respect for diversity, and to use critical knowledge to challenge the status quo and promote social change" (Williams & Zlotowitz, 2013, p. 23).

Similar to our work within services, as researchers we often gain the privilege of access to people's lives, their stories and experiences. Traditional paradigms that we are taught throughout our undergraduate education and beyond, and against which our research skills are typically measured, encourage researchers to adopt positions of neutrality, and to strive for objectivity (Kemmis & McTaggart, 2005). However, many now consider that these guidelines were defined by scientists typically located within a Western culture and worldview (Bergold & Thomas, 2012), and would argue that there are possibilities to adopt a reflectively subjective role, that gives appreciation to a diversity of perspectives.

In our everyday practices, we encourage that consideration be given to our use of language in how research is thought about, fulfilled, disseminated and talked about, and in particular the implication that psychologists do research 'on', and conduct studies claiming to 'give voice' to, other groups. Language use can confer a difference in power and status, in which the researcher assumes benevolence, whilst implying that the researched group is disempowered. One way to address such power imbalance is by incorporating principles from 'participatory research' (Hall, 1992) where partnerships are forged with community members to carry out research *alongside*, and position participants as equal architects and authors of research projects (Nelson & Prilleltensky, 2004). Such collaborations with marginalised communities are often only possible through the establishment of trust

(Rath, 2012) that comes about through time, honesty and emotional investment. This makes important the balance between engagement in such projects with potential costs of commitment, time and energy, and the value and benefit that communities perceive these result in. For example, Romena reflects on her own story of involving her community in research in the *In focus* box below.

In focus: Faces of Westminster

"My father and I worked alongside the first- and second-generation British Bangladeshi people from our community. The aim was to replace negative narratives told about immigration through the media, with stories of 'resilience' and 'courage'. A key part of our project was to train the young people in conducting their own research; this allowed them to take ownership of the project and motivated them to share their findings widely. We then compiled a book with our findings that was then launched by the local MP at the Houses of Parliament. To help draw public attention we also invited other members of the local Labour Party and the media, thus allowing the publication to be broadcast on TV. Our book *Faces in Westminster* was printed and launched in November 2016. The freedom of doing this work as part of my community as a community worker, outside of the discipline of psychology, reminds me of how constrained we are within the profession".

Romena Toki (for more information see Toki and Rahman (2016) or visit: www.facesinwestminster.co.uk)

Through such collaborations with communities, and investment in the ethics of our work that values an outcome useful to communities – not just academic interests – our research will be enriched by the lived experience offered by diverse communities (Russo, 2012), and will bring authenticity to the resulting recommendations.

Conclusions

As authors, the writing of this chapter entailed confronting some of our own blind-spots to privilege, and drew attention to the times when we perhaps failed to act, or transgressed our own values. This teaches us that there are many layers to the work, and that most importantly, this work requires us to develop self-awareness, reflexivity, and both the capacity and tolerance to understand our own biases; to hear when we have hurt or offended, to take responsibility for this and apologise, and then to change our actions. Despite the difficulties, learning to stand alongside can be liberating as well as painful, and can enable closer connections to others as well as to our own ethics.

We reflect that there are many opportunities for change within our practice, and this chapter is an invitation to find and consider those opportunities when they become available. But also, there is a reality within certain contexts that we may find restrictive: there are elements to working in the NHS, for example, or fulfilling the requirements of training, that make some positions hard to take. We reflected on our privilege to be training within a course framework that has allowed us a large degree of freedom to pursue topics and research areas of our choice. We would like to see more freedom, more collaboration and more encouragement to pursue projects aligned with the values of trainees, just as we, in turn, aspire to support each other in finding creative and necessary ways to enact values of social justice.

Acknowledgements

We would like to thank the many people who provided advice, encouragement, experience, and personal reflections for writing the chapter: Noreen Dera, Pamela Akemu and Christabel Adebayo; Orla Gormley; a university friend who wished to remain anonymous; Genevieve Wallace; Dr Nina Browne; Dr Lizette Nolte; and all of the people we have worked with and learned from in our practice, research and communities over the years.

References

Arnstein, S. R. (1969). A ladder of citizen participation. *Journal of the American Institute of planners, 35*(4), 216–224. doi:10.1080/01944366908977225

Beresford, P. (2002). Participation and social policy: Transformation, liberation or regulation? In R. Sykes, C. Bochel, & N. Ellison (Eds.), *Social policy review 14: Developments and debates* (pp. 265–290). Bristol: The Policy Press.

Bergold, J., & Thomas, S. (2012). Participatory research methods: A methodological approach in motion. *Historical Social Research/Historische Sozialforschung, 37*(4), 191–222. doi:10.12759/hsr.37.2012.4.191-222

Bishop, A. (2002). *Becoming an ally: Breaking the cycle of oppression in people.* London: Zed Books.

BPS. (2018). *Psychologists and the media: Opportunities and challenges.* Retrieved from https://thepsychologist.bps.org.uk/volume-31/april-2018/psychologists-and-media-opportunities-and-challenges

Browne, N. (2017). *Practice to policy: Clinical psychologists' experiences of macro-level work* (Doctoral dissertation), UCL University College London.

Browne, N., Zlotowitz, S., Alcock, K., & Barker, C. (2019). *Practice to policy: Clinical psychologists' experiences of macro-level work.* Manuscript submitted for publication.

Burton & Kagan. (2008). *Societal case formulation.* Retrieved from www.compsy.org.uk/Societal%20case%20formulation%20expanded%20version%202008.pdf

Clearing House. (2019). *Equal opportunities.* Retrieved from www.leeds.ac.uk/chpccp/equalopps2017.html

Daiches, A., & Anderson, D. (2012). The experiences of training as a clinical psychologist with a minority sexual orientation. *Clinical Psychology Forum, 232*, 14–20.

Freire, P. (1970). *Cultural action for freedom*. Retrieved from www.thinkingtogether.org/rcream/archive/110/CulturalAction.pdf

Gay, R. (2016). *On making black lives matter*. Retrieved from www.marieclaire.com/culture/a21423/roxane-gay-philando-castile-alton-sterling/

Hagan, T., & Smail, D. (1997). Power-mapping: I. Background and basic methodology. *Journal of Community & Applied Social Psychology, 7*(4), 257–267.

Hall, B. L. (1992). From margins to center? The development and purpose of participatory research. *The American Sociologist, 23*(4), 15–28. doi:10.1007/bf02691928

Innes, A., Macpherson, S., & McCabe, L. (2006). *Promoting person-centred care at the front line*. York: Joseph Rowntree Foundation.

Kagan, C., Burton, M., Duckett, P., Lawthom, R., & Siddiquee, A. (2011). *Critical community psychology: Critical action and social change*. Chichester: BPS Blackwell.

Kemmis, S., & McTaggart, R. (2005). *Participatory action research: Communicative action and the public sphere*. Thousand Oaks, CA: Sage Publications.

Kessi, S. (2016). *Decolonising psychology creates possibilities for social change*. Retrieved from https://theconversation.com/decolonising-psychology-creates-possibilities-for-social-change-65902

Kinouani, G., Tserpeli, E., Nicholas, J., Neumann-May, B., Stamatopoulou, V., & Ibrahim-Özlü, J. (2015). Minorities in clinical psychology training: Reflections on the journey to finding a voice. *Clinical Psychology Forum, Special Issue*, 22–25.

Leonard, P. (1984). *Personality and ideology: Towards a materialist understanding of the individual*. London: Macmillan.

MAC-UK. (n.d.). *Our approach*. Retrieved from www.mac-uk.org/our-approach

Martín-Baró, I. (1994). *Writings for a liberation psychology*. London: Harvard University Press.

McClelland, L. (2014). Reformulating the impact of social inequalities. In L. Johnstone & R. Dallos (Eds.), *Formulation in psychology and psychotherapy* (2nd ed., pp. 121–144). London: Routledge.

McIntosh, P. (1988). *White privilege: Unpacking the invisible knapsack*. Retrieved from www.racialequitytools.org/resourcefiles/mcintosh.pdf

Nelson, G. B., & Prilleltensky, I. (2004). *Community psychology: In pursuit of liberation and well-being*. Basingstoke: Palgrave Macmillan.

NHS England. (2016). *The five year forward view for mental health*. Retrieved from www.england.nhs.uk/wp-content/uploads/2016/02/Mental-Health-Taskforce-FYFV-final.pdf

Odusanya, S. O. E., Winter, D., Nolte, L., & Shah, S. (2017). The experience of being a qualified female BME clinical psychologist in a national health service: An interpretative phenomenological and repertory grid analysis. *Journal of Constructivist Psychology, 31*(3), 273–291. doi:10.1080/10720537.2017.1304301

Orford, J. (2008). *Community psychology: Challenges, controversies and emerging consensus*. Chichester: Wiley. doi:10.1002/9780470773154

Pantic, I. (2014). Online social networking and mental health. *Cyberpsychology, Behavior, and Social Networking, 17*(10), 652–657.

Rath, J. (2012). Poetry and participation: Scripting a meaningful research text with rape crisis workers. *Forum: Qualitative Social Research, 13*(1/22). http://dx.doi.org/10.17169/fqs-13.1.1791

Reynolds, V. (2011). Resisting burnout with justice-doing. *International Journal of Narrative Therapy & Community Work*, (4), 27–45.

Reynolds, V. (2013). "Leaning in" as imperfect Allies in community work. *Narrative and Conflict: Explorations in Theory and Practice, 1*(1), 53–75.

Rhodes, E. (2016). *Are we punching our weight?* Retrieved from https://thepsychologist. bps.org.uk/volume-29/may-2016/are-we-punching-our-weight

Richardson, C., & Reynolds, V. (2012). "Here we are, amazingly alive": Holding ourselves together with an ethic of social justice in community work. *International Journal of Child, Youth and Family Studies, 1*, 1–19.

Russo, J. (2012). Survivor-controlled research: A new foundation for thinking about psychiatry and mental health. *Forum: Qualitative Social Research, 13*(1). http://nbn-resolving.de/urn:nbn:de:0114-fqs120187

Saffer, J. (2018). *How changes to disability benefits harm claimants' well-being and sense of identity.* Retrieved from https://theconversation.com/amp/how-changes-to-disability-benefits-harm-claimants-well-being-and-sense-of-identity-91951

Saffer, J. (2019). Providing a humanising service for our dehumanised clients. *Context, 164*, 34–36.

Saffer, J., Nolte, L., & Duffy, S. (2018). Living on a knife edge: The responses of people with physical health conditions to changes in disability benefits. *Disability & Society*, 1–24.

Shah, S., Wood, N., Nolte, L., & Goodbody, L. (2012). The experience of being a trainee clinical psychologist from a black and minority ethnic group: A qualitative study. *Clinical Psychology Forum, 232*, 32–35.

Smail, D. (2005). *Power, interest and psychology: Elements of a social materialist understanding of distress.* Ross-on-Wye: PCCS Books.

Sue, D. W., Capodilupo, C. M., Torino, G. C., Bucceri, J. M., Holder, A., Nadal, K. L., & Esquilin, M. (2007). Racial microaggressions in everyday life: Implications for clinical practice. *American psychologist, 62*(4), 271–284.

Tisdall, E. K. M. (2017). Conceptualising children and young people's participation: Examining vulnerability, social accountability and co-production. *The International Journal of Human Rights, 21*(1), 59–75.

Toki, R., & Rahman, A. (2016). *Faces in Westminster.* London: Central London Youth Development Trust.

Wallcraft, J., Rose, D., Reid, J. J. A., & Sweeney, A. (2003). *On our own terms: Users and survivors of mental health services working together for support and change.* London, UK: Sainsbury Centre for Mental Health.

White, M., & Epston, D. (1990). *Narrative means to therapeutic ends.* London: Norton.

Williams, G. A., & Zlotowitz, S. (2013). Using a community psychology approach in your research. *PsyPAG Quarterly*, (86), 21–25.

Chapter 8

Reflections on the therapeutic journey

Opening up dialogues around personal therapy

Amy Lyons and Elizabeth Malpass, with thanks to Silan Gyane

Introduction

As the authors of this chapter we believe in the value of being open about ourselves and who we are. To us, this is important both personally and professionally in our role as psychologists. One way in which we have felt able to understand and be open about ourselves is via our journeys within our own personal therapy, which we briefly describe in this chapter. Sometimes beginning the therapeutic journey can be daunting, particularly when facing decisions about what would be most useful to you. We have come together to write this as an invitation to you to consider your own therapeutic journeys, wherever you find yourselves within this. Some of the discussions throughout come from research completed by the two of us, who are interested in understanding differing methods of personal development and how these may create impact on practice (Lyons, Mason, Nutt, & Keville, 2019; Malpass, 2018). One of the ideas that sparked our interest in these areas was the debate around whether clinical psychologists should engage in mandatory personal therapy.

Unlike other psychologists in training (e.g., counselling psychologists), personal therapy is not a mandatory requirement for trainee clinical psychologists in the UK (Wilson, Weatherhead, & Davies, 2015). There are no clear accounts or indicators within the professional body on how this decision was and continues to be made. The British Psychological Society (BPS) Division of Clinical Psychology (DCP) website states that the decision is largely due to the historical routes and foundation upon which the clinical psychology training programmes were developed, as well as the varied role of clinical psychologists who do not work solely as therapists (Duncan, 2012; Wilson et al., 2015). Some argue that there is little conclusive evidence that completing therapy whilst training impacts on clinical practice (Murphy, Irfan, Barnett, Castledine, & Enescu, 2018). This lack of evidence may impact justifications for making personal therapy mandatory. There continues to be debate relating to whether the culture of the profession may impact on how therapy and experiences of distress are talked about (Davidson & Patel, 2009).

There are ideas embedded within the profession that suggest that in order to prac-tice, clinical psychologists should be immune to their own difficulties (Davidson & Patel, 2009). Richards (2010) talks of the distinction between 'us' and 'them', which may give the idea that individuals seeking support are somehow different to the professionals they visit. The desire, or perceived need, to engage with therapy may suggest vulnerability, or movement towards the position of client. This may make open discussion difficult for those of us who experience distress or vulnerability.

Therefore, discussions around the use of and experiences of therapy may be challenging. These challenges may also reflect broader perspectives of aspiring psychologists to discuss personal experiences and expressions of distress that can make us feel vulnerable (Aina, 2015; Davidson & Patel, 2009). This is despite a widely accepted understanding that distress often influences us to embark upon the journey to becoming a psychologist in the first place (Jackson, 2001). The journey arguably requires much self-reflexivity. This can refer to a process of reflecting on the self – our presence, contribution, power and interests (for discussion see Chinn, 2007; Holland, 1999). It has been referred to as the 'internal conversation' we have with ourselves (Archer, & Archer, 2003; Wiley, 1994), which involves both self-knowledge and self-monitoring (Gecas & Burke, 1995; Pagis, 2009).

To begin reflections on these issues this chapter will explore what we mean by personal therapy and how we might use it as part of becoming a psychologist. We provide our own reflections on experiences of therapy before and during training as psychologists. We hope the chapter provides a reflective space to consider what therapy is and how it may relate to your personal and professional journeys. We hope that this also opens up conversations about experiences of distress and ways that these might be understood and managed.

The wounded healer

The idea of the 'wounded healer' suggests that those experiencing psychologi-cal 'wounds' may come to the profession as a method of drawing on our own 'wounds' to assist the healing of others (Guggenbühl-Craig, 1971; Jackson, 2001; Nouwen, 1972; Sedgwick, 1994). We understand the definition of wounds to be broad; relating to any experience that results in distress. There is suggestion that the more a 'wounded healer' understands their 'wounds', the better able they may be to guide others through this process (Gelson & Hayes, 2007). It may then be important for those of us hoping to become psychologists to be able to reflect on our own 'wounds' so that we may be better able to help others.

What is therapy and what do we mean by it?

In this chapter, we refer to personal therapy as a form of therapy of any theoretical kind or format (Norcross & Guy, 2005). Each of us will have differing under-standings of what we consider to be therapy. Some may only consider traditional self-defined methods, which would include particular models or modalities with a trained therapist or counsellor. This may be provided by the National Health

Service (NHS), or be privately funded or commissioned by services acting on behalf of an individual (e.g., social services). The modes of therapy would be exhaustive but may include psychotherapy, humanistic therapy, counselling, systemic therapy or cognitive behaviour therapy. Sometimes, therapists may integrate different ways of working, which would be described as integrative practice (Lazarus, 2005). Cognitive analytical therapy (CAT) would be an example of a defined integrative therapy (Ryle, 1990), whilst other integrative ways of working are more loosely defined.

Less prescribed or conventional forms of therapy may include models based on peer support, such as the Hearing Voices Network. We would also like to extend this definition to include any therapeutic activity or endeavour that allows a space for reflecting on oneself, and perhaps providing some form of psychological healing. This may include artistic pursuits, reflective groups, or yoga and dance, all activities that might allow a connection and an exploration of the self (Colbert, Cooke, Camic, & Springham, 2013; Croom, 2015; Stuckey & Nobel, 2010).

Thinking space

Take a few minutes to reflect on experiences which you have found therapeutic. What is it that you may have learnt about yourself from this, what was it about this interaction that made it feel therapeutic? If you were to talk about this experience with a friend, how would you describe it? If you feel that you have not had an experience of something therapeutic, then have a think about what might have stopped you (e.g., was there something about you, the other person, or the environment at the time?).

Why use personal therapy?

Personal and professional development (PPD) is the way in which we gain knowledge about ourselves personally and professionally and is central to working as a psychologist (BPS, 2006). One important way in which PPD is developed is through reflecting on how we work, which may include thinking about how our personal selves impact our professional work as well as how our work impacts who we are. This way of reflecting is often called reflective practice, a process through which "we learn by doing and realising what came of what we did" (Dewey, 1938, p. 367).

There are many ways to develop reflective ways of practicing (Cushway & Gatherer, 2003; Lavender, 2003; Stedmon, Mitchell, Johnstone, & Staite, 2003). Personal therapy has been suggested as one of these, because it has been linked to the development of self-awareness, reflective skills, and personal development (Nel, Pezzolesi, & Stott, 2012; Grimmer & Tribe, 2001; Lavender, 2003; Rizq & Target, 2008a, 2008b; Timms, 2010; Wigg, Cushway, & Neal, 2011; Wilson et al., 2015).

Apart from being a method to assist in the development of self-reflection, therapy may assist in helping and understanding our own distress, another important aspect of our profession. It is however important to note that some research has demonstrated that although therapy can be helpful, it can also be experienced as challenging and can at times lead to distress (Murphy et al., 2018; Rizq & Target, 2008a, 2008b; Wilson et al., 2015). For many, this distress was felt to be justifiable given the eventual outcome, for others this is not the case (Malpass, 2018; Murphy et al., 2018).

We have discussed some reasons to use personal therapy, as well as some of the potential barriers or problems faced in doing so. We now move to an exploration of the authors' experiences of using personal therapy, and how these experiences were understood by an aspiring clinical psychologist.

Curious conversations: *what is therapy really like?*

In thinking about how to write this chapter we collaborated with an assistant psychologist who interviewed us about what therapy was like. The excerpts below are taken from our conversations, and are grouped together into themes. We have added references along the way for further reading and ideas. An introduction from the interviewer provides the context for the interview.

An introduction from the interviewer

Silan: *Prior to this interview, I had had conversations with more and more psychologists in professional settings who told me of their decision to go to personal therapy before or during their training. This sparked my curiosity in their choices to pursue therapy, the timing of these choices in their professional journeys and what sorts of things they took to therapy. These conversations were also a catalyst to me in considering whether or not personal therapy would be something I would want to pursue.*

When the opportunity to interview Amy and Liz arose, I chose to ask questions that would give me insight into their personal reasons to pursue therapy and some detail about their experiences of it, particularly whilst training to be psychologists. I was interested in finding out how they balanced attending to and processing their own therapy during clinical training, whilst at the same time supporting clients to improve their own emotional wellbeing. I also wanted to find out how open they felt they could be with their fellow trainees, course staff, friends and family about engaging in personal therapy.

Making the decision to use therapy

The beginning of our conversation explored how we came to use therapy both before and during training. Our conversations highlight that we were both drawn to use therapy as a way of making sense of times of distress.

Needing to make sense of distress

Liz: *I've used therapy a few times in my life. The reason I went to see a therapist for the first time (prior to training) is that I had a really difficult relationship breakdown, and I was just really struggling emotionally and it was impacting my day to day life. The therapy was relatively brief, and I think I did about 24 sessions with an integrative therapist. It was really helpful, and I felt a lot better, and more able to reengage with things I had stopped doing.*

Amy: *I had a similar experience – I had a relationship breakdown. And I wasn't coping very well. Going through that experience opened up Pandora's box a little bit. So that's where my therapy journey began. Initially I had some counselling, and then accessed an Increasing Access to Psychological Therapies (IAPT) service and had cognitive behaviour therapy (CBT). I later started schema therapy, which ended the month before I started training. I then had about a six month break from therapy before starting again.*

Working out the unanswered

As we both began training, there was a continued sense of curiosity in further understanding ourselves, and perhaps arguably, the feeling that understanding ourselves may be an important aspect of our training. One way in which we felt we could do this was by accessing our own therapy.

Liz: *One of the reasons I went back to therapy was because of the process of training; I became more aware that there were lots of things that had happened to me throughout my life that I hadn't addressed. I hadn't really thought that I needed to until I started training, I then began wondering if some of my experiences were unresolved and how these may impact on my work if not addressed.*

I also remember one of my tutors saying to me something like, "how can you ask other people to be vulnerable with you if you can't take steps to be vulnerable with others?" And I was really struck by this, and by my lack of willingness to take risks with my own vulnerability, yet that is what I asked of others. Then in my second placement, I had a client who I found really challenging to work with and I wanted a space to work out why, as I felt I couldn't do that with my supervisor. So that's how I came to consider going back to therapy whilst training.

Amy: *I started private therapy, an attachment-based psychodynamic psychotherapy in the second term of training. I've been seeing this therapist for over four years now. Another relationship breakdown made me realise there was a lot of stuff there that I hadn't looked at before; it was present before the breakup, but the actual breakup itself was almost like a catalyst for thinking about it. I sometimes look back and wonder whether, if I was in a different career, I would have sought different ways to cope with what was going on, as opposed to taking it to the therapy room?*

Every person's decision to access a talking therapy at different points in their life will be based on a unique set of circumstances. As we have outlined above however, there can be common themes that can link these experiences. Above, we demonstrated how both of us had significant life events causing distress that led us to start using personal therapy and that we both used therapy during training to support our personal and professional development, as well as to help in managing difficult aspects of training. For further explorations of trainee clinical psychologists' experiences of using personal therapy whilst training see Malpass (2018) and Wilson et al. (2015).

Choosing a type of therapy

Liz: *I actually looked at a few different types of therapy; I didn't want something practical, I wanted something exploratory, I wanted to think about my childhood and how it linked to where I'm at now.*

Amy: *For me, CBT didn't scratch the surface, and counselling didn't either. It needed to go deeper, and I think my difficulties are related to my attachment style and the patterns in my relationships. I needed longer-term therapy that focused on relationships. I wondered if I wasn't doing this for a job and making a career out of this, would I know how to access the right support? I perhaps wouldn't have been able to pinpoint the type of support I really needed, which makes me feel really sad, that I might never have had the opportunity to work through some of that stuff. It's really quite a privilege. Not that the process is finished – I think I'll be in the process of resolving, or working towards resolving, and examining those relational difficulties, probably for the rest of my life.*

The decision as to what kind of therapy may be a good fit for you is very personal. As we have shown, both of us sought out analytical forms of therapy. These models and other models derived from psychoanalysis are often the most common forms of therapies accessed by training therapists (Malpass, 2018; Murphy et al., 2018; Nel et al., 2012; Wilson et al., 2015). This may be because these models are more exploratory, typically longer term, and focus on identity and self-exploration. It is of course worth noting that decisions around what type of therapy to engage with could reflect personal preferences, curiosities, the purpose of seeking supports, or the perceived nature of 'the problem' or the situation at hand. Take for example, the editor of this book decided to engage in CBT before training due to his hopes of creating a greater sense of certainty about 'what to do' with his dwindling sense of self at the time.

Being a trainee psychologist in therapy

These extracts explore our feelings about being in the position of a trainee psychologist and a person in therapy at the same time, and dilemmas that may have come with this.

Liz: I actually think accessing therapy whilst training was useful. I felt like I had a genuine window into what therapy was like from the perspective of clients – not just an intellectual sense of what it was like but I felt I had a better emotional understanding of the process. Of course, your experiences are not the same as your clients', but I felt that it gave me a better understanding of things that I felt might be helpful or not so helpful in my own practice.

However, there were times when I found therapy incredibly emotionally challenging. I would say I found it more difficult to go to university at these times. Perhaps because university was a really safe space for me, and so then if I was upset, I guess it would all come out. At these times it was more difficult to concentrate on lectures because my mind would just be elsewhere. However, overall, I think the gains outweighed the challenges.

Amy: I think it enabled me to connect more with my clients. And it allowed me to be a bit more forgiving about my practice as a therapist. Sometimes I'd walked into my own therapy and think, you know what, I can't be bothered! I can't be bothered to go and talk. And it made me realise that probably some of my clients probably felt the same sometimes, and that's okay. And it was all about recognising that, which was important.

Sometimes I'd be really hard on myself as a therapist after a particular session, and think, I've not done well today. But then there'd be a parallel process in my own therapy, like sometimes I'd think that wasn't a great session; we were just treading water. But what it taught me was that actually that is part of the wider process, and to trust in that process. So, you might start putting pieces of the jigsaw together in your mind about a session that you had weeks ago, and suddenly it's like, I can make sense of that now, which again has allowed me to be more forgiving to myself as a therapist. I learned that not every session will lead to huge revelations, but every session is still important in its own way.

Liz: It made me realise the extent of the impact I could have on others. I've had sessions in which my therapist had really upset me. Either by using humour, but just at the wrong sort of times, or by getting something wrong and me feeling that I hadn't been understood. Looking back, these moments were actually helpful. Not only did they make me understand that I had the power to potentially hurt the clients I worked with in the same way, but it allowed me to understand the process of therapeutic repair.

What's common to both of our reflections here is that a lot of useful information can be taken away from the experience of being a client and a lot can be learned on both a personal and professional level. This fits with other research that suggests that one of the most important parts of the experience of using personal therapy whilst training is that experiences in one's own personal therapy allow a deeper and more substantial understanding of how therapy may be for our clients, which is sometimes called experiential learning (Malpass, 2018; Wilson et al., 2015).

Can I train to do this if I haven't even got myself 'together'?

An interesting question that came out of this interview was how one may feel about being a trainee at times when they may not feel very 'together' themselves. It speaks to the question of whether we can be responsible for helping others at times of our own distress.

Liz: *Someone did say to me once, if you're a psychologist, aren't you supposed to know how it works? I took from this that they meant that I should be emotionally stable at all times. I would guess that other people think this too. I used to think it myself, sometimes I still do. Sometimes I worried my therapist would judge my professional capacity. Even now I sometimes wonder whether they're thinking 'how the hell are you giving other people therapy'. The key is, I would say this to them, and only then could we think and talk about it, and work out why I was feeling that way.*

      Through therapy I have become more comfortable with owning the idea that everybody can be distressed. So, if I said to my therapist, I feel "mad" they'd say, isn't everybody mad? Isn't that just being human? Everybody is depressed sometimes, everybody is anxious sometimes, everybody is angry sometimes, so they'd helped me to appreciate that life comes with ups and downs for everybody. I guess what is important is through using therapy I know my limitations and when perhaps I do need to take a day off.

Amy: *Yeah, definitely, through darker times I would despair at myself, absolutely. And sometimes, I do the same now, actually! When I'm having a wobbler, I have that thought still. But I don't think I've experienced that from other people, it's more from myself and the pressure and expectations I put on myself, which doesn't necessarily match other people's expectations. I think for a lot of us, before getting onto training, we thought that everyone that gets on is perfect and amazing, and I think we were quite fortunate that we were in a cohort that sent the message that it's okay, it's part of being a human to sometimes not be okay. I think part of our role is to advocate that we all have mental health. If we aren't able to send that message, then what hope have we got for advocating for the people we work with?*

As you can see, we have had experiences where we question our competence, particularly at times when we have felt emotionally vulnerable. In addition, there were worries about how our own therapists might view us given our feelings. As we have discussed, within the British context of clinical psychology, experiences of distress can be difficult to talk about due to the 'us and them' divide – the idea that professionals should be different from the clients they are working with. Indeed, when James (the editor) accessed CBT as a health care assistant, he held back from mentioning his degree and work for quite some time – fearing exposure as someone who 'ought to know better'. For further discussion of these ideas see Aina (2015), Davidson and Patel (2009); Malpass (2018), and Richards (2010).

In closing the interview, we asked the interviewer to reflect upon the process.

Reflections from the interviewer

Silan: *Being part of a conversation about personal therapy with Liz and Amy brought to light a number of benefits of pursuing personal therapy. They both spoke of it enhancing their work with clients in the therapy chair, having been in that position themselves. Through what they shared, I got the sense that receiving personal therapy gave them a unique perspective through which they can now relate to clients in ways that are more empathetic, warm and thoughtful. They also commented that balancing the demands of personal therapy, university and placement workloads was manageable, but I wonder whether this can change at particular points in one's journey?*

    Amy and Liz talked of the challenges faced in committing to personal therapy before and/or during training, but also of how personal therapy could enhance their work with clients. Their perspectives gave me insight into how transparency about one's pursuit of personal therapy as a psychologist can be perceived in different ways, and can depend on, for example, the culture of the service or university one works in, or the cohort that individuals train with. It was interesting to hear that some of the stigma they feel is attached to the idea of psychologists speaking openly about their pursuits of therapy in the profession.

    In terms of my position on pursuing therapy as someone about to embark on training, I would say that this conversation has highlighted how helpful personal therapy can be both personally and professionally, with balance of some of the challenges. I would be open to pursuing therapy in the future if I felt it would be helpful, even more so in light of this conversation with Amy and Liz.

To use therapy, or not to use therapy? Some concluding thoughts

Throughout this chapter, we have provided you as our reader an introduction to how therapy might be used as part of your journey to becoming a clinical psychologist. As we have described, both of us came to write this chapter as we had a particular interest, and personal experience of accessing different types of therapies throughout our journeys to becoming clinical psychologists. We therefore advocate for its use: from our perspective, we believe that all aspiring clinical psychologists should experience some form of therapy either prior to or during their training.

As we have shared with you, we believe that therapy can be a useful experience in relation to our personal and professional development. This is supported by the

BPS (2006), who acknowledge that PPD is the range of ways in which we gain knowledge about ourselves personally and professionally and is central to working as a psychologist. Perhaps more importantly, we think that having the experience of being a client in therapy can help to expel some of the myths related to the 'us and them' idea, and can embody the message that it is okay to not to be okay.

We hope this chapter has helped you to consider your own position about seeking therapy, and has challenged some of the perspectives and ideas that you might have held prior to reading it.

Finally, we want to stress that the accounts presented here are related to *our* experience of therapy, and that this will be different for each and every one of us. We hope that we have instilled the idea that therapeutic activities are not limited to a 'formal' therapy process; that there are a rainbow of ways in which we can engage in a therapeutic encounter, and each one will be unique to us all.

Reflective activity: debating the need for personal therapy

Find a friend or group of peers, and assign yourself into roles: those in agreement and arguing *for* a point, and those in disagreement, arguing *against*. Then discuss the following statement: *Personal therapy should be compulsory for those training to become clinical psychologists. Debate.*

You could arrange to discuss this at a later date, so that you and your peers can do some wider reading. Could you invite someone else, perhaps a supervisor or someone not associated with psychology, to join as your audience and see whose argument they are most convinced by?

References

Aina, O. (2015). *Clinical psychologists' personal experiences of psychological distress.* (Doctoral dissertation), University of East London. Retrieved from http://roar.uel.ac.uk/4547/1/Olumayowa%20Aina.pdf

Archer, M. S., & Archer, M. S. (2003). *Structure, agency and the internal conversation.* Cambridge: Cambridge University Press.

British Psychological Society (BPS). (2006). *Generic professional practice guidelines.* Leicester, England: British Psychological Society.

Chinn, D. (2007). Reflection and reflexivity. *Clinical Psychology Forum, 178,* 13–16.

Colbert, S., Cooke, A., Camic, P. M., & Springham, N. (2013). The art-gallery as a resource for recovery for people who have experienced psychosis. *The Arts in Psychotherapy, 40*(2), 250–256.

Croom, A. M. (2015). The practice of poetry and the psychology of wellbeing. *Journal of Poetry Therapy, 28*(1), 24–41.

Cushway, D., & Gatherer, A. (2003). Reflecting on reflection. *Clinical Psychology*, *27*, 6–10.

Davidson, S., & Patel, N. (2009). Power and identity: Considerations for personal and professional development. In J. Hughes & S. Youngson (Eds.), *Personal development and clinical psychology*. Leicester: British Psychological Society.

Dewey, J. (1938). *Experience and education*. New York: Palgrave Macmillan.

Duncan, A. C. (2012). *Intra and interpersonal factors in the use of personal therapy by trainee clinical psychologists*. (Doctoral dissertation). Retrieved from http://hdl.handle.net/2299/7621

Gecas, V., & Burke, P. J. (1995). Self and identity. In K. S. Cook, G. Fine, & J. S. House (Eds.), *Sociological perspectives on social psychology* (pp. 41–67). Boston, MA: Allyn & Bacon.

Gelson, C. J., & Hayes, J. (2007). *Countertransference and the therapist's inner experience: Perils and possibilities*. New York: Routledge and Taylor & Francis Group.

Grimmer, A., & Tribe, R. (2001). Counselling psychologists' perceptions of the impact of mandatory PT on professional development: An exploratory study. *Counselling Psychology Quarterly*, *14*(4), 287–301.

Guggenbühl-Craig, A. (1971). *Power in the helping professions*. Ohio, USA: Spring Publications.

Holland, R. (1999). Reflexivity. *Human Relations*, *52*, 463–483.

Jackson, S. W. (2001). The wounded healer. *Bulletin of the History of Medicine*, *75*, 1–36.

Lavender, T. (2003). Redressing the balance: The place, history and future of reflective practice in clinical training. *Clinical Psychology*, *27*, 11–15.

Lazarus, A. A. (2005). Multimodal therapy. In J. C. Norcross & M. R. Goldfried (Eds.), *Handbook of psychotherapy integration*. New York: Oxford University Press.

Lyons, A., Mason, B., Nutt, K., & Keville, S. (2019). Inside it was orange squash concentrate: Trainees' experiences of reflective practice groups within clinical psychology training. *Reflective Practice*, *20*(1), 70–84.

Malpass, E. (2018). *Trainee clinical psychologists' experiences of personal therapy and its relationship to development across training: A grounded theory study*. (Doctoral Dissertation). University of Hertfordshire, Hatfield, UK.

Murphy, D., Irfan, N., Barnett, H., Castledine, E., & Enescu, L. (2018). A systematic review and meta-analysis of qualitative research into mandatory personal psychotherapy during training. *Counselling and Psychotherapy Research*, *18*(2), 199–214.

Nel, P. W., Pezzolesi, C., & Stott, D. J. (2012). How did we learn best? A retrospective survey of clinical psychology training in the United Kingdom. *Journal of Clinical Psychology*, *68*(9), 1058–1073.

Norcross, J. C., & Guy, J. D. (2005). The prevalence and parameters of personal therapy in the United States. *The Psychotherapist's Own Psychotherapy: Patient and Clinician Perspectives*, 165–176.

Nouwen, J. M. (1972). *The wounded healer: Ministry in contemporary society*. New York, USA: Doubleday Publishing.

Pagis, M. (2009). Embodied self-reflexivity. *Social Psychology Quarterly*, *72*(3), 265–283.

Richards, D. (2010). Low-intensity CBT. *Oxford Guide to Surviving as a CBT Therapist*, 123.

Rizq, R., & Target, M. (2008a). "The power of being seen": An interpretative phenomenological analysis of how experienced counselling psychologists describe the meaning and significance of personal therapy in clinical practice. *British Journal of Guidance & Counselling, 36*(2), 131–153.

Rizq, R., & Target, M. (2008b). "Not a little Mickey Mouse thing": How experienced counselling psychologists describe the significance of personal therapy in clinical practice and training. Some results from an interpretative phenomenological analysis. *Counselling Psychology Quarterly, 21*(1), 29–48.

Ryle, A. (1990). Cognitive analytic therapy. In J. C. Norcross & M. R. Goldfried (Eds.), *Handbook of psychotherapy integration*. Oxford: Oxford University Press.

Sedgwick, D. (1994). *The wounded healer: Countertransference from a Jungian perspective*. New York, NY: Routledge.

Stedmon, J., Mitchell, A., Johnstone, L., & Staite, S. (2003). Making reflective practice real: Problems and solutions in the South West. *Clinical Psychology, 27*(7), 30–33.

Stuckey, H. L., & Nobel, J. (2010). The connection between art, healing, and public health: A review of current literature. *American journal of public health, 100*(2), 254–263.

Timms, J. (2010). A taste of our own . . . therapy: Trainees' rationales for, and experiences of, personal therapy'. *Clinical Psychology Forum, 213*, 34–39.

Wigg, R., Cushway, D., & Neal, A. (2011). Personal therapy for therapists and trainees: A theory of reflective practice from a review of the literature. *Reflective Practice, 12*(3), 347–359.

Wiley, N. (1994). *The semiotic self*. Chicago: University of Chicago University Press.

Wilson, H., Weatherhead, S. J., & Davies, J. S. (2015). Clinical psychologists' experiences of accessing personal therapy during training: A narrative analysis. *International Journal of Practice-based Learning in Health and Social Care, 3*(2), 32–47.

Chapter 9

On the reconciliation
of selves

Reflections on navigating
professional domains

Danielle Chadderton and Marta Isibor

In aspiring to become clinical psychologists, we are faced with many challenges. The competitive nature of applying to training means that we will often spend many years in lower paid roles to gain relevant experience, with no guarantee of progression. This can lead to high levels of stress and burnout, even before considering the difficult nature of working in mental health at a time when resources are extremely limited. For many of us, we will have our own personal mental health experiences that have led us to pursue this career. This brings further questions: how do I reconcile my own vulnerabilities with a role that requires me to provide a support to others? In what way can I authentically bring all of who I am to my work, in order to benefit others?

Here, we share our thoughts, experiences and reflections on the interface of the personal and professional – a place where we find ourselves faced with the daily nuances of the political. As individuals hoping to one day train as clinical psychologists, we hope that sharing our own accounts of navigating our personal distress within professional terrains, can offer something different for you as our reader, but also, for our wider profession – recognising, naming and reflecting on the often invisible and/or unvoiced experiences of those pre-qualified clinicians with lived experience of mental health difficulties.

Disclosure of our own mental health problems, as discussed in previous chapters, brings with it a range of concerns over fitness to practice and questions around how we will be perceived by others on hearing of our experiences. Stigma and discrimination remain rife in mental health settings and this can affect our own attitudes toward self-disclosure. Conversely, by disclosing we are likely to go some way towards tackling the prejudices and myths that exist. By sharing, as individuals and collectively, we acknowledge the shared humanity in mental distress and go some way in breaking down the 'us and them' barriers that continue to harm those who use the services we work in. The profession of clinical psychology is harmed when people who would diversify it are dissuaded from even applying, and when we do not see ourselves in the spaces we would like to enter. Though the impetus should be on creating the contexts for which lived experience can be heard and be visible, and not on the individuals themselves. As authors, we each have experiences of disclosing our mental health difficulties as psychology graduates working in mental health services – though they are not necessarily through choice and are in very different settings.

Living with dermatillomania is difficult. Skin picking has a visible physical manifestation. This makes it tricky to hide it from the outside world – the stuff doesn't happen only in your head but it ravages your skin. It's like a virus or like an obsession. Is it a disease to combat or a part of me to accept? And what does this mean for an aspiring clinical psychologist working in mental health? First of all, it presents me with a number of issues and decisions to make. One of the chief ones concerns disclosure. Do I remain silent about my mental health, do I talk about it openly, do I try to conceal it and only address it if directly asked? What's more – am I in a position to support others while I myself at times require support? Are mental health professionals not meant to be the emotionally well-rounded role models? How far in the healing process should we be before engaging in a therapeutic work with people? Am I going to be criticised as a wounded healer? Does having a mental health diagnosis constitute vulnerability or strength in a therapeutic role? Does this give me a unique insight? Does this change how I relate to clients? As an aspiring clinical psychologist, I am only beginning to appreciate the complexities of these issues.

It is widely known that psychology is a very popular choice for prospective students, with many psychology graduates aspiring to practice within clinical psychology. The reality also is that the clinical training route is heavily oversubscribed. Many graduates, including myself, attempt to gather adequate experience in order to get on the training. This can be a challenging and draining time, given the limited opportunities available to those at the pre-qualification stage. This is certainly the case in Edinburgh, where I work as honorary assistant psychologist in Psychiatric Rehabilitation Service. A context of restricted resources leads to a climate of 'fighting for resources', which can generate a toxic atmosphere of competition. Understandably, this poses numerous problems. Given the caring nature of the mental health profession, characterised by high rates of burnout and emotional burden, we should not underestimate the possible impact of all of this on the wellbeing of aspiring psychologists, even at this early stage of their career.

Marta

As someone in a lived experience role (a peer recovery worker in a community mental health team), I do not get to choose whether or not I disclose my mental illness to colleagues and people under the care of our team. I work very specifically as part of the 'personality disorder' pathway, and explaining what I do means explaining that I have a diagnosis of Borderline Personality Disorder. I'm not currently using mental health services but have received treatment from the NHS Trust I now work for. I feel like I'm often put in the position of giving the 'service user' perspective, which is not only impossible to do with just one person's input, but also feels very far from my experience given that I spent many more years just trying to access mental health services at all, than I did actually receiving them.

It's difficult to try to be learning from colleagues and building myself into a team, whilst also trying to retain my identity as someone whose work is about having a shared understanding with the people we care for.

It often feels like I am residing in this liminal space where there are no certainties, and I have to learn to become comfortable with the tensions between where people think I should be, where I would like to be, and where I am. At the same time, I have to be aware that if I am to progress in a mental health career, I will have to re-train in another role, have different boundaries and make different choices than I do now when it comes to disclosure, because I will be using a professional 'expertise' and not 'myself' as someone who has personal experience of living with mental health issues. It's a very confusing place to be and having to constantly reflect on my position in relation to others is incredibly challenging.

Dani

The typical 'recovery story' that is often shared will follow the narrative of unwellness to wellness, from struggle to success, in a way that makes the darker times seem more meaningful. For many of us, though, the struggle goes on. We can't box away our difficulties. While they may not lead our lives, they still play a vital role in shaping who we are and how we respond to ourselves, and those around us. Accepting our personal struggles can help us to hold conflicting ideas alongside one another, to be both one who suffers and one who supports others.

When I am with someone who is in crisis, allowing myself to feel what they are feeling is painful and reminds me of my own experiences, but it also allows me to understand and appreciate what they are going through. What I hope I am also beginning to be able to do is to communicate that to the other person, that I'm trying to hold both of our pain and treat it with the respect and care it deserves. Even if it is just looking or nodding or saying a word, I trust that the genuineness and authenticity of those moments is felt and provides an opportunity to feel something different from another person than what has come before: your pain is real, and important, and deserving of attention. I feel that is what I got from my own experience of therapy with a final year trainee clinical psychologist, and it transformed my relationship with myself and made me want to pursue clinical psychology as a career. I see my emotions as a valuable part of how I interact with others in my role now, and the pain of that as the price for being trusted to support people when they are at their most vulnerable. If we don't feel in any way affected by being with someone who feels suicidal, how can we say we have really cared for them?

I have often wondered if it might be somehow easier when I am not in a role that displays some of my vulnerabilities and defines me by them, but over time I have realised that whatever I do, my experiences will inform my relationships with people. Becoming familiar with discomfort and accepting it as part of a process of growth, rather than of punishment, feels like the right (if not the easiest) way forward. I've also learned to appreciate that there are others who will be judged on sight, for their class/ethnicity/gender/sexuality, and those people do not have a choice about changing those characteristics and avoiding the preconceptions. Nor do the people who have spent their lives having others define them by the state of their mental health. My goal as I move forward is to make sure I can hold on to how my vulnerabilities connect me to others instead of separating me from them.

Dani

I doubt myself constantly. I question whether clinical psychology is a place for me. There are some amazing people around me who have shown me incredible support and I would not be where I am today without them, perhaps turning away from this path long ago. There are times when others believe in you more than you believe in yourself. This is precious and can make all the difference because despite much talk of increasing inclusiveness and diversity of the profession, and of the value of lived experience, this does not translate into reality all too often. There are still so many obstacles to openness and acceptance in this field. I come from Poland, I am a mother, carer, survivor, I use mental health services – and I feel underrepresented in both the pre-qualification as well as the post-qualification sections of clinical psychology.

In the midst of this, relating back to some of the previously posed dilemmas and particularly the issue of disclosure, I turn to reflecting on core values. Here, I feel special connection to integrity. It is integrity that drives to be true to oneself. It is integrity that prompts honesty and transparency. So often we are supportive towards others, but at the same time we forget to look after ourselves. It is integrity that made me realise I have to value myself and has helped me to find the courage to challenge shame and doubt, and make difficult life decisions. We have one life and I cannot imagine a worse way to spend it than forsaking my own truth.

Marta

Ultimately, how we approach and use our personal experiences as we move forwards in our lives and our careers, is deeply personal. It may change at different times, but it must sit with our value systems, as humans and as practitioners, and for the good of those who are seen by the services we work in. Whether we disclose, use our experiences to inform our clinical practice, or feel 'othered' from the profession, we must manage personal, professional and political struggles even whilst dealing with the stress of applying to (or going through) training. For both of us, our evolving relationship to ourselves and ways of managing any related struggles, have been very different and our experiences are across very different roles. These experiences have shaped the psychologists we see ourselves becoming in the future, but have also highlighted some of the ways in which our professional body and training communities will need to address in terms of access, structure, supports and mentorship for those living with mental health difficulties, who wish also, to pursue a career in clinical psychology.

The professional

The use of self in clinical psychology

Part III

The professional
The use of self in clinical psychology

Chapter 10

'Taking the plunge'

How reflecting on your personal and social GgRRAAAACCEEESSSS can tame your restraints and refresh your resources

John Burnham and Lizette Nolte

Introduction

We both feel that it is refreshing that this book is exploring and promoting the 'use of personal self' as a 'good thing' during professional training. It is not a simple matter. Any person approaching a training in the helping profession may well have been encouraged by significant others that they already have an aptitude for helping others. Approaching a training necessary to qualify, they may also have doubts/curiosities about whether they will be good enough to do it professionally ('imposter syndrome'; Brookfield, 1994). They may also wonder whether who they are and the life experience they had so far, will be regarded as a resource or a restraint in their training. They may have encountered many messages about what the 'correct' ways are to get onto a training programme and may have wondered whether they 'fit' the criteria. In some modest ways, this chapter will explore this complex issue from a number of perspectives and offer a way of critically appreciating your experiences so that you can both maintain a sense of coherence of 'who I am now', as well as extending yourself through coordinating (creating a relationship) with the experience of others who are both similar and different to you; 'who I am becoming'.

This contribution is based on a mnemonic which began as DISGRRACCE (Burnham, 1992, 1993) and then developed, in collaboration with Alison Roper-Hall (1998, 2008) into what is known as the Social GgRRAAAACCEEESSSS. Its history and development is described more fully in Burnham (2012). I (JB) initiated this when I became increasingly aware of, but found it difficult to remember the many broad distinctions and finer nuances that can be made when considering how to understand oneself as well as 'others'. Both authors, in different ways, find that the mnemonic can serve as a heuristic prompt to trigger ourselves to routinely consider multiple aspects of a person's situation, and not to be so restrained by our current resources, including our own limited views, experience, or what we may be currently reading or inspired by. The letters in the mnemonic stands for *Gender, Geography, Race, Religion, Age, Ability, Appearance, Accent, Class, Culture, Ethnicity, Employment, Education, Sexuality, Sexual orientation, Spirituality.* Its intent was and remains to help us to constantly be reminded of the multiple experiences that contribute to the creation of identity. This list has grown over the years, enhancing its usefulness, which has been recognised by its inclusion on many training courses, practitioners' daily practice and in the Association for Family Therapy training criteria (2015). One of the criticisms/frustrations of some users is that aspects of experience that do not fit into the mnemonic may be neglected and so John recently added a 'final letter' which is an 'S' which stands for 'Something else', opening space for other aspects of identity that are yet to be included.

One of the advantages of diversity and difference in any culture, including our professional cultures, is that it enhances the range of resources available to the people in that culture. These resources may be in many forms, including different ideas about life and different practices of living. Totsuka (2014) describes an excellent group training exercise entitled: 'Which aspects of social GGRRAAAACCEEESSS grab you most?' Totsuka (2014) invites you to identify which are your 'go to Graces'; that you feel most familiar/passionate about, and to also consider the ones that you feel least familiar/knowledgeable about and may overlook or neglect. Using the group as a mutual learning community, you are then invited to find others who favour what you overlook, and to mutually support one another to use these differences to develop and extend one another's ability to be more inclusively curious.

The mnemonic may be prefaced by 'social' or 'personal', may be visible/invisible or voiced/unvoiced and developed by exploring the interplay between the personal and the social (Burnham, 2012). The social has been explored in a range of other publications, including Roper-Hall (1998, 2008). A special edition of *Context* in 2017 represented its 25th birthday and included a number of articles demonstrating the range of ways in which a variety of practitioners debate and use the framework (see Helps, 2017).

In this chapter we each 'take the plunge' and share our personal experiences to demonstrate how reflexive processes in training and beyond can be used to 'tame' our restraints and 'refresh' our resources. Along the way, we invite you to reflect on the evolving story and consider how your own experiences might be reflexively explored. Thereafter, Lizette will reflect on John's account, and link this to her own and to some theoretical positions, while inviting you to do the same. We will conclude by drawing out some of the ways that we and our students have found it helpful to manage this demanding yet potentially rewarding experience.

The beginnings of John's career: pride and prejudice

READER ALERT: Some of the material might be considered by some to be quite raw. I am grateful to one colleague (Karen Partridge, personal communication, 2019) who advised that I 'warmed the context'

(Burnham, 2005) for readers. So, reader, these are some of the fragments from my (inter)-personal experiences that helped to shape me as a person and restrain/resource me as a professional. They are not an expression of current suffering or problem, but as a transparency/sharing that might encourage readers to transform their own (inter)-personal experiences into resources available to them in surviving and thriving in professional training and beyond.

As a trainer I (JB) have tried to remain faithful to the maxim that I would not ask a trainee to do something that I was not prepared to do myself. For example, in workshops and other training events, if I ask trainees to disclose some aspect of their personal experience, then I usually go first to 'warm the context' for them to contribute. And so, with this chapter, I will express aspects of my experience in the context of social GgRRAAAACCEEESSSS as an example, and Lizette and I will relate/expand these to some of the theories in the text as the chapter proceeds. As an exercise for the reader (as well as myself), I will express this aspect of my early narrative 'as it comes' and then use the GgRRAAAACCEEESSSS to see which aspects were bolder and took up more space and which aspects were subtler, and which I may have missed out altogether. So here goes:

I began training to become a professional (paid) helper when I was 23–24 years old. By that st(age) some of the personal life experiences I had been through/collected and influenced my choice of career included:

Born into a working class extended family in Newcastle upon Tyne (3 families in 3 bed terraced, railway house, with an outside toilet).

Moving into a council flat aged 5 and raised as an only child (though sharing a bed with my grandmother until she died when I was 8).

Experiencing the juxtaposition (inter-sectionality?) of working/middle class cultures. Our Council flat was in the middle of a street of owner occupiers who regularly reminded the council flat dwellers that they were 'superior' and we 'owed' them. Some felt entitled to use our back yard to dump rubbish as they paid council tax.

Attending a grammar school and being told a range of things:

- *"You can't help it (not doing well) Burnham, it's your working class background".*
- *"Burnham has many admirable qualities, unfortunately none of which he applies to his academic work. He will need to work hard if he is to salvage something from the wreck".*

- *Suspended from school and being taken back, largely due to the fact that the Head said, "Well Burnham, I don't know if one word of what you have told me is true or not, but you do tell a good story". (It was true!)*
- *After failing and then excelling at an A level exam: "I didn't really believe that you could do it, but you have".*

Acting as a mediator between my parents during their marital arguments, separations and reconciliations.

Using humour and being humorous was a valuable/essential way to de-escalate arguments, even those that included verbal/physical violence.

Attending a few sessions with a GP regarding my dad's excessive drinking and participating in some kind of family based therapy (progressive GP!).

Learning how to drink a lot of alcohol as part of performing a particular form of (northern?) masculinity.

Physical fight with my dad that became a transformational moment in our relationship and in my life. We both realised that things had gone too far and the relationship took a turn for the better. This positive outcome continues to be an inspiration to my professional thinking/practice.

Leaving school at 16 to work as a trainee salesman in a department store, being one week early for the start of my job. Back to sixth form at school for beginning of term 2 of the new year. I had passed more exams than I had imagined I would and . . . work was hard and I missed sport. Being good at sport was one of the reasons they took me back, I think.

Going to college, (first in the family) despite never believing I could (I'm still not sure it really happened!).

Getting married in church (for the first time) aged 21 to a woman from my local area/class.

Leaving home and Newcastle aged 21 to go to university.

Discovering a different world outside Newcastle which was, at that time, largely a monocultural city.

These experiences occurred before I ever (formally) considered helping/therapy as a paid professional career.

Thinking space: pausing for reflection 1

In doing this exercise I was tempted to go back and change what I had written to make it look better in the eyes of the reader by: inserting ones I had left out; editing what I had written to smooth out the rougher edges. Instead, I decided to 'keep it real'. How could I expect readers to do likewise?

Taking a self-reflective position, I might pose the following to myself: 'I notice that you seem to have mentioned mainly difficult experiences as significant influences. What were the inspirational moments that you drew from your pre-training experiences that sustained you? What did you gain from being raised in that family; that regional culture; that particular time in the UK?

Invitation

You may choose to do this exercise now, later, or never.

Take some time, if you will, to write down a few of the fragments of your personal GgRRAAAACCEEESSSS emerging from your own lived experience and which you think influences/contextualises your current position in becoming a professional helper/psychologist.

Back in the room/chapter

On my reading, I think I have shared, to different degrees, 9 of 15 of my personal GgRRAAAACCEEESSSS that you might be able to identify from what I have written. If I had been speaking to you in person you might have been able to hear my accent, *(voiced)* and see my appearance, *(visible)*. In person, you could have followed your curiosity and asked me questions about the *unvoiced* and the *invisible*.

These fragments from my earlier life experiences could be considered within the context of a model I (JB) have developed into a quadrant known as Problems-Possibilities & Resources – Restraints (PPRR; Burnham, 2019 in preparation). These resources and restraints were generated in the context of life events/problems that I faced, and each one opened up some possibilities and closed down others. Each of them, and the inter-action between them, influence the kind of professional helper I am always in the process of becoming.

As I engaged in training to become a professional helper some of these issues seemed like a tremendous resource and I experienced others as a restraint (but did not necessarily recognise at the time). Over time, and with the help of compassionately critical others, I came to view each one, as potentially, both a resource and a restraint, and this has changed over the years. For the moment/purposes of this book, let's focus on the initial stage of training. These experiences led me to:

- Believe I understood the experience of working-class families (useful chip on my shoulder!);
- Believe that colleagues with a middle-class background couldn't;
- Feel confident in managing relationships even when there was shouting and potential violence;

- Have a belief/faith that change can happen, surprisingly, even in the most adverse of circumstances;
- Believe that middle class people could not, ought not to have difficulties since they had so much 'going for them';
- Be able to listen to stories about very disturbing events without becoming too disturbed/disabled myself;
- Be able to tell stories with the potential to change a situation not only for myself but for others also.

These are the ones that occurred to me initially and perhaps further on in the chapter I may remember others. These aspects of my personal and social GgRRAAAACCEEESSSS have changed reflexively over the years but remain a significant part of my personal/professional identity, not always in the same way as they were originally.

Thinking space: pausing for reflection 2

You may choose to do this exercise now, later, or never.

Consider how the fragments of your personal GgRRAAAACCEEESSSS that you generated earlier maybe have helped you to develop beliefs, abilities and the faith/confidence (however fragile!) that you can survive and flourish in professional training. Which of these, currently seem like a resource and which ones seem like a restraint?

Below, I briefly outline some of the transformative changes that these beliefs and passions underwent, not all at the same time or at the same pace. Some of the restraints responded to change quite quickly whilst others were surprisingly resilient and it took a lot of persistence to reduce their presence, and need regular maintenance in regulating their influence on my practice. Others which began as personal resources became more versatile across contexts, as I was able to relate them to theoretical principles, which extended their utility.

Initial personal ggRRAAAACCEEESSSS	Changed in context of a social process
Believe I understood the experience of working-class families (useful chip on my shoulder!).	This personal resource became a restraint when it positioned me as the kind of 'expert' who has suffered a 'curiosity bypass'.
Believe that colleagues with a middle-class background couldn't understand the experience of working-class families.	I saw middle class colleagues bringing forth different information than I was anticipating, through a genuine curiosity. My own curiosity underwent a revival.

Initial personal ggRRAAAACCEEESSSS	Changed in context of a social process
Feel confident in managing relationships even when there was shouting and potential violence.	This continues to be a personal resource. I became a better team member/trainer when I became more compassionate to colleagues and trainees who couldn't tolerate this so much.
A belief/faith that change can happen, surprisingly, even in the most adverse of circumstances.	This belief became a more versatile resource when I stopped allowing it to push me into pushing people into changes they didn't relate to personally.
Middle class people could not, ought not to have difficulties since they had so much 'going for them'.	This restraint was undermined when I was helped to step aside from it long enough to listen to and appreciate the lived experience of middle-class peers and clients.
An ability to listen to stories about very disturbing events without becoming too disturbed myself.	This has continued being a resource to my clients and trainees. It became more aesthetic when I ensured it didn't appear as indifference to the profound effects of the events.
An ability to tell stories with the potential to change a situation not only for myself but for others also.	The extension of my repertoire to include abilities to 'bring forth' clients' stories through systemic questioning, from a posture of curiosity made me less reliant on this resource and a more versatile professional.

Practice examples

It is important to emphasise that these personal changes are social achievements generated, amplified, and sustained in relationships with colleagues, trainees and clients. I am grateful for their generosity in their candidness, compliments, compassion, criticism and tolerance during this continuing process. Brief examples of these processes are described below.

Context: With colleagues
Practice: I worked for 25 years in therapy and training with Dr Queenie Harris, a child psychiatrist who was Indian, female, Christian and middle-class. We saw many families and ran training courses, together as a team. In the very early days of our working partnership, Queenie would often say that the working-class families were mine and I would say the Asian families were hers. We initially regarded this as respecting one another's expertise by virtue of identity (race/culture/ethnicity). Gradually, we each took risks in appreciating the other's curiosity about assumed areas of our own expertise. This enabled each of us to extend our ability to practice across contexts.
Reflexive Learning: Stepping outside our own cultural 'insider knowledge' allows us to see/glimpse ourselves as others see us. This can allow for and extend the second order curiosity of both 'insiders' and 'outsiders'.

Context: With trainees

Practice: A *trainee* systemic psychotherapist from Finland said that as a *young woman* it felt *culturally* inappropriate for her to interrupt an *older man* who was 'holding forth' in the family conversation and closing down the possibilities for others to contribute. These beliefs were deconstructed in our supervisory conversations. At the beginning of the next session she re-positioned herself in relation to the family: *'Growing up as a young woman, I was raised to believe that it is impolite to interrupt family members, especially if they are older than me. However, as a professional person providing you with a service, I must overcome that dis-ability in order to offer you the help you are requesting'*. This re-positioning was effective in that it gave each participant an opportunity to speak, including the therapist.

Reflexive Learning: Supervision can be used by trainees to understand/step outside the influence of their personal GgRRAAAACCEEESSSS in order to develop their agility to move between their GgRRAAAACCEEESSSS and develop a mutually influential relationship between the personal and professional.

Context: With clients

Practice: Working with an Asian family, I was keen to be careful, and not do anything wrong. I began in the spirit of relational reflexivity (Burnham, 1993, 2005) *'It looks like we are from difficult cultures and so if I say or do anything that is inappropriate, would you please let me know?'* They smiled and said they would let me know. Nevertheless, I continued to behave hesitantly and request permission at every turn in the session. They sometimes sighed and looked at each other with raised eyebrows. I viewed their sighs and looks as signs I had done something wrong, I redoubled my 'checking out'. Eventually the father said *'The GP said you could help us with our child's difficulties. Please would you 'get on with it' and stop asking permission so much. We already told you that we will tell you if something is not OK'*.

Reflexive Learning: *Relational reflexivity (Burnham, 1993, 2005) has its limitations and may sometimes lead to 'unsafe uncertainty' (Mason, 1993).*

Why am I telling you about this?
What use might this be to you?

People apply for and commit to professional training for various reasons. It is likely that aspects of your personal GgRRAAAACCEEESSSS will have influenced your choice of profession, alongside the opinions of people who have already benefitted from your pre-course abilities. It is important, as Cecchin (Cecchin & Radovanovic, 1993) advised against becoming a 'prisoner of identity'; that is, to only depend on/play to those resources that led you towards your profession of choice (for now, anyway!). Also, it is important to re-evaluate those personal GGRRAAAACCEEESSSS that you regard as restraints.

This is a reflexive process that involves self and relational reflexivity (see Burnham, 2005). I have outlined, briefly some of the processes I engaged in, as an invitation to you to do likewise. The differences between us may be profound, and it is the process which may be helpful; empowering even?

Lizette's reflections

As I (LN) read John's reflections, I notice myself firstly responding as a reader, feeling curious and noticing many questions coming to mind. I also feel moved by the relational risk-taking (Mason, 2005) I see in the telling, something I deeply value and respect in others and strive for in myself. Elsewhere I have reflected on how I have felt encouraged by the mnemonic of the social GgRRAAAAC-CEEESSSS to consider my own privilege(s) in many areas of my life (including my whiteness, my middle-class and educated appearance, etc.); to consider my personal values and what I wish to stand for as a clinical psychologist; and to consider how I wish to take action (i.e., what I can personally do to remain in line with my values and to respond to inequality) (Nolte, 2017). I read in John's reflections a reminder of these aspects that have become important to me.

Then I see an invitation to us all to consider for ourselves two key questions, already highlighted in the reflective moments above: firstly, which of our own personal or social GGRRAAAACCEEESSS are readily available to us in therapy and which are consciously or unconsciously left outside the work/training/therapy door (or come in with us unnoticed and unacknowledged); and secondly, how, when and where do our personal or social GGRRAAAACCEEESSS become resources for us in our work and how, when and where do they become restraints? So, let us consider these two questions, and also consider how theory and further reflective spaces might help us to answer these questions.

Finding a place for our selves:
counter-practices to 'desirability'

It is the end of a one-day workshop for final year trainees on a Doctorate in Clinical Psychology programme. I ask for some feedback about the workshop and what trainees will be taking away. One trainee comments, "this was the first time I felt that all parts of myself were invited into my work as clinical psychologist". I am left wondering: What has it been like for this trainee until now to find that not all parts of her self were welcome in clinical psychology? What have the implications been for this trainee of doing the work to keep her uninvited selves outside of her work up to this point? What might the implications have been for her clinical work and for her clients? I am also considering: What might change for this trainee if she continues to feel that all aspects of identity are welcome and seen as useful within her clinical psychologist self? How will her therapeutic work change if all aspects of self become more available to her in her clinical work?

Thinking space

When you were responding to John's *Reflection 1* earlier, which of your own personal or social GGRRAAACCEEESSS came to mind first and which ones did not present themselves? Why might some aspects be bolder or louder in John's words, and others more shy or quiet? How do different aspects of our selves intersect to make up who we become in different professional situations?

Let us first consider 'desirability' in our evolving professional identities. Getting onto a clinical training course can be an extremely gruelling process, one that can become very competitive. Once a training place is obtained, you find yourself constantly 'observed' and assessed. These processes often invite us into a position of figuring out what the 'right' way is to be a clinical psychologist, which bits of our selves 'fit' and which bits might not be 'right' for getting ahead. We might even conclude that we need to leave our personal selves and all the life experiences that have shaped and continue to shape these selves, at the professional door; that we need to find a whole new 'professional' self. As Noreen Dera writes about composing her personal statement when first applying for clinical psychology training, "I passed my personal statement from pillar to post, from psychologists to business analysts to career advisors – I was invested in creating the perfect magnum opus. With each correction and value judgement imposed by each rater, I lost my narrative. My personal statement became mechanised to the point where I could not recognise myself" (Dera, 2019).

Michael White (1997) wrote an important critique of professional disciplines like clinical psychology. He described how, when we enter/try to enter these professional disciplines, we encounter a change in what counts as (valuable) knowledge. The more local and personal knowledges that have been gained in our lived experiences throughout our lives are often displaced by more formal and 'expert' knowledges. We are told that these formal and professional knowledges of our discipline are superior to those ways of knowing "that have been generated in the immediate contexts and intimate communities of (our) daily life" (White, 1997, p. 11). This process invites us to become observers and assessors of our selves, to begin to judge how we are doing in attaining this desirable professional identity. Often, the essential knowledge and skills required to obtain this professional identity can feel always out of reach. Also, we might be invited into a comparison to others – are we doing better or worse than everyone else in attaining this identity? This sense might encourage us to hide any struggles, vulnerabilities and differences from peers and colleagues, further perpetuating this sense that everyone else has 'their act together' and know the 'right way' to be a clinical psychologist (Winslade, 2002). The outcome of this can be that we are left with a persistent sense that we have not managed to know what we need to know yet, that is that we are failing at becoming the 'correct' or 'good enough' sort of clinical psychologist (White, 2002).

Reflective activity

Take a moment to consider how you would respond to the following statement at this point in your journey:

> "This is who I am as an aspiring clinical psychologist and this is what I am trying to do in the world".
>
> (adapted from Winslade, 2002)

Towards responding to this statement, take some time to consider:

- Which aspects of my self-hood brought me into this work?
- What are the ways of being in my work that I particularly value?
- What did my family and friends say about me that made me think that it was worth spending all this time training in order to do this kind of work?
- What are the histories of these aspects of self and ways of being in my life and work? Who have been important in shaping these?
- What have I noticed about which of these aspects of self and ways of being my clients have particularly appreciated or valued?

'Desirability' goes beyond our views of what is desirable within our profession. We might experience parts of self as a potential obstacle in our relationships with colleagues or clients. My Afrikaner background has always been one such social grace for me. When I first arrived in the United Kingdom as an immigrant from South Africa in the mid-1990s, my clients often guessed that I was French. There was always that moment of reluctance to correct them, bracing myself for the anticipated spoken or unspoken response when I informed them that I was from South Africa. Other times my awareness of personal privilege has also been in the forefront of my mind, potentially becoming an obstacle in my work. I remember for example, when doing home visits in the housing estates in deprived areas of Hackney in London, I always had an underlying sense of discomfort with my middle-class clothing and way of talking and the obvious education I had, wondering how clients could ever imagine that I could understand and relate to their circumstances and experiences.

We can learn from the dominant discourses in the society and communities we find ourselves in to feel either pride or shame in relation to certain personal or social GGRRAAACCEEESSS. Whether we are considering interactions in wider Western society, our therapeutic work, our supervision relationships, or our professional relationships with peers, colleagues and employers, our similarities and differences in relation to the social GGRRAAACCEEESSS are not 'neutral' (Pendry, 2017). We might have experienced marginalisation or discrimination in response to aspects of self (e.g., racism, homophobia, sexism, xenophobia, etc.). Or we might have felt excluded or unwelcome in professional spaces because of our 'difference'. In such circumstances we might find that we face a choice of either foregrounding our 'difference' and remaining an outsider and/or taking on the responsibility of being a flagbearer; or alternatively conforming and avoiding emphasising our 'difference' and put in the hard work to adapt to a way of being that is perceived to be more 'suitable' and that tries to leave aspects of our selves outside the door (Odusanya, Winter, Nolte, & Shah, 2018; Ragaven, 2018; Shah, Wood, Nolte, & Goodbody, 2012). For some with invisible differences there can be a significant conflict about sharing what is viewed as less desirable or 'different' parts of self (Randall, 2018; Twist, 2017). We can come to leave (or try to leave) these parts of our selves outside the clinical psychology door and therefore, we are not able to draw upon and use these parts of our identities in our work (Roberts, 2005).

Here I would like to extend an invitation to consider bringing the personal and the professional closer together. Instead of aspiring to a theoretical ideal of what a clinical psychologist should be and leaving (or trying to leave) parts of our selves at the door, consider what might become possible if we can work towards fully integrating our individual experiences, values, and relationships into who we are as clinical psychologists. I invite you to reclaim left-behind and/or un(der)-valued aspects of self, and to consider the possibilities for your life and work of incorporating these selves, and their relational contexts, into your emerging professional identity. I invite you to engage in gaining a clear and rich sense of "the history that stands behind" (White, 1997, p. 81) the ways you wish to be (as) a clinical psychologist. I also invite you to consider the relationships you wish to be central in shaping this emerging professional identity.

Reflective activity

Revisit the statement and questions above:

"This is who I am as an aspiring clinical psychologist and this is what I am trying to do in the world".

(adapted from Winslade, 2002)

Towards responding to this statement on this second reflection, take some time to consider:

- How do I bring my self to my work? Which selves are appropriately invited in and which selves are left at the door (but sneak in anyway)?
- What are the histories and contexts of leaving/trying to leave these parts of self outside the professional door?
- What might get in the way of me beginning to bring these parts of self more into professional contexts? What/who might support me beginning to bring these parts of self more into professional contexts?
- How can I let my trainers, supervisors and peers know about these aspects so that together we can protect and polish them as part of my professional self?
- How do these realisations influence how I hope to act in different contexts, e.g., in selection interviews, in meetings with my supervisor, in role plays and class discussions, in reflective conversations, in my written work?

Returning to Noreen Dera's blog, mentioned previously, she goes on to state about her second attempt at composing a personal statement for application to clinical psychology training, "I poignantly remember pulling up a word document and literally writing, in my own words, in a true felt sense why I wanted to do the doctorate. No part of the form was adulterated by external raters . . . This time round, I surrendered my application in faith that I'd somehow captured my truth . . ." (Dera, 2019).

What then might happen if we decide to 'take the plunge' to resist the pull to strive for what is deemed a 'desirable' professional self and instead consider all parts of our selves as parts of our professional identities? Firstly, it is important to acknowledge that taking the plunge can be a daunting experience and brings with it challenges. However, some clinical psychologists who have gone before describe not only the challenges, but also the surprises this process may bring (see e.g. Randall, 2018; Twist, 2017).

Let us now consider what might follow 'taking this plunge'.

Considering how our personal or social GGRRAAACCEEESSS become resources or restraints

John described above how each of our personal or social GGRRAAACCEEESSS can at times open up possibilities, and at other times close them down. Earlier I mentioned how acutely aware I was of my middle-class clothing and my level of education when working with families from deprived areas of Hackney. I saw these parts of my self as possible barriers to forming a trusting therapeutic connection, and I am sure at times they were. I identify with John's account above of permission asking and 'checking out', possibly bringing an unhelpful tentativeness to my work. However, soon I learned that for many families this part of my self was (also) a resource that they hoped I would make available in our work together, e.g., when the housing association had to be contacted or when they needed a letter of support for capability assessment as part of a review of their benefits. I therefore find it helpful to remember John's perspective that each of our personal or social GGRRAAACCEEESSS are both a resource and a restraint.

One outcome of bringing all of our selves into the therapeutic environment could be the potential of "finding bridges across difference" (Barry Mason, in interview with Hardman, 2006, p. 18), that is, that we may stand more chance of finding similarities and useful connections. Jos Twist (2017) beautifully describes how their own gender transition during clinical psychology training led to them having gender identity in the forefront of their mind in terms of its potential impact on the therapeutic relationship (e.g., wondering whether young clients might feel confused about their gender or whether they might experience the therapeutic space as less safe). However, they then describe how a young person they were working with felt able to relate to them due to similarities in their class and age, aspects of self maybe more out of view for Jos at that time. Similarly, practitioners from minority backgrounds describe using their difference as a way to join with families, elicit new ideas and perceptions and enrich the therapeutic conversation, e.g., through using curiosity and unique perspectives as described by John earlier (Shah et al., 2012). Thomas (2002, p. 67) points out that therapists from minority backgrounds have particular vantage points that they bring into the profession and their therapeutic work; and also, that they bring with them their experiences of living both in their personal contexts and in wider society, and that this enables them to bring useful skills to their work and the profession.

Reflective activity: a re-membering exercise*

Take some time to consider the last time you experienced yourself as 'knowledged' and skilled in your work.

- What ways of being in the world were championed in this situation?
- What knowledges were you drawing on in this situation? Which values are implicit in these knowledges? What do these values mean to you?
- What is the history of these knowledges and ways of being in the world in your life and work? Who or what was/is influential in your development of these knowledges?
- How can you continue to keep these knowledges alive in your life and work? Who can support the commitment to the further development of these knowledges?

*Activity inspired by Michael White (1997, p. 59)

It might also be that bringing all of our selves into the therapeutic environment could potentially bring barriers into our work and relationships. Rather than concluding that we should try and hide, exclude or ignore these aspects of self, we might instead invest in doing the work individually, with trusted peers and in supervision, to continue to become ever more aware, reflective/reflexive and skilled in navigating these barriers (even while acknowledging that there is no final point of 'arrival'.

John models a number of important practices in the practical examples above, including *naming the difference* and asking clients to *let us know when we get it wrong* as John describes doing in his work with the Asian family (Burnham, 1993); *positioning ourselves in the identity we are speaking from* as the Finish trainee did (see Messent, 2017 for a rich description of this practice); and *taking relational risks* in our relationships with colleagues and clients as John describes in his work with his colleague Dr Queenie Harris (Burnham, 1993; Mason, 2005). In relation to my own personal or social GGRRAAACCEEESSS I have experimented with these different practices, and also with *humour and playfulness* and with *humbly apologising and trying again*. I believe that I will continue to learn.

Reflective activity

Consider one of the Personal or Social GGRRAAACCEEESSS/aspect of your evolving professional identity (consider using John's table above to inspire your thinking):

What problems might [aspect of self] resolve? What problems might [aspect of self] create?

How and when is [aspect of self] a resource? How and when is [aspect of self] a restraint?

What possibilities might [aspect of self] create? What possibilities might [aspect of self] close down?

What skills do you currently have to support you in your work, when an aspect of your evolving professional identity becomes a constraint? Which other skills are you interested in developing? Who might support this process?

All of John's practice examples also demonstrate finding those who can guide and support our learning and be a 'critical friend' along this journey, and I will now consider how we might do this.

Considering relational and contextual processes that transform Personal or Social GGRRAAACCEEESSS

It is clear from John's reflections that our relationships with our personal or social GGRRAAACCEEESSS are not fixed, but rather continue to evolve and respond to the contexts and relationships we find ourselves in. Let us consider how we can keep this process alive for ourselves and how we can sustain ourselves as we continue on this journey.

Building a supportive community

Finding a community that can "shoulder [us] up" (Reynolds, 2013, p. 5) as we discover the gifts and find ways to share these gifts on our journey to becoming a clinical psychologist can significantly enrich this journey. This 'community of practice' (Winslade, 2002), or 'club of life' (White, 1997), are those who we see standing around us, cheering us on, but also challenging us with kindness. It is those who shape and guide our thinking; those who offer us space to reflect and learn, and whose critique we can hear and accept because it is offered with care and safety (e.g. Mason & Sawyerr, 2002). As Jos Twist (2017) says, "through seeing the self in the eyes of the other (mirroring) and being seen and validated by others (witnessing), one's identity becomes solidified" (p. 27). This awareness of the importance of finding a supportive community can be influential in our decision about which courses to apply for. Also, our club of life can include role models or mentors we meet or find for ourselves along the way. Sometimes, these mentors or role models can be in the papers or books we read. Sara Ahmed (2017) says, "I often think of reading . . . books as like making friends, realising that others have been here before" (p. 31). Maybe this book can become such a friend for you.

Making the most of supervisory relationships

Supervision relationships can be some of the most influential relationships on the journey to becoming a clinical psychologist. How can we guide our supervisors to supervise us in ways that allow all parts of our selves to be acknowledged, appreciated and available to us in our work; supervision that allows us to take relational risks? Vikki Reynolds (2013) promotes 'safe-enough' supervisory relationships; that is, relationships where we can "(resist) innocent positions, and (problematise) the politics of politeness" (p. 1). She suggests that this requires "supervision that is profoundly collaborative" (p. 2), which provides the scaffolding for critiques that are expansive, relational and dignified. These 'safe-enough' contexts might allow us to make use of moments of what Phillip Messent calls "relational danger" (Messent, 2017, p. 45). He suggests we can linger a little "in the dangerous territory . . .perhaps taking the risk to deepen discussion" (p. 45), which can become rich conversations of learning. Zhao-O'Brian (2014) describes how, as such safety was established between herself and her supervisor and as she grew in confidence, she was "able to offer perspectives from (her) Chinese or Eastern contexts which (her) supervisors found refreshing and stimulating" (p. 45). She and her supervisor were moving towards a supervisory relationship where "their cultural heritage and qualities (brought) out novel things in each other, helping each other achieve 'personal bests' and creating 'synergy', thus leading to a relationship that (was) mutually enriching" (p. 45).

In it together – looking beyond our selves

While we are focusing here on what each of us can do individually to enrich our journey and include more of our selves into our professional identity, this is not to imply that that is all that needs to happen. While gaining a training place on a clinical psychology course in the United Kingdom is a challenge for everyone, we know that for those of us from minority identities (e.g. applicants from minority cultural and ethnic backgrounds, LGBTQIA+ applicants, applicants from a working-class background or applicants living with a disability) there are additional challenges and obstacles to navigate. Once a training place has been obtained, all trainees find training challenging, albeit hopefully also rewarding. However, we know that trainees from minority backgrounds also face additional challenges (Shah et al., 2012, etc.). The Division of Clinical Psychology's Minorities in Clinical Training Group recently stated that the causes of these additional challenges are not with minority applicants, and therefore, the solutions should in the first place, be structural; the responsibility for such structural changes lies with leaders in the profession, with the British Psychological Society, the Division of Clinical Psychology, the Association of Clinical Psychologists-UK, and training courses. However, all of us share the responsibility to tirelessly work to remove obstacles faced by our colleagues and friends and to contribute to a fair and inclusive profession.

Reflective activity

Consider your areas of privilege and how you may use these to take actions to build an inclusive and diverse profession that is a welcome and safe-enough space for all.

Use these questions to guide your thinking:

- How can you open up your reading and discovery in the profession of clinical psychology by including work by authors writing from non-traditional viewpoints, e.g. post-colonial, decolonizing, critical or liberation psychology perspectives?
- How do you use your influence (e.g. in your workplace; on committees; etc.) to work for a more inclusive environment and profession?
- How do you contribute to making spaces welcoming and safe-enough for all colleagues, e.g. during CPD events, at conferences, in classrooms, in your workplace, etc.
- Do you persistently challenge discriminatory practices within the profession, including for each of us, our own?
- When you have contact with leaders in the profession, including lecturers, supervisors, etc., how can you invite them to hold inclusivity in mind within their role and use their power to work for a more inclusive profession?

- If you were to obtain a leadership position in the profession one day, what would your hopes and dreams be for how you will use the power that will come with this position?

Conclusion

Throughout this chapter we have invited readers to contemplate 'taking the plunge' into self-reflexivity, using the Social GgRRAAAACCCEEESSSS as significant contexts for reflexion. Each of the authors has offered fragments of their own experience of engaging in this process. Not to indicate 'this is the way to do it', but rather as a way of creating possible connections with the reader and to show that it is a career long process, not a once off exercise. We also realise that this is not necessarily an easy process to begin or continue, and you as reader, may worry that you could become flooded or even drown! As Myerhoff and Ruby (1982) express:

> Reflexivity generates heightened awareness and vertigo, the creative intensity of a possibility that loosens us from habit and custom and turns us back to contemplate ourselves just as we may be beginning to realise that we have no clear idea of what we are doing. The experience may be exhilarating or frightening or both, but it is generally irreversible
>
> (Myerhoff & Ruby, 1982, pp. 1–2)

There are many potential challenges in 'taking the plunge'. Authors such as Burnham and Harris (2002), Roberts (2005) and Vetere and Stratton (2016) offer helpful suggestions to navigate this process. In addition to these we would like to end with a few 'top tips'.

'Top tips' on 'taking the plunge'

Self-compassion: bell hooks (1994) describes 'education as the practice of freedom'. As we take the plunge into our personal GgRRAAAACCEEESSSS, our contexts, and the people who constitute them will respond to the changes we are making, sometimes in helpful and sometimes in unhelpful ways. As hooks highlights, it helps to embark on this process with self-compassion, taking it at a pace that works for us and the contexts in which we are living our lives.

Relational-compassion: As we travel this – in turn, exciting, exasperating and hopefully expansive process for our 'selves' – we do so in the company of 'others'. The spirit of relational reflexivity (Burnham, 1993, 2005), involves explicitly negotiating and re-negotiating the relational context in which personal positions can be spoken of. Relational compassion leads

people to feel glad they have spoken out because the way they are listened
to allows the exploration of their current personal position(s) and promotes the potential for re-positioning in relation to themselves and others.

Dipping and diving: Trainees often find it useful to consider if they are 'dip-
pers' or 'divers' when they approach difficult issues or experiment with
difference. This gives the trainee and the trainer some sense of how to
pace the process of reflexion on current positioning and experimentation.
One person extended this metaphor and described themselves as 'wading
in the shallow end'. Choose a metaphor that describes your approach and
let those around you know this.

Gentle 'nudging': Sometimes people on the edge of change may benefit
from a gentle nudge, which may take a number of acceptable and agreed
forms. We encourage you to be watchful for and open to such 'nudges',
and where possible, to embrace them.

References

Ahmed, S. (2017). *Living a feminist life*. London: Duke University Press.

Association for Family Therapy. (2015). *The blue book: Training standards and course accreditation* (4th ed.). Retrieved from https://www.aft.org.uk/SpringboardWebApp/userfiles/aft/file/CRED/AFTBlueBook%204th%20Ed%20Final%20PDF.pdf

Brookfield, S. (1994). Tales from the dark side: A phenomenography of adult critical reflec-tion. International Journal of Lifelong Education, *13*(3), 203–216.

Burnham, J. (1992). Approach-method-technique: Creating distinctions and creating con-nections. *Human Systems, 3*, 3–27.

Burnham, J. (1993). Systemic supervision: The evolution of reflexivity in the context of the supervisory relationship. *Human Systems: The Journal of Systemic Consultation and Management, 4*(3&4), 349–381.

Burnham, J. (2005). Relational reflexivity: A tool for socially constructing therapeutic relationships. In C. Flaskas, B. Mason, & A. Perlesz (Eds.), *The space between: Experi-ence, context, and process in the therapeutic relationships* (pp. 1–18). London: Karnac Publications.

Burnham, J. (2012). Developments in social GRRRAAACCEEESSS: Visible-invisible and voiced-unvoiced. In I.-B. Kraus (Ed.), *Mutual perspectives: Culture and reflexivity in contemporary systemic psychotherapy* (pp. 139–162). London: Karnac Publications.

Burnham, J. (2019 in preparation). *From problem to possibility through taming restraints and generating resources*.

Burnham, J., & Harris, Q. (2002). Emerging ethnicity: A tale of three cultures. In K. N. Dwivedi & V. P. Varma (Eds.), *Meeting the needs of ethnic minority children* (2nd ed., pp. 170–199). London: Jessica Kingsley Publications.

Cecchin, G., & Radovanovic, D. (1993). Prisoners of identity: A conversation with Dr Gianfranco Cecchin. *Human Systems; The Journal of Systemic Consultation and Man-agement, 4*, 3–18.

Dera, N. (2019). I finally got onto the doctorate! Tears, tribulations and triumphs. *Psychre-flections Blog*. Retrieved April 6, 2019, from https://psychreflectionsblog.wordpress.com/2019/02/11/i-finally-go-onto-the-doctorate-tears-tribulations-and-triumphs/

Hardman, V. (2006). Bridges to safe uncertainty: An interview with Barry Mason. *Australian and New Zealand Journal of Family Therapy*, *27*(1), 16–21.

Helps, S. (Ed.). (2017, July). The social graces. *Context*, *151*.

hooks, b. (1994). *Teaching to transgress: Education as the practice of freedom*. New York: Routledge.

Mason, B. (1993). Towards positions of safe uncertainty. *Human Systems*, *4*, 189–200.

Mason, B. (2005). Relational risk-taking and the therapeutic relationship. In C. Flaskas, A. Perlesz, & B. Mason (Eds.), *The space between: Experience, context and process in the therapeutic relationship* (pp. 157–170). London: Karnac.

Mason, B., & Sawyerr, A. (2002). Introduction. In B. Mason & A. Sawyerr (Eds.), *Exploring the unsaid: Creativity, risks, and dilemmas in working cross-culturally* (pp. xvii–xxii). London: Karnac.

Messent, P. (2017). Supervision across ethnic difference: Learning of a White supervisor and manager. In J. Bownas & G. Fredman (Eds.), *Working with embodiment in supervision: A systemic approach* (pp. 34–48). London: Routledge.

Myerhoff, B., & Ruby, J. (1982). Introduction. In J. Ruby (Ed.), *A crack in the mirror: Reflexive perspectives in anthropology*. Philadelphia: University of Pennsylvania Press.

Nolte, L. (2017). (Dis)gracefully navigating the challenges of diversity learning and teaching: Reflections on the Social Graces as a diversity training tool. *Context*, *151*, 4–6.

Odusanya, S. O. E., Winter, D., Nolte, L., & Shah, S. (2018). The experience of being a qualified female BME clinical psychologist in a national health service: An interpretative phenomenological and repertory grid analysis. *Journal of Constructivist Psychology*, *31*(3), 273–291.

Pendry, N. (2017). The construction of racial identity: Implications for clinical supervision. In J. Bownas & G. Fredman (Eds.), *Working with embodiment in supervision: A systemic approach* (pp. 19–33). London: Routledge.

Ragaven, R. (2018). *Experiences of Black, Asian and minority ethnic clinical psychology doctorate applicants within the UK*. (Unpublished doctoral thesis), University of Hertfordshire.

Randall, J. (2018). The personal politics of becoming a visibly tattooed psychologist: Participating in a chosen social grace of appearance. *Context*, *158*, 21–24.

Reynolds, V. (2013). Centering ethics in group supervision: Fostering cultures of critique and structuring safety. *International Journal of Narrative Therapy and Community Work*, *4*, 1–13.

Roberts, J. (2005). Transparency and self-disclosure in family therapy: Dangers and possibilities. *Family Process*, *44*(1), 45–63.

Roper-Hall, A. (1998). Working systemically with older people and their families who have "come to grief". In P. Sutcliffe, G. Tufnell, & U. Cornish (Eds.), *Working with the dying and bereaved*. New York: Routledge.

Roper-Hall, A. (2008). Systemic interventions and older people. Chapter 29 In R. Woods & L. Clare (Eds.), *Handbook of the clinical psychology of ageing* (2nd ed., pp. 489–504). Chichester: John Wiley and Sons.

Shah, S., Wood, N., Nolte, L., & Goodbody, L. (2012). The experience of being a trainee clinical psychologist from a black and minority ethnic group: A qualitative study. *Clinical Psychology Forum*, *232*(4), 32–35.

Thomas, K. L. (2002). Ethnic sameness and difference in family and systemic therapy. In B. Mason & A. Sawyerr (Eds.), *Exploring the unsaid creativity, risks and dilemmas in working cross-culturally* (pp. 49–68). London: Karnac.

Totsuka, Y. (2014). "Which aspects of social GGRRAAACCEEESSS grab you most?" The social GGRRAAACCEEESSS exercise for a supervision group to promote therapists' self-reflexivity. *Journal of Family Therapy, 36*(S1), 86–106.

Twist, J. (2017). Putting the pieces together. *Context, 151*, 26–29.

Vetere, A., & Stratton, P. (2016). *Interacting selves: Systemic solutions for personal and professional development in counselling and psychotherapy.* Abingdon: Routledge.

White, M. (1997). *Narratives of therapists' lives.* Adelaide: Dulwich Centre Publications.

White, M. (2002). Addressing personal failure. *International Journal of Narrative Therapy and Community Work, 3*, 33–76.

Winslade, J. (2002). Storying professional identity: From an interview with John Winslade. *International Journal of Narrative Therapy and Community Work, 4*, 33–38.

Zhao-O'Brian, J. (2014). Stranger on the shore: On becoming a clinical psychologist as a British-Chinese trainee. *Clinical Psychology Forum, 262*, 44–48.

Chapter 11

Self-formulation

Making sense of your own experiences

James Randall, Emma Johnson and Lucy Johnstone

Introduction

A key practice for clinical psychologists is the process of developing psycho-logical formulations in collaboration with service users (Division of Clinical Psychology, 2011) and more recently, with colleagues and teams (Johnstone, 2014). Aspiring psychologists will be expected to use a range of psychological theories and evidence in order to develop skills in making sense of unique, complex, and often challenging struggles and situations. Alongside this, the psychologist facili-tates a collaborative process of identifying personal and social resources and sup-ports for service users, based on an individual intervention plan. Thus, the person is supported to change something about their current environment and/or the ways in which they relate to past events and significant others.

At the crux of psychological formulation is a desire for meaningful change and a search for how to make this a reality. With these ideas in mind, what we intro-duce here is a potential task of familiarisation, personal discovery and develop-ment through applying the principles of formulation to oneself. Readers will be shown what psychological formulation looks like in practice and to begin to con-sider the ways they can formulate their own stories, as people working towards a career in clinical psychology. We will illustrate this through examples of our own self-formulations.

We now invite you to start a reflective process of self-formulation and discover what can be learned from 'practising what psychology preaches'. In welcoming you to explore and learn from formulating yourself rather than the 'other', we hope your practice will be enriched and changed for the better.

What is meant by a psychological formulation?

Clinical psychologists draw upon and integrate a wide range of interpersonal, biological, social and cultural factors in order to conceptualise distress (Division of Clinical Psychology, 2011). Psychological formulations should be developed collaboratively with service users. In formulating, we offer summaries of core difficulties and experiences, drawing on psychological theory to explain how experiences link and relate to one another, as well as how they developed over time and may be maintaining the individual's current distress (or indeed, prosperity). Psychological formulations should also lead to plans about how to adapt to, or change, the circumstances that people find themselves in (Johnstone & Dallos, 2013).

Psychological formulation "is the lynchpin that holds theory and practice together . . . [and formulations] can best be understood as hypotheses to be tested" (Butler, 1998, p. 2). As such, they are always tentative and incomplete – open to review and re-formulation. Formulations then, are never static and only ever a cross-sectional glance, snapshot or momentary understanding – evolving and developing in a dynamic process of experimenting with different ways of being, relating and doing. In order to keep open possibilities for change, practitioners need to be careful not to 'marry their hypotheses' (Cecchin, Lane, & Ray, 1992).

Working formulations can take very different forms and formats, but generally speaking, some predominantly focus on the 'here and now', whereas others may focus on early life experiences as the key explanatory factors in making sense of someone's experience. Some formulation traditions also use visual representation to summarise a person's experiences, though not all. For an overview of a range of different approaches to formulation, see Johnstone and Dallos (2013).

Thinking space

When next in practice, be curious about the preferences of the people you work with – could a change of tack in how we 'use' and construct psychological formulations (e.g., more visually) support the person to describe and develop their story as is most helpful for them, at that time?

Differences *within* approaches to formulation

Psychological formulation can look very different, depending on the evidence-base, the skill set and theoretical persuasions of the professional involved, the particular set of issues at hand, and the broader systemic influences. For example, it can be argued that clinical psychology as a profession has sought to explain distress as "largely an *interior* matter; i.e., a question of psychological causes originating in individual's heads that have, so to speak, escaped out into the real world by way of their actions" (Smail, 2005, p. 5).

Clinical psychology, like many helping professions, incorporates a broad range of theoretical approaches – often with differing assumptions about how we can understand the ways in which we gather, create or discover truths, knowledges, and facts (i.e., epistemological assumptions). The reflective activity below is designed to help you explore these factors further.

Reflective activity: exploring therapeutic assumptions*

We invite you to consider your own understanding of psychological theories and therapies across the individual and social domains (you could draw this out, like Figure 11.1). Think of a model of therapy, cognitive behaviour therapy (CBT) for example, and place this along the line indicating the individual-social spectrum below in a way that indicates your understanding of what that model says about change. If you place the model nearer or on the 'individual' end, you are indicating that you believe the model sees the individual as the agent of change. At the 'social' end, you are indicating that the model focuses predominantly on environmental/contextual and social/political change. Think of as many models as you can and that you are familiar with. For example, you might place acceptance and commitment therapy (ACT), cognitive analytic therapy (CAT), psychodynamic therapies, systemic therapy, narrative therapy, schema therapy, all at very different places on the continuum.

Individual ◄─────────────► Social

Figure 11.1 Exploring therapeutic assumptions through the individual-social spectrum

What factors influenced your decisions during this task? Were there any models that you struggled to place along this line? Why do you think that is? Can models conceptualise distress from both individual and social viewpoints? Can they also intervene across both domains? If you have had your own personal therapy, where do you think this experience would fit along this individual-social spectrum? Once you have completed this task, perhaps you could share your responses with someone else who has also done the exercise – how similar or different are your responses? Why do you think this is?

You can extend this exercise further, through considering other factors relevant to psychological formulation, such as areas of power through a personal-political spectrum, or for further thinking around epistemological positions such as a positivist-constructivist spectrum (i.e., theories of how we discover or develop knowledges). There are, of course, many other options that we invite you to consider along the way.

*This activity was inspired by David Smail's 'conceptual space of therapy' figure in the book *Power, Interest and Psychology* (2005)

Formulating yourself

Psychological formulation provides a framework and way of understanding your situation, in a way that enables change through a greater degree of clarity and direction. This understanding can then provide us with workable ways forward and invites us to begin a new relationship with ourselves and our circumstances. Formulating yourself then, can invite different ways of thinking, feeling, behaving and being oneself.

There will be a range of reasons why someone would want to formulate themselves – from the more pragmatic, personal development angle, to reasons more aligned to survival, and/or curiosity about one's own mental health and wellbeing. We have, for example, found self-formulation key to navigating the grey area between service user and mental health professional. Self-formulation provides us with a meaningful framework with which to guide us in inhabiting professional roles, whilst also managing our own challenges; it encourages us to be mindful of how we use or are influenced by our own experiences of adversity responsibly within our role; it guides our future actions and aspirations; and it can help us to reflect on difference, diversity and our evolving privileges as professionals. Self-formulation can also help us to manage the very real challenges that we all face simply through being human.

Planning how to formulate yourself

Beginning to formulate oneself is not necessarily an easy task, and so it can be useful to consider what 'tools' we have available in order to make sense of the ways in which we relate to ourselves, others and the world. In doing so, we can begin to bring meaning to the adversities we have faced and become more aware of the resources, strengths and abilities developed along the way.

Formulating our own stories might raise some difficult questions or memories that remain confusing or difficult to process. As such, it is important to spend some time thinking about how best to engage with the self-formulation process in a way that is rewarding and helpful. The *Reflective activity* below suggests one way of looking after yourself throughout the process.

Reflective activity: internalised others

Pause for a moment; looking back – bring to mind a trusted and reliable friend, colleague or family member – someone you can visualise quite easily. When thinking about the task ahead, what would be this individual's personal qualities that help you along the way? What encouraging words would they say? In what ways would they bring out curiosity within you? Perhaps you'd like to write down some of their words of encouragement, to keep with you?

Now think of that trusted individual's words as your very own. In what ways could you embody that same kindness, compassion and curiosity when reflecting on your own experiences, in questioning your own understanding of distress and/or life story? In what way could you remind yourself of inner support for the times in which you find yourself stuck, or struggling with the process of formulating yourself?

Sometimes it can feel confusing to think about ourselves in largely unstructured ways, and this is why it can be useful to use a range of tools that can elaborate, guide, and/or challenge our thinking. The possibilities are endless and the ideas presented in the *In focus* box below are only suggestions about what we have found useful along the way – you may have many others that have helped you to make sense of your difficulties in the past.

In focus: some useful tools for self-formulation

- Keeping a diary or journal to log your experiences and reflections over time.
- Completing some of the psychometrics, questionnaires and screening tools we would ask of our service users, to help inform our thinking and understanding. For example, some of the authors have completed 'psychotherapy files' used as part of the CAT approach, in order to elaborate on our own relational patterns.
- Developing our own family trees and genograms, and thinking about the stories that family members tell about ourselves, others and the world (i.e., family scripts) – noting ideas around identity, difference and intergenerational patterns of coping (e.g., the ways in which your family deals with loss, bereavement and transitions).
- Looking back over photographs from across the lifespan; reminiscing with others about our lives.

Now we turn to two examples by Emma and James of using psychological formulation to make sense of our own stories. Firstly, Emma explores her own experiences using the Power Threat Meaning Framework (Johnstone et al. 2018) and then James uses a reformulation approach drawn from the cognitive analytic therapy (Ryle & Kerr, 2003).

Emma's account using the Power Threat Meaning Framework (PTMF)

> *"Rather than asking what is wrong with a person, the PTMF considers what [has] happened to the individual and what they had to do in order to survive. This empowers people to create stories about their unique life experiences, and the adversities they may have, or may still be facing".*
>
> *(Griffiths, 2019, pp. 9–11)*

As a social worker, perhaps it is not surprising that I have always viewed my experiences of distress through a 'social/trauma' lens, very aware of the impact of power, structural oppression and interpersonal trauma within my early life. My way of surviving mainly involved food, or the restriction of it, as well as other patterns of control. The Framework is designed to be used both within formal therapy and as a peer support/self-help tool. I wonder whether it can be useful as a reflective supervision tool also. I have used it here as a self-help tool to formulate my experiences and the sense I make of these as someone who has experienced various forms of early life adversity, and who also had a range of fortuitous protective factors in place. I have used this understanding in therapy and I hope this extends to other areas of life, relationships and the various roles I inhabit as a partner, friend and colleague. The PTM Framework talks people through the key questions below, which I have illustrated with my own answers.

'What has happened to you?' (How is power operating in your life?)

This question recognises the impact of power and how various forms of power can intersect. Most people recognise that children are relatively powerless due to being reliant on the adults around them for provision, love and nurture, because they are still developing emotionally and physically and because as humans, we are designed to seek out care and attention and to attach to the people offering us this. The Framework describes 'coercive power' as that of aggression, violence or intimidation, including domestic abuse. My late childhood and early adolescence took place against a background of a general 'chaos' and threat, punctuated by incidents of aggression, often fuelled by alcohol. I didn't feel safe, and this was frequently ignored, dismissed or seeming not to be heard or taken in by members of my extended family, teachers, the parents of friends. I think I gradually lost trust in how I experienced the world around me. 'I must be wrong'. Maybe overarching discourses that 'adults know better than children', old but tenacious narratives surrounding gender – 'girls should be nice', 'being quiet and compliant is desirable and 'good'' and in my growing up world, a religious (Roman Catholic) narrative

intensified these things. Such narratives hold immense power to silence, trivi-
alise or intimidate. Another commonly held attitude at the time was that both
addiction and inter-familial violence were 'family matters'. This ideology
shored up the secrecy and created another barrier to speaking out. It meant
that when I did ask for help, aged fourteen, by calling the police in the middle
of an aggressive dispute, my story was brushed aside by the (male) police
officer as exaggeration.

There were social and economic 'threats' too. Not unusually, my mum had
few material resources available to only her, and this meant that escaping from
a relentlessly threatening situation felt impossible. Later, unstable and inconsis-
tent housing and the fragile sense of safety that brings, maintained this sense of
threat.

I think the cumulative effect of this was that when other things that were equally
serious but different in nature occurred at a later time, I did not consider asking
for help to be an option. So, the impact of power in one area left me vulnerable in
another, as often happens with young people who grow up with parents who are
preoccupied with their own difficulties in a world that tends not to want to help
them.

'How did it affect you?' (What kind of threats does this pose?)

Domestic abuse often creates a range of threats, some of which are more visible
than others. Bodily and relational threats, isolation from social networks, lack
of financial and material resources and separation from sources of potential
support within the local community. Shame fuels secrecy. I think a big threat
for me involved simply not feeling safe, either physically or psychologically,
and therefore feeling very easily overwhelmed in situations which otherwise
I might have managed relatively easily. I had already used up my resources
at home and they didn't get replenished very often. This meant that although
school offered a degree of safety and predictability (I loved learning), 'fun'
and playfulness felt pointless, and navigating friendships was fraught with
difficulty (how can you invite someone home, when you are unsure what you
will be bringing them home to?). I felt aware from a young age of how alco-
holism was perceived and the fact that having an alcoholic parent made me
different and somehow 'less than'. I tried to make up for this with relent-
less striving – to achieve academically, to please, and to be as 'clean' and
'ordered' as possible.

So domestic abuse and the impact of addiction were key threats, 'witness-
ing' aggression, but also directly being the target of it (is it accurate to ever
say that children only 'witness' domestic abuse?). Being left in unsafe situ-
ations, with unsafe people (or to use the proper, stronger word, neglect) and
being given a level of responsibility incompatible with the stage of devel-
opment I was at. I was acutely aware from a young age of existing within

intergenerational patterns of addiction. And in trying desperately to resist what seemed like an inevitable fate by maintaining 'control', I fell into the compulsivity of anorexia. The way in which the anorexic state of mind takes a person over and divorces them from their sense of self means that it can be conceptualised both as a threat and a threat response. Anorexia left me confused about who I believed myself to me, mirrored the confusion I felt about the validity of my needs and the reasonableness of taking up space in the world. It was augmented of course by the subtle and ever-present scrutiny that comes with living in a woman's body in a world seeking to create dissatisfaction in all of us.

What sense did you make of it? (What is the meaning of these situations and experiences to you?)

Unsurprisingly, the meaning I took from my experiences was fairly bleak. Mainly a sense of difference, inadequacy, 'unlikeable-ness'. Often this was focused upon my body but it really extended to my core sense of myself. 'I am not okay as I am but maybe if I try hard enough, I can compensate for that'. Conditional acceptance.

I also developed a strong, unforgiving sense of responsibility. 'I'm responsible'. 'I have to hold things together or everything will fall apart'. I think until beginning to discover feminist literature, and meeting others who were unapologetically vocal, I felt that I must exist solely to meet others' needs and having little sense of being seen, valid or deserving of space, opinions, care.

And the 'anorexic' denial of needs, which functioned to cut off from all feelings and manage the sense of overwhelm I often experienced. 'My needs don't matter'. 'Good things don't last, stability doesn't last and I don't deserve it to'. And a sense of being tainted by my experience, and (interacting with that sense of responsibility), 'the people I love might get dragged into that too.' I was, sometimes quite literally, frozen.

What did you have to do to survive? (What kinds of threat response are you using?)

I like this question because (similarly to CAT) the responses to threat are not conceptualised as symptoms but rather as understandable (if not always helpful) responses to threat. Responses which were at one time reasonable survival strategies.

My major threat response described in the Framework was, until recently, that of restrictive eating, coupled with striving, 'drive' based strategies such as overwork and perfectionism. These strategies are described as to a degree conscious or 'deliberate', in contrast with autonomic, bodily responses such as flashbacks, panic, nightmares. Restrictive patterns around food make

*sense as a means of gaining a sense of control and 'coping' whilst also func-
tioning as a way to disconnect from some of the more intrusive symptoms of
trauma. In that sense, the two responses could be seen as feeding each other.
Once I regained some control back from restrictive patterns around food and
re-gaining weight, other threat responses became more prominent, mainly
anxiety-based responses such as flight/freeze in response to reminders of earlier experiences, nightmares, and compulsions aimed at appeasing intrusive
thoughts. I have found that the PTMF can help to make sense of shifts, in
particular 'symptoms' or behaviour patterns. If the impact of the core threat
is not addressed, it makes sense that symptoms will shift and change as a
person seeks to manage this in whatever way feels most accessible to them
at the time.*

*Another key strategy involved trying to desperately keep the people I
depended on as emotionally 'together' as possible (by being compliant,
appeasing, trying to anticipate and meet their needs, trying to not get in the
way or make things more difficult – and therefore automatically dismissing
what I might feel, need or want because it was too much and in any case, there
was no space for this). Again, this left me vulnerable. Looking back, I was a
painfully compliant young person, terrified of doing something 'wrong' and
working very hard to please and appease the adults around me. This probably
set me up for limited friendships with peers because it took a great deal of
energy and – frankly – I wasn't very 'fun'.*

What are your strengths? (What access to power resources do you have?)

*My formulation has been somewhat bleak up to now; however, there were some
really quite powerful positive influences in my life and I'd like to think that they
mitigated against some of my most difficult experiences. I had a wonderful grandmother and an equally kind, 'comfortable', fun aunt. What this meant was that my
sibling and I had a refuge away from the chaos, and in this warm environment were
able to feel safe and relaxed enough to have fun, to play, to develop our interests.
I think this was vital and really provided a sense of stability from which to build.*

*From a young age I read vociferously. This rapidly became a soothing strategy
but also one that helped me to learn. The striving pattern gave me the motivation
to work hard and complete my education to postgraduate level. This opened up
opportunities for me, and new ways of thinking and seeing the world. I realised
that there were other, more compassionate, hopeful ways of viewing the world. I
had access to other perspectives. I also (very importantly) had a sister who was
a source of solidarity and validation, particularly as we grew older – 'this isn't
right, is it', 'this doesn't happen at so and so's house', 'I felt sad when that happened too'.*

*The Framework mentions the phenomenon of 'revictimisation', including
by mental health services. I consider myself fortunate to have largely had an*

experience of services (and therapy) that has been kind, restorative and has offered a framework for something new. I know this is not everyone's experience. I have for some time worked in mental health services, and I want to do all I can to help services and practitioners to be trauma-informed, and to break down the 'us and them' attitude that can persist within services. We are all human, we are all 'us'.

And what about the way out?

When thinking about changing or revising these (now largely unhelpful) survival strategies, one huge thing for me has been a relationship with someone who is kind, and has remained kind and continued to see 'me' even after knowing the 'really bad stuff'. Contact with services that have on the whole been compassionate, understanding and really, really tried to help has also been important. Over the last couple of years, I've felt genuinely listened to, people have taken the time to map out patterns with me, helped me to tolerate the risk of beginning to change those, and have validated that it is okay to need help with that process. I think there was something powerful about my partner, therapist and the service I attended all being on the same page. Fighting that relentless anorexic mindset can feel so confusing. Having someone bravely say 'yes, they are right' when I was raging against having to eat yet another 'unnecessary' meal was actually really helpful. Someone I trusted told me, 'this is what you need to do, and you can do it', and I replayed that in my mind over and over as an anchor. I couldn't always talk (I froze), so I wrote sentences and handed them over to be read, drew doodles and sketches, and wrote blog posts – all perhaps attempts to find my voice and put words to experiences that had always felt too big to tolerate.

A while ago, I wrote myself a note that 'Whatever happens, the bravest thing I can do is to step away from the critical, dismissive, punishing patterns as much as I can each day.' This commitment has helped me to take what are actually quite significant risks to me, even though they may not look like that to others. I've started reading for pleasure again – novels, poetry, children's books. I take risks with food, and slowly they stop becoming risks and begin to become normal. My motto for a while was 'be more reckless and less rigid'. Some days I try out the idea of being tolerable and 'okay', not broken or contaminated. I am trying out ways of attending to myself, trying to carve out moments of calm, reminding myself that as a result of my 'back story', I might need different things to others sometimes.

Survival strategies can turn on you and trap you and that is what restrictive and controlling patterns do. 'Anorexia' was my way of surviving horrible things, but it became tangled into almost every aspect of my life and sense of self. It began as a form of resistance to and a barrier against oppression but then I found myself in a position of needing to resist it and finding allies around me, and within me, to help me to do that. So, when I think about power, I also think about resistance.

Resistance, for me, involves risking kindness towards myself and others, risking allowing more, both physically and psychologically. It means risking stillness and finding ways to calm the relentless thoughts and mental pictures. The kindness of many other people – my husband, friends, services and strangers on the internet has been a huge part of this beginning to shift. It's a slow chipping away but the more of those kind interactions I have, the more my cynical, jaded, terrified world-view is challenged.

I think the final piece of resistance for me involves the power of finally telling my story. Telling it, validating it, daring to speak it, daring to use the words, daring to sit in a room and look at it, taking risk after risk. I hope I am finding a space to tell mine. Slowly, haltingly, but telling it. In words and pictures and silences. "Liberation is always in part a storytelling process: breaking stories breaking silences, making new stories. A free person tells her own story. A valued person lives in a society in which her story has a place" (Solnit, 2017).

A visual representation of Emma's account can be found in Figure 11.2. For anyone who wishes to try this for themselves, the PTMF resources are available for free at www.bps.org.uk/news-and-policy/introducing-power-threat-meaning-framework. A guided discussion with prompts to help you think through the key questions can be found in Appendix 1 of the PTM overview.

James' account using the cognitive analytic therapy (CAT)

Formulations using CAT have not only consistently pulled me in (i.e., interesting-interested: I'll explain in a moment), but have managed to capture an emotional salience that many other therapeutic approaches fail to achieve (in my experience). I am the first to admit that I can easily fall into an intellectualising trap of emotional disconnection under the guise of my meandering wonderings that have served me quite well in my academic endeavours. However, when I accessed CBT to address the social anxieties I masked through avoidance, I still only really connected at the intellectual level. Through counselling and Jungian therapies, I found myself feeling something – but lacking a clarity of thought or having any clue as to what on earth I was doing, or what was being done to me. Through my training, I started self-formulating, challenging myself to re-formulate and embrace the difference that comes with using alternative psychological theories. As I described earlier, I have found thinking about myself in terms of CAT the most unnervingly revealing, yet reassuringly helpful; the most effective in communicating and challenging, and the most dynamic – a continual curious and evolving way of making sense of yourself. So below, I briefly describe the basic tenets of CAT. Following this, I introduce you to my 'CAT map' that I have used to make sense of the impact of difficulties in social communication as a child – and how this has shaped the person I am today.

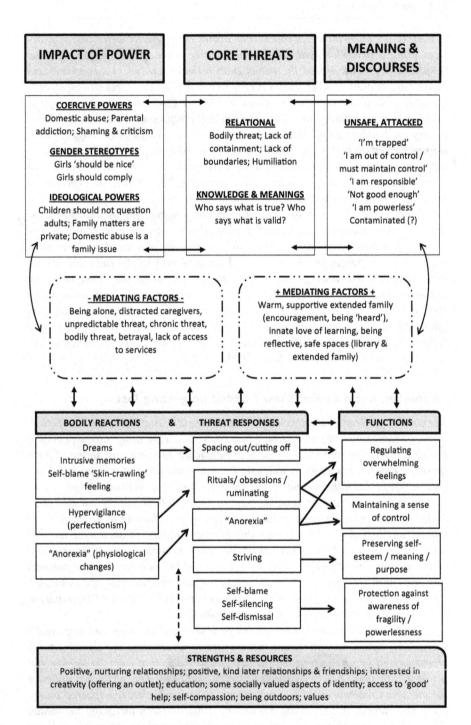

Figure 11.2 Emma's account using the Power Threat Meaning Framework

CAT is an integrative approach that draws on cognitive-behavioural practices using a psychoanalytic lens – particularly around attachment styles and
relational processes within the therapeutic relationship (i.e., transference and
counter-transference). CAT invites people to become aware of 'reciprocal roles' –
patterns of how we experience others around us (other-self reciprocal roles),
and our way of relating to ourselves (self-self reciprocal roles). Here, I focus
mainly on building something the literature terms a 'sequential diagrammatic
reformulation' (Ryle & Kerr, 2003), but which is informally referred to as a 'CAT
map'. Mapping relational patterns using CAT begins to draw out the reciprocal
roles and patterns that lead to frequently occurring 'states' (i.e., an experiential
state that comprises of a complex configuration of emotions, thoughts, memories,
and behaviours). This process will also identify sticking points and impasses;
namely, traps, dilemmas and snags. Traps symbolise particular behavioural patterns we fall into, which although they may seem to help in the short-term, often
keep our main 'target problems' going. Dilemmas present the false choices we
give ourselves, where we get stuck in 'either/or' situations that leave us losing
out every time. Finally, snags relate to what people often call 'self- sabotage' –
though I would argue that this is not necessarily a conscious act (as snags can
often activate the blaming-blamed reciprocal role, due to the sense that people
'choose' to stay in distress). Curious readers can seek out further reading on CAT
(e.g., McCormick, 2017; Ryle & Kerr, 2003).

"A thinker, not a talker": how I ended up getting lost

It is not always clear what triggers off my state of helplessness, eerie disconnection,
and a general sense of feeling lost. I just know that 'something' has happened –
I have experienced someone or others as 'silencing' in some way, shape or form
(perhaps they do not seem to welcome the back-and-forth of conversations, or
they interrupt and talk over me). I will often get caught up in over-thinking, rumi-
nating, and self-correcting thoughts (setting myself lots of traps!). I would often
buffer against these feelings of disconnection, by proclaiming to be nomadic in
nature; an 'outsider' – but perhaps this is really a snag, masked as a survival
strategy, or perhaps both. What I describe here represents some of the dynamic
shifts and altering of patterns over time. I can still fall into very similar patterns
to when I was younger, but how the relational patterns manifest are somewhat
different. CAT has allowed me to do some digging – and build a CAT map that for
me, seems to represent a process from my youth to now.

Systemic theory informs much of my practice, and in understanding myself
using CAT, this is no different. I have come to understand my earlier life as
characterised by a particular family script about me; that I am "a thinker, not
a talker". In part, I internalised this script about me. The script has salience
for me, due to memories of how my struggles to speak clearly impacted on my
early experiences in life: being mocked by other children for going to "beach
therapy" (i.e., speech therapy); hiding under coats out of the shame of not being

able to communicate clearly; regularly getting lost in supermarkets; becoming a 'missing child' on Bournemouth beach for several hours, being found by the life guards, realising they could not understand me and thus, could then not help me. Compounding the ways in which I made sense of these experiences, I also had a changing relationship to the 'thinker, not a talker' script – as I found myself on the peripheral at family gatherings (with other children being of a different age) and at times, in friendship groups (possibly due to the snag of self-doubt). As such, through others describing me in this way, when young I would experience them as disempowering: leaving me feeling silenced, voiceless and muted. At earlier stages of the process, and the initial stages of sense-making and mapping, I understood the script to reflect a snag imposed upon me by others. As Tony Ryle suggests: "sometimes the snags come from the important people in our lives" (Ryle, Leighton, & Pollock, 1997, p. 301), albeit, not necessarily intentionally, I would add. In this light, I would like to draw your attention to my initial mapping of this silencing-to-voiceless and muted positions, as illustrated in Figure 11.3.

When I experienced others as silencing, I would find myself voiceless and muted. I perceived myself to be peripheral to the conversation, and would be left feeling disconnected, helpless and lost. Naturally, these states could be emotionally toxic for me – these are the very factors that left me terrified and alone on a beach with strangers as a child, led to me feeling ashamed and unable to ask for help when I made mistakes, and so on. As such, I would get caught up in particular patterns: a trap of trying to please others, which would either actively or implicitly entail a suppression of my needs – needs that would remain unmet over time, and thus crafted the conditions in which a gradual and incremental building of discontentment/resentment would lead to the surface, eventually. The surfacing of bottled up needs would often look like an explosion, either a desperate neediness and pleading for response, or a stroppy onslaught (i.e., 'pushing forwards'). The more I pushed, the more others would pull back; feeling challenged, confused and failing to understand what I am trying to communicate (pushing-forwards-to-pulling-back reciprocal role). I was then faced with a dilemma: either I express myself, but people don't understand, or I gag myself to avoid the confusion, but feel forgotten and lost in translation. If I expressed myself, I found myself more often than not falling back into 'pushing forwards' type behaviours that perpetuated that sense of misunderstanding, disconnection and loneliness, as others 'pulled back' – or I gagged myself; a resistance through mutism (i.e., a snag). As described and illustrated, all of these patterns continued my experiences of others as silencing, but ultimately, also led to an internalised pattern of silencing myself.

The mindful observer: the reformulation process in action

In formulating myself here, I am aware of the potential to look back with rose-tinted spectacles. As described earlier, I have reformulated myself several times over the years, using different models, and various tools from psychology (e.g., the psychotherapy file, self-help books, psychometrics, reflective diaries); all in

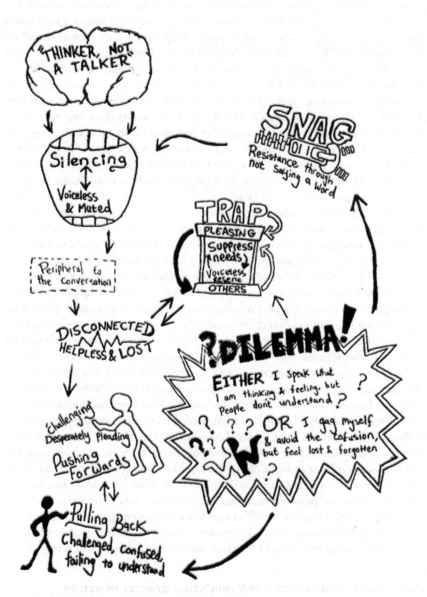

Figure 11.3 A CAT map of silencing-to-voiceless and muted.

hope of getting my formulation 'as right as possible'. The problem here is, that 'right' is such a nonsense of a word – other than as far I can say it is 'right' for me, at this particular moment in my life. Perhaps during more difficult times, I could look back relating to my journey in a blaming-to-blamed fashion, whilst at other times, risk falling into an idealising-to-idealised pattern (e.g., "look at how effectively I changed!"). In formulating yourself, this latter pattern of idealising brings with it a 'neatness' and a coherence to the process itself. However, self-formulation is a process that I rarely find is anything other than messy in practice. If I haven't been clear: self-formulations are changeable, evolving, and not a 'thing' to achieve. As such, the thoughts and conversations we have, each and every time we look back on our formulations are relevant and key to the process of making-sense of our distress or development over time. Before I explore my exits below, I have interrupted my presentation in part, to reflect on the 'live' reformulation of my account. A significant proportion of my childhood years were spent overweight, coming from a family context of 'eagerly striving and dieting to disappointed and staying the same'. Indeed, on the one hand, I had a very stable and loving family home, protecting and nourishing me – leaving me feeling secure and safe, yet on the other, I had a questionable sense of worth, a distaste for my body, and a great sense of fear about letting my loved ones down (even though they constantly reassured me: "We will love you, whatever you do, whoever you are"). That fear would often play out in perfectionist drives that boded well for my exams, but not for the intense stress I experienced, which seemed to cause a grey patch to appear within my hair (though I am curious as to any other hypotheses for its appearance?). Two things helped to bring about change here: I had always felt alienated from physical sports, cowering and covering my body in the changing rooms – yet one day in my late teens, I tried a rowing machine in a lesson and achieved the best time, receiving praise and feedback for something I had never succeeded in before. I craved more of this feedback, but feared making a fool of myself. Around this time, I went to the orthodontist and had braces put on – which I found would ache, a stagnant, dull, yet heavy tension throughout. I began to restrict my food and naturally, after a while, I started to lose weight. I saw the potential to finally be slim – something I had aspired to almost my whole life. This became a reality as I started to go to the gym for hours each day, and if not restricting my food intake, at least minimising and avoiding meals where I could. Later, I had my body tattooed, telling people when I was younger, that "perhaps a blue and orange belly will stop me from getting fat again".

During the reformulation process, therapists often write to their clients, exploring the reciprocal roles and patterns that present themselves in the therapy; using prose and a personal approach to make sense of the person's adversities in a new light. Perhaps I could have written to myself:

James,

I was just as surprised as you – when you realised such an engrained and embodied experience just seemed to slip your mind. Being so defined by your weight when younger, just happened to slip your mind. I know that you once were searching, hoping and looking to be somebody else. I wonder whether you found that somebody, when you kept on finding your voice over time? When those kids would jump you, you would get straight back up and shout at them, despite risking their return: you found your voice. When you started writing poetry, although you admit it was rather melodramatic and melancholic in nature, you will be the first to admit: you found your voice. When you wrote to yourself in a kind, observing and listening way: you found your voice.

"Finding my voice": how I used creative means to feel connected

In finding my voice, I want to make clear that my family nourished and supported my developing self; they offered me a playful, loving, accepting, curious, and empathic PLACE (Hughes, 2007) to grow up. Looking back, I would say that this was the key catalyst in my story developing in a way that enabled me to find a voice, which eventually became my own voice. My subsequent mapping of potential exits from voiceless and muted position is illustrated in Figure 11.4, with an overall sequential diagrammatic reformulation illustrated in Figure 11.5.

Over time, entrusting the people and systems around me gave permission to relate to family scripts in a new and different way. Instead of automatically feeling silenced by the "thinker, not a talker" script, I started to observe myself and others in a more mindful, thoughtful and less reactive way (perhaps maturing somewhat); a reclaiming of the "thinker, not a talker" identity as something empowering, liberating even. As such, I felt more accepted and hopeful about myself (as a result of empowering and liberating to accepted and hopeful reciprocal roles).

Being referred to speech and language therapy enabled me, over time, to quite literally find my voice and begin to increase my confidence and ability to communicate with others. Through this, I felt more connected with others and could experience myself as more accepting and hopeful. The creative platforms in which my voice could be heard then became compelling outlets for my own self-discovery, release and validation. In finding my voice, I found a home with the music style heavy metal – often subjugated as angry and 'noise for noise's sake' – I learned who I was, who I could become, and what other 'disconnected' souls I could share the journey with. Similarly, writing poetry and playing guitar created new avenues for expression, escaping the need to rely on voice alone – whereas heavy metal gave me a forum to protest in the loudest of ways about injustice and express myself to a captive and listening audience. Similarly, a natural exit from states of disconnection for me, as a younger James, seemed to be through shifting mindsets: escaping into imaginary worlds, apocalyptic fantasies of heroic endeavours, and day-dreams of the absurd and frankly peculiar. Even back then, I began to write all of these things down, creating stories and long tales of adventure.

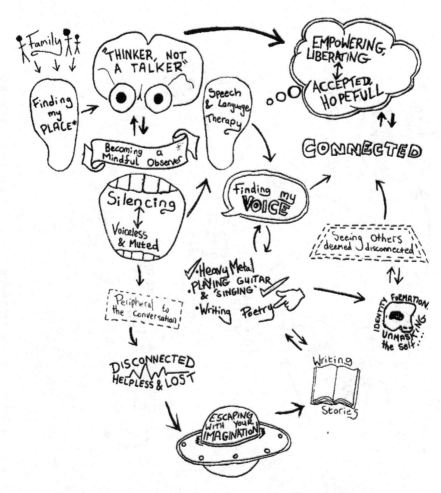

Figure 11.4 A CAT map of exits that lead to 'empowering and liberating to accepted and hopeful' reciprocal roles.

An ending-to-beginning letter to myself

CAT therapists often write ending letters to service users with a personal acknowledgement of their relationship and recognition of the changes made over time. During this self-formulation process, I again, wrote to myself:

> James,
>   I know that you didn't expect this to last as long as it did – and you certainly didn't think it would feel so liberating to put your experiences down

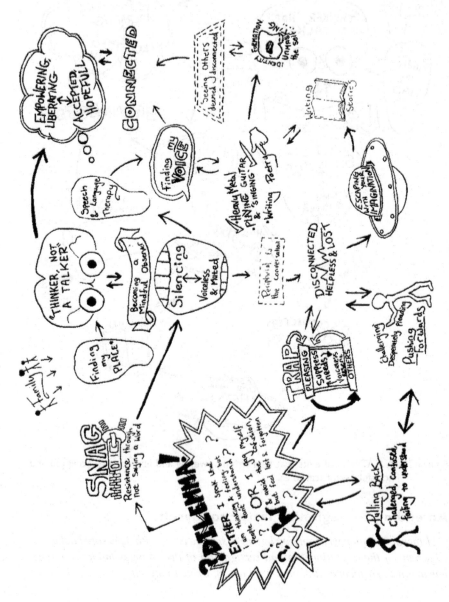

Figure 11.5 A CAT map of 'silencing to voiceless and muted' to 'empowering and liberating to accepted and hopeful'.

on paper. Although at times you felt silly drawing out that spaceship, your mouth, the theatre mask, and so many other things, the moment in which you accepted this as an important part of the process – letting yourself experience how you uniquely make sense of your own history and patterns, well, this really resonated for me – looking back, thinking about the time you put into this. In fact, there was a sense of irony in some ways, it was almost like you had created those playful, loving, accepting, curious, and empathetic conditions for yourself – through self-formulating how you found your voice, and in the process, you seemed to find your PLACE. I imagine you will look back on this chapter with pride, you know? New ways of talking about our personal selves in clinical psychology are still very much emerging and an evolving area of interest – for you personally, but also for the profession as a whole. I can hear the words of your family and some of your most trusted supervisors; you have taken some risks here James, and you should remember, this is not easy – talking about the fragility of being a human within that 9–5 psychology job (though we all know it never stays within those temporal confines!). So, we end our work here James, with new beginnings really – as we've said all along, self-formulating is a process and not an end point, so I'll see you in a while – perhaps something to celebrate next time, and not just the hurdles? All the best pal x

Beyond these pages: developing your own self-formulation

Mapping out distress and trying to make sense of your current or past distress can be empowering and liberating in many ways. Not every discovery, revelation and resolution is necessarily about the *content* of your formulation though. The power of simply creating time and space amongst a hectic schedule, in order to consider your own experiences and story, should not be underestimated. We continue to learn from our experiences, as each retelling involves an older self, with a slightly different take on things. You would not think that taking the time to write or draw out perceived difficulties, relational patterns and significant experiences would make too much of a difference. However, perhaps like mindful focusing, spending time narrating and/or drawing out your experiences can help to establish new relational patterns.

Reflective activity: creating your own self-formulation

Pick a familiar model or therapeutic approach. Try and formulate yourself or a situation using this.

If you are stuck, try using the 5 Ps (i.e., presenting, predisposing, precipitating, perpetuating, protective) and just make a list of information to start with. Then have a break. Take another look and stand back: See if some of your experiences can be linked. In what way? Does one appear to lead to another? What influences this?

Find a trusted friend or colleague and see if you can bring your formulation into a conversation. How has it felt to discuss this with someone else? Are there pros and cons of talking and not talking to others about your formulation?

In light of this process of self-formulating, we now invite you to reflect on our accounts and consider:

• What lessons might we draw from thinking about our two examples, particularly about the process of self-formulation?
• What thoughts and ideas might our two examples of self-formulation have sparked in you? Which approach makes most sense to you personally?
• What questions might you have asked at different points in your life? How might others have formulated your story differently, do you think?
• In what ways does our sharing of self-formulations make us *resourceful*, and in what ways does our openness *restrain* us? What become the *problems* and *possibilities* of speaking about ourselves in this way, as professionals? See Chapter 10 for further discussion on Burnham's 'problems-possibilities, resources-restraints' framework.
• What are the factors that have supported you in opening yourself up to self-formulation? And what are the things that have made it more difficult for you to spend time exploring your own account?
• What then, do you need to change in order to improve your chances of committing to self-formulation in the coming weeks?

Owning your self-formulation

We hope that you reach this point in the chapter with a clear sense of why formulating ourselves matters not only for the people we see within our practice, but also as an important process for ourselves as individuals pursuing a career in clinical psychology. There is no monopoly on psychological formulation, just as there is no monopoly on your testimony and personal account – anyone can begin to formulate their lived experience.

Personal accounts are inherently political; the ways we choose to speak about ourselves and others have implications for the ways in which we act towards ourselves and others. Telling our own stories matters, because powerful others can 'step in' and impose their own accounts of what is going on – which leads many to argue for the need to reclaim 'ordinary language': "Reclaiming ordinary language that is grounded in people's lived, subjective experience, which restores meaning, context and agency – just saying it as it is – is quite simply, a liberatory act"(Dillon, 2013, p. 18).

Concluding thoughts

In drawing this chapter to a close, it is important to emphasize that psychological formulation is just one part of a broader package of personal and professional development – and as many readers may attest to, can never replace the act of committing oneself to personal therapy. However, self-formulation is unique in that it is accessible to all, has endless possibilities, and can inform your practice indirectly. Through learning and experimenting with the ways in which we tell our own stories, we can become more mindful about the ways in which we support others in our clinical practice.

Lastly, and by no means least, we wonder what other possibilities there are in experimenting with the medium of self-formulations. Thousands of people now choose to blog about their experiences of mental distress, others write poetry or design comic book strips, and many other stories can be seen in the artwork individuals choose to hang upon their walls or ink upon their skin. The creative ways in which you choose to enrich your own journey and the ways in which you experiment with formulating yourself are a testament to who you are. Through using the tools most appropriate for you, you can discover the most useful way of making sense of yourself, your work and the clinical psychologist that you wish to become.

References

Butler, G. (1998). Clinical formulation. In A. Beck & M. Hersen (Eds.), *Comprehensive clinical psychology* (pp. 1–24). Oxford: Pergamon.

Cecchin, G., Lane, G., & Ray, W. A. (1992). *Irreverence: A strategy for therapists' survival*. London: Karnac Books.

Dillon, J. (2013). Just saying it as it is: Names matter; language matters; truth matters. *Clinical Psychology Forum, 243*, 15–19.

Division of Clinical Psychology. (2011). *Good practice guidelines on the use of psychological formulation*. Leicester: The British Psychological Society.

Griffiths, A. (2019). Reflections on using the power threat meaning framework in peer-led systems. *Clinical Psychology Forum, 313*, 9–14.

Hughes, D. (2007). Creating PLACE: Parenting to create a sense of safety. In J. MacLeod & S. Macrae (Eds.), *Adoption parenting: Creating a toolbox, building connections: More than 100 contributors create a practical, hands-on approach to parenting your adopted child* (pp. 57–61). Warren, NJ: EMK Press.

Johnstone, L. (2014). Using formulation in teams. In L. Johnstone & R. Dallos (Eds.), *Formulation in psychology and psychotherapy: Making sense of people's problems* (2nd ed., pp. 216–242). East Sussex: Routledge.

Johnstone, L., Boyle, M., Cromby, J., Dillon, J., Harper, D., Kinderman, P., Longden, E., Pilgrim, D., & Read, J. (2018). *The power threat meaning framework: Overview*. Leicester, UK: British Psychological Society.

Johnstone, L., & Dallos, R. (2013). *Formulation in psychology and psychotherapy: Making sense of people's problems*. London: Routledge.

McCormick, E. W. (2017). *Change for the better: Self-help through practical psychotherapy* (5th ed.). London: Sage Publishing.

Ryle, A., & Kerr, I. B. (2003). *Introducing cognitive analytic therapy: Principles and practice*. Hoboken, NJ: John Wiley & Sons.

Ryle, A., Leighton, T., & Pollock, P. (1997). *Cognitive analytic therapy and borderline personality disorder: The model and the method*. Hoboken, NJ: John Wiley & Sons Inc.

Smail, D. J. (2005). *Power, interest and psychology: Elements of a social materialist understanding of distress*. Ross-on-Wye: PCCS Books.

Solnit, R. (2017). Silence and powerlessness go hand in hand–women's voices must be heard. *The Guardian Newspaper*. Retrieved March 28, 2019, from www.theguardian.com/commentisfree/2017/mar/08/silence-powerlessness-womens-voices-rebecca-solnit

Chapter 12

Pebbles in palms

Sustaining practices through training

*Sarah Oliver, Hannah Morgan, James Randall,
Amy Lyons, Jessica Saffer, Jacqui Scott
and Lizette Nolte*

Clinical psychology training can offer an extensive range of opportunities for both personal and professional development. The teaching methods offered by different courses can be diverse, but they aim to ensure that trainees develop the competencies they need for working with the communities in which they serve. The process of training provides an exciting space to define your own questions and learning, as you interact with qualified professionals, a diverse peer group and a range of client groups. The opportunity to be part of a group of knowledgeable trainees allows you to learn from each other, share ideas, and be inspired by those alongside you. This chapter aims to explore these, the training journey and considers different ideas on making the most of these opportunities whilst juggling the multiple demands of being a trainee. We invite the reader to consider how to sustain themselves in times of hopelessness and embrace the experiences offered to them during training.

Training methods and opportunities

The British Psychological Society (2014) guidelines on the standards for doctoral programmes in clinical psychology emphasise the need for courses to combine evidence-based and practice-based approaches, develop the trainee's ability to synthesise knowledge and experiences, and apply these critically and creatively. Furthermore, they highlight the importance of reflective practise through supervision, co-working and collaboration with service users; and in doing so they emphasise the importance of having an awareness of diversity issues. There is some variation in the teaching methods that are adopted in different training programmes, although all courses expect trainees to juggle the demands of academic, research and clinical skills, whilst going on a challenging journey of personal and professional reflection and development.

Identifying and overcoming the challenges of training

Despite offering a unique and enriching experience, training is not without its challenges and many trainee clinical psychologists express high levels of stress (Hannigan, Edwards, & Burnard, 2004). Our experiences of training can parallel some of the processes within our therapeutic work, as we move between three different domains: personal domain, domain of production, domain of reflection (Lang, Little, & Cronen, 1990). The *personal domain* requires us to consider the personal challenges and experiences that we become aware of. The *domain of production* requires us to take action, through completing assignments, or thinking about a treatment plan for an individual. The *domain of reflection* requires us to question our assumptions and relationship with different diversity factors, and our relationship with different theories and knowledges. As we experience some of the demands of training, we develop the skills and resilience to cope with the challenging field that we have chosen. Here, we will explore some of the more challenging aspects of training that have been reported in the literature. We will invite you to explore your own relationship to some of these challenges, and ways in which you can ensure that you take steps to sustain yourself through the process and find support from those around you.

Managing the practical pressures of training

The academic component of the course can involve an element of didactic teaching, experiential learning (e.g., role plays), peer-assisted learning (Nel, Canade, Kelly, & Thomson, 2014), reflective practise groups (Lyons, Mason, Nutt, & Keville, 2019), and problem-based learning – a group learning exercise which encourages members to share and discuss material related to a "problem", whilst reflect on their individual and group process (Stedmon, Wood, Curle, & Haslam, 2006; Nel et al., 2008; Keville et al., 2009). Trainees are examined using a variety of methods including examinations, presentations, debates and written assignments, including clinical practice reports, reflective accounts and literature reviews. These learning methods ensure trainees receive robust and holistic training that allows them to meet their core competencies. However, the workload can lead to an increase in stress in trainees (Hannigan et al., 2004) and it has been reported that it is hard to maintain a healthy work life balance on training due to the academic and clinical demands of the course (Pakenham & Stafford-Brown, 2012).

In addition to the workload, the process of adapting to life as a trainee psychologist can lead to a sense of discomfort. It is not uncommon for many to report feeling in competition with their peers, after having faced a challenging journey to secure a place on the course – triggering a tendency among trainees to compare themselves to others. Trainees can find themselves in unfamiliar territory, and feel as though others know more than them, leading to an uncomfortable feeling of being deskilled (Kumary & Baker, 2008; McElhinney, 2008) – battling with 'imposter syndrome' (Clance & Imes, 1978). However, it is important to acknowledge that every trainee has had their own individual journey, and therefore has a unique contribution to the group.

Trainees consistently emphasise the active component of learning and report benefits from having a chance to practise their skills, and observe others doing so (Nel, Pezzolesi, & Stott, 2012). These experiences can sometimes feel quite exposing and lead to feelings of vulnerability and fears of being judged by others. However, upon reflection, it can be said that this feeling can provide an example of how it must feel for some of our clients when they come into a therapeutic session and discuss their experiences.

Furthermore, as clinical work is, by its very nature, ambiguous, learning to sit with uncertainty is an uncomfortable yet necessary part of training – which can create high levels of anxiety (Pica, 1998). However, it is these challenges that can help prepare us for the road ahead. Clinical training provides a setting to reflect on our relationship with uncertainty, to help prepare us for the realities of our clinical work, when clients do not fit neatly into diagnostic categories or treatment protocols, and we are forced to cope with the experience of 'not knowing'.

The benefits of being able to identify our own strengths and value our own perspective, knowledge base, and contribution to the group, whilst being open to the ideas of others, can help to reduce the discomfort caused by starting this journey. Recognising and valuing the unique contribution that members of the group bring to the discussion and being open to listening to and learning from colleagues can be a way of sharing some of the tasks of training. It is also helpful to set realistic goals and be aware of any perfectionistic ways, which are common in clinical psychology trainees (Grice, Alcock, & Scior, 2018).

Embarking on a journey of research and contribution to the field

Clinical psychology trainees are also required to develop their competencies in research, in order to gain the skills to be able to complete audits, service evaluations and contribute to the growing evidence-base – and where appropriate, to challenge the established or routine procedures of psychological practices. This process is recognised to be a particularly demanding process (Thomas, Turpin, & Meyer, 2002).

Before carrying out research, there are a number of important yet challenging steps that trainees are expected to carry out. Initially, choosing a topic of interest from a vast array of areas, whilst ensuring your contribution to the field is unique. Following this, trainees are required to find a supervisory team who are able to provide further insight into this area and together, develop an appropriate design for the study. Gaining ethical approval, especially when working with client groups can also be time consuming and create extra pressures (Brindley, 2012; Brindley, Nolte, & Nel, *in prep*). Finally, finding enough participants to agree to take part in the research, to allow you to have sufficient time to analyse and write up the final project. No two trainee's journey is the same, with many facing different barriers along the way. Again, comparisons with others can lead to increased anxiety, as people's progress depends on their own journey.

In focus: surviving research during training – interview with a clinical psychologist

What was your initial reaction to the thought of completing a research project?

I was quite overwhelmed by the enormity of the task. However, I felt my research skills were acceptable and I welcomed the opportunity to look in depth at an area I found interesting. However, I didn't know where to start or what area that I wanted to study. We had a research day where different people presented their ideas. This helped me to gather my thoughts about areas of interest. Further discussion with the course team helped me to consider my ideas.

What are your top tips for completing your major research project?

There were a number of factors that helped me to survive the process:

1   Consider what your hopes are for the project – I wanted to do something that I felt added to the research base and focused on an area that I was passionate about, as I was going to be working on this project for a while. However, I was also aware of the pressures of the course and the need to pick a topic that was achievable, given the time constraints.
2   Seeking supervision – My supervisor's enthusiasm always brought a lot of passion to our conversations, as well as providing priceless support and advice.
3   Utilising peer support – My fellow trainees were a huge source of support. They helped me by joining me during study sessions at the library, helping me to review my data and the analysis, providing me with examples of the work they had done e.g., sharing sample consent forms and ethics applications.
4   Planning and goal setting – I wasn't always good at staying focused. However, having a rough plan and guide to work towards helped me make progress. For example, giving myself regular chapter deadlines.
5   Self-care – I found it important to take breaks from my project, when other aspects of training became overwhelming. Allowing myself the space to get away and take a break helped to re-centre me.
6   Not comparing – I learnt that it was important not to compare myself with other trainees. Everyone had different challenges along the way – others were able to recruit faster than me and collect their data early on.

However, other people's analysis took longer than mine, or they had to organise for translators, etc. No one person was at the same stage of the journey at any one time, and we all had very different styles of working. Each person's journey was their own.

Personal and relational challenges of training

Clinical psychology training emphasises the importance of reflective practise in the personal and professional development of clinical psychology trainees (Sheikh, Milne, & MacGregor, 2007). Models of reflective practice recognise the importance of the awareness of the 'personal self' in our therapeutic work (Lavender, 2003). However, this can present a challenge, as one considers how to integrate and/or assimilate their personal and professional identities, whilst embarking on a journey of personal development and self-discovery (Delany et al., 2015). Trainees have reported looking to others whilst negotiating this process (Woodward, 2014). However, there is a danger that trainees could have the tendency to minimise their differences, in order to feel part of the homogenous group (Shah, Wood, Nolte, & Goodbody, 2012). Furthermore, individuals may struggle to know how much of their personal selves they should bring into the training process, as this can leave individuals to feel quite exposed and vulnerable (Woodward, 2014).

When able to find a way to voice our differences within our cultural heritage, geography, religion, ability, appearance, class and spirituality, this can provide a space of greater learning and reflection (Burnham, 2012). The process of doing so can provide an opportunity to reflect on our personal and relational aspects of difference and allow us to consider alternative narratives about our backgrounds, journeys to training, professional perspectives, and political views, in order to broaden our curiosity.

Reflective activity: power, interest and clinical training

When considering the personal and relational challenges of clinical training, it is important to continually question and evaluate your practice and the contexts within which your presence is called upon. Below, we have adapted five questions posed by David Smail in his book *Power, Interest and Psychology* (2005). Once you have answered these, perhaps you can find a friend or colleague to discuss your answers to these.

1   What resources are available to you in clinical training?
2   What material, social and economic power is accessible to you at this time?

3   What are your experiences of organisations, services and systems?
4   What possibilities for change are afforded by your situations and environments throughout clinical training?
5   In whose interests is your clinical training? Will potential change for you be affected by the interests of others?

Contextual challenges and ethical dilemmas

There are many ethical dilemmas that you have the opportunity to reflect upon and learn from during clinical training. For example, applying knowledge to complex settings; working in over-stretched services facing cuts to funding; and the high level of adversity facing some clients. For example, as clinicians working in times of spending cuts and increased pressure on funding for health and social care services, we can find ourselves having to grapple with large caseloads and little flexibility in terms of the support that we can offer (Morgan et al., 2019). Many individuals we hope to support are left struggling to access the support they require (Cummins, 2018) and marginalised groups have been found to be the most vulnerable, with the hardest hit being from the most socially deprived areas (Mattheys, 2015). We can be left at odds with the medical model of mental illness, as it often ignores the social causes of psychological distress, with the emphasis of change being placed on the individual (Mattheys, 2015).

As trainee psychologists working as individual therapists, we can feel overwhelmed by the complex systems that interact with the problem in front of us. This can invite a sense of hopelessness, which can lead to positions of disempowerment, impacting on our levels of commitment and energy (Weingarten, 2010). Our relationship to and awareness of this position can be important in reducing burnout. Weingarten (2000) identified four different positions of empowerment (aware and empowered; unaware and empowered; unaware and disempowered; aware and disempowered). As a group of trainee psychologists, we reflected on the positions we found ourselves in at different points on the course and considered the active process of holding onto hope, to maintain our energy (Weingarten, 2010).

Overcoming these obstacles and holding onto hope

Completing the tasks of training can require trainees to find ways to cope with the personal, practical and contextual challenges that they face. At times this process may invite feelings of hopelessness or disempowerment but by reflecting on these processes and using the resources that we have, it is possible to use these experiences as tools in our learning. Bronfenbrenner's (1977) ecological systems theory highlights the influence of different contexts on individuals' lives, and how

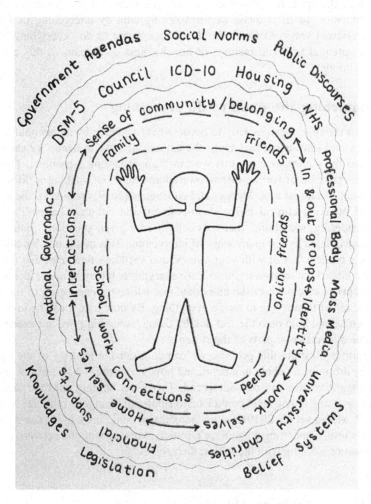

Figure 12.1 An example of Bronfenbrenner's (1977) Ecological Systems Theory

these can influence one another. This model considers the influence of the people that directly surround an individual (micro-level; e.g., family, school/work, peer groups); the relationships between these people (meso-level; e.g., relationship with services); systems that a person does not have direct contact with but still have an influence on those within their microsystem (exo-level; e.g., mass media); and finally, the wider cultural systems in which a person lives (macro-level; e.g., societal norms, political policies, etc.). An example has been included above in Figure 12.1.

As psychologists, we exist within our own set of influential systems. The skills that we develop through our training, allow us to work in a number of different roles (e.g., therapist, researcher, consultant and trainer). These positions enable us to influence the individuals we are working with by intervening in a number of different ways. At times this leads to a desire to do "everything". This has the potential to invite feelings of hopelessness or despair, as this can feel overwhelming.

Relinquishing the need to do *everything*

Whilst on training, it can be easy to become overwhelmed by the amount of theory one could learn about and apply, the amount of ways in which we can intervene, and the numerous ways that we can think regarding a problem. This can invite our position of feeling disempowered and hopeless, making it difficult to know what to address first. Morgan and colleagues (2019) considered the importance of breaking clinical tasks, socio-political and cultural challenges down, and considering 'something' that we could do in a given situation – rather than feel overwhelmed by too many ways of intervening. This might involve thinking about the models that fit with your values, and spending time applying these to certain contexts, rather than trying to learn everything. It may be about identifying an appropriate care plan for the individual that addresses one aspect of their difficulties, rather than trying to tackle everything. By doing so, it can be important to recognise and hold onto the fact that by doing 'something' we are exerting an influence over different parts of the system.

To further illustrate this process, we can consider the analogy of the ripples made by dropping a pebble in a pond, and how, no matter the size of the pebble, the change it creates can be widespread. Therefore, holding onto the idea that doing something at one level could lead to ripples of change at other levels (Figure 12.2, Morgan et al., 2019). Doing 'something' could include speaking up in a team meeting, completing an audit or research, working with the network around the person or working with the person themselves.

Reflective activity: pebbles in palms

We wish to invite you to consider what you can do to hold onto hope and consider what pebbles you can bring to the field.

Spend some time thinking about one hope, ambition or value you wish to share through the way you approach your clinical work.

How could you capture this on a pebble? Could you paint a symbol that represents a memory of a time when you felt listened to, or a time in which you gave someone a helping hand?

What are the benefits of having tangible reminders and objects within your home, on your desk or in your pocket? Could you take this and start a conversation with a friend or even a stranger?

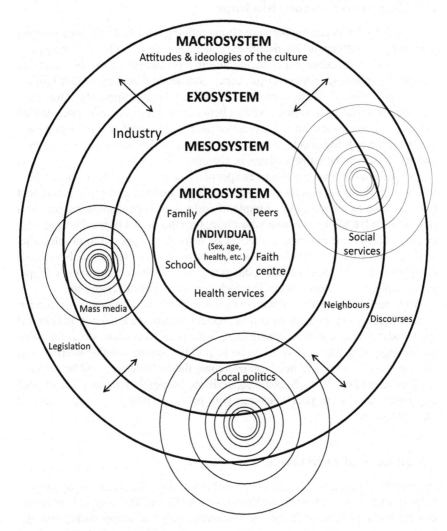

Figure 12.2 Pebbles in palms analogy

Source: Morgan et al., 2019

Through our own reflections on the process of training, we considered the following 'survival strategies' and counter-practices to despair that helped sustain us through our experience of training. We identified four factors that empowered us during our journey. These are reasonable hope; small acts of resistance, being stronger together and sustaining ourselves over time (Morgan et al., 2019). By considering these factors, we were able to cope with the demands of training, in addition to the challenges that we faced whilst working with families facing multiple problems.

Holding onto 'reasonable hope'

When faced with increasing pressure during training – for example, when feeling overwhelmed with upcoming deadlines, when being faced with the complexities of working with families experiencing multiple problems – it can be helpful to hold onto a grounded, more practical, hope – something Weingarten (2010) coined as 'reasonable hope'. Weingarten (2010) identified three components of this idea: that hope is relational in nature (existing between people rather than solely within individuals); that hope is an active practice (helping to identify actions that people can work towards together); and that hope maintains that the future is unknown, uncertain, and can be influenced and/or changed.

As hope is an act that exists between people, it can be helpful to consider where feelings of disempowerment can originate from, and the collective action that one may take as a result. For example, if feelings of hopelessness are part of a (hypothesised) transference from your client, then this arguably provides you with an insight into their experience and can be helpful, as opposed to problematic. Thus, a pebble that you might throw might be an effort to reflect on this experience and think with the client about things that provide them with a sense of hope, for example, future events, times in which they overcame adversity, etc.

When feeling overwhelmed with personal or relational experiences of training (e.g., struggling to cope with the conflicting pressures of the academic and clinical workloads; having a difficult relationship with your supervisor; struggling with comparing yourself to others), it can be helpful to consider whether sharing your dilemmas with others will help you overcome these challenges, and help you to see a different possibility. Seeking supervision, keeping a reflective log of your experience, or sharing your dilemmas with peers can help to alleviate some of these pressures.

Small acts of resistance

Wade (1997) recognised the importance of any action that people engage in that helps them to cope with or prevent forms of oppression. This way of intervening can be viewed as an act of resistance. On starting new placements during training, trainees are often faced with unfamiliar contexts, cultures, and team members. This can mean that they tend to be more cautious about contributing, critiquing or challenging practices across a range of situations. As such, resistance or protests can be disabled by their training and personal contexts. However, it is important to be able to stay true to our own values within our practise and not become overwhelmed – risking feeling disingenuous or inauthentic in our practice.

Small acts of resistance can not only sustain the self during challenging times, when we would otherwise feel silenced, unheard or invisible, but can also provide a foundation for more visible and effective action in the future – even if our initial behaviours may at first seem inconsequential (Wade, 1997). By doing so we can question existing discourses, enabling us to advocate for the people we seek to support. This, at times, requires us to be critical of existing knowledge in order to expand and develop ideas. In doing so, the importance of developing independent thought, being critical in approach and giving oneself permission to disagree with the status quo becomes imperative (Nel et al., 2012).

Throughout this book, the importance of reflecting on aspects of diversity within ourselves, our peers, trainers, supervisors and clients, reminds us about the dangers of making assumptions in relation to how we 'should' be, or how others 'should' fit into care pathways. The assumptions we make can shape our actions or interact with power structures within society. For example, Randall (2018) explored differences in appearance, made out of personal choice, and how these can sometimes lead to others making assumptions. He describes taking a personal risk, to become a visibly tattooed psychologist, which may challenge the status quo of identity within the clinical psychology and the helping professions more broadly. Such challenges can help to increase the diversity within the profession. The alternative would be to continue to shy away from 'difference', reducing our ability to challenge some of the dominant discourses that exist within our society.

We wonder whether other forms of resistance can include, for example, listing International Classification of Diseases (ICD) codes that represent social-determinants of ill-health above those deemed more individualising in an unhelpful manner (Kinderman, Allsopp, & Cooke, 2017); using humour when feeling confined by bureaucracy or forced into actions by those in more powerful, managerial positions (Griffiths, 1998). In what ways could you envision resisting in small ways?

Growing together

Reynolds (2010) introduces the concept of being an imperfect ally, in which we stand alongside each other to take a collective ownership of issues that we believe should not be made to reside within individuals. For example, the *Psychologists Against Austerity* movement (Harper et al., 2015) has successfully united psychology professionals from all over the UK together, to speak out against the impact of austerity on people's wellbeing and to challenge political discourses. As discussed above, training provides you with an opportunity to work with fellow trainees that have a wealth of knowledge and experiences, which can challenge you to think outside the box. Drawing on the skills from the collective group can help to share out the responsibility to do "everything" – not only making it more manageable, but more connecting and personally nourishing (Morgan et al., 2019).

We are shaped into the clinical psychologists that we become through the people that we meet on our journey, both professionals and clients, their friends and family. White (1997) introduced the concept of *re-membering* which referred to the way our identities are shaped by the influential people we share our lives with (whether presently or historically; physically or symbolically). He referred to these people as a 'club of life'. He acknowledged that each person within our 'club of life' is attributed a different status, and therefore we place more or less weight on this person's contribution to our lives, depending on how highly we value their contributions in particular contexts (Carey & Russell, 2002). We carry their presence and/or these voices with us along our journey and can call upon them in times of need. Sometimes, 'members' of our club of life, may not even be 'people' as such, and can be animals, items and objects, and fictional characters. For example, during the interview process, one of the authors carried a pebble with him that symbolised the courage of his fellow authors – and through bringing this particular club of life to mind, he was able to use this courage in order to conquer difficult and testing situations. It is the process of holding onto these voices, that can sustain us through training and beyond.

Reflective activity: club of life exercise, as adapted from White (1997)

In thinking about your own club of life, you may find it useful to write your initial answers to these questions down and then revisit the questions afterwards. This will help you to fully immerse yourself in the activity and to reflect on those who have influenced, and continue to influence, your life and practice. At the same time, you may find it useful and enriching to draw out your club of life in response to these questions, or to use photographs, materials or mediums that resonate or mean something to you – thus, using creative means to make this exercise as meaningful as possible and help bring these important others to mind as fully as possible.

Who is in your club of life? Do you have any objects, things, or animals in your club of life?
How do you think you came to be the clinician you are today?
Was there anyone in particular that introduced you to this way of being/thinking/acting?
What has this person (or object) contributed to your life? What did they do that made a difference in your life?
How did the actions of this person/these people make a difference in how you understood yourself and your life? How did they make you feel and think about yourself?
How did you contribute to that person's life? What difference do you think you may have made to how they thought about themselves and their life?

In completing the club of life exercise, perhaps you may wish to consider what your 'club' will have looked like at different points in your life? A useful exercise when working with children and young people, for example, is to take yourself back to a similar age and try and consider who or what would have occupied key positions in your club of life back then. Importantly, this might help you to consider the ways in which you supported yourself at the time – through staying connected to important others, whilst at the same time perhaps assist in understanding and relating to those that you see in your practice. By reconnecting with a younger you, for example, what creative and playful ways of surviving training are revealed?

Sustaining ourselves

Given the challenges faced in pursuing a career in clinical psychology, it is important that we are able to sustain ourselves through the training process (Morgan et al., 2019). Reflecting on the words of Vikki Reynolds, it is important to continually reflectively work to remain in line with our values in our practice in order to resist burnout; to identify the practices that allow us to hold onto hope; and to stay connected to others (Reynolds, 2010), valuing the social net of care that can easily become eroded in our current working contexts (Reynolds, 2019). However, despite clinical psychologists being trained on the importance of such practices, we might not always apply these practices on ourselves. Along with ways we develop to take care of ourselves, collective care (Reynolds, 2019) invites us to consider how finding those we can stand in solidarity with and that can shoulder us up in challenging times can be central to how we sustain ourselves through training.

The things that help us take steps towards other important aspects of life, are those that essentially help sustain our sense of self during training – that is, those things that help us to 'survive' the process. Reflecting on some of the strategies that helped to sustain us through our journey, we identified a variety of such ways, but these differed for each of us:

- Applying psychological ideas and strategies to ourselves can allow us to develop an understanding of our strengths and difficulties, realise the potential resources available to us, and highlight potential solutions and ways forward available to us.
- In our experience, for some, sustaining ourselves could also be about things that we could do outside of psychology – to allow us to connect to 'other parts' of our selves (e.g., engaging in social activities with each other; physical activities, such as exercise, yoga, and outdoor pursuits that refresh us).
- For some, sustaining ourselves was about feeling 'part of something' – such as engaging in a community activity (e.g., volunteering, campaigning, becoming part of local neighbourhood initiatives).
- For some, sustaining ourselves was through continuing to connect with and develop our psychological knowledge through exploring professional areas of interest and attending conferences or contributing to working groups.
- For some, sustaining ourselves was about providing ourselves with opportunities to have some 'down-time' (or indeed, *up-time*!) – such as ensuring we get good-enough sleep, or taking time-out from work.

- And finally, but by no means least, for most of us, sustaining ourselves was about nurturing our 'inner child' by reconnecting with our playful sides; allowing ourselves to laugh and connect through silliness in and outside of work; or reconnecting with our sense of adventure and creative expression – fostering creativity by playing music, writing, going to ballet classes or singing lessons, knitting, baking or making art; and continuing to make time for those relationships that are most important to us – remembering to ask "how are you?" and to say "thank you".

From outlining some of the challenges that we faced during the training process, and how we came to reflect, learn and grow from these experiences, we have invited you to consider your own personal qualities, values and hopes that you will take with you through the training journey. Although both applying to and completing training can at times feel uncertain, there are ways to strengthen our alternative discourses and stories of resourcefulness, independence of thought, connectedness and the ability to hold on to hope in times of despair.

For us, reflecting on content and processes along the way have allowed for an enriching process, for development and growth, but also development within the field. Through building a sense of selfhood, we have also experienced an evolving sense of trust in and connection to others, sometimes developed through hostile times that leave us vulnerable and exposed – and yet we manage to survive, *together*. This emphasizes the importance of holding onto the people that have contributed to shaping our identities. We can also begin to consider the ways in which we have influenced the lives of others and be mindful of the legacy of our contributions in other's lives both in and outside of our work.

Conclusion

The journey to becoming a clinical psychologist is a meandering and unclear path – one that is constantly evolving and developing. Once we arrive at the gates of clinical training, there are several barriers and obstacles that we are yet to face. Finding ways to cope with these, and finding ways to stay true to the values that drive us, are important factors in maintaining the hope that gives us the energy to continue supporting others in our work. Important aspects of survival include being able to resist the temptation to do everything, despite the complexity of the problems or situations we face. Therefore, recognising the importance of a small act, intervention, or pebble within your palm, is key to realising the potential for influence across different levels of the system. Being able to acknowledge who you are as a clinical psychologist in order to find a voice that can challenge dominant discourses, is not just for our own survival, but also as a way of giving voice to those that are most ostracised. In crafting the way for your own survival as a critical- and community-minded clinical psychologist, for example, is an important stepping stone to creating the conditions in which we can support one another to act in line with our values and for greater, more ethical and moral causes.

Finally, practising what we preach, and ensuring that we engage in activities that sustain ourselves outside of our field will help prevent burnout. We do not believe this journey to be complete, but rather the start of an enriching path that enables us to work alongside those that we seek to support.

References

Brindley, R. (2012). *"We were in one place and the ethics committee in another": Trainee clinical psychologists' experiences of research ethics processes.* (Doctoral dissertation), University of Hertfordshire, UK. Retrieved from https://ethos.bl.uk/OrderDetails. do?uin=uk.bl.ethos.573326

Brindley, R., Nolte, L., & Nel, P. W. (2019). We were in one place, and the ethics committee another: Experiences of going through the research ethics application process. *Clinical Ethics.* Manuscript submitted for publication.

The British Psychological Society. (2014). *Guidelines on the standards for doctoral programmes in clinical psychology.* Retrieved from www.ucl.ac.uk/clinical-psychology-doctorate/sites/clinical-psychology-doctorate/files/Appendix4r2010.pdf

Bronfenbrenner, U. (1977). Toward an experimental ecology of human development. *American Psychologist, 32*(7), 513–531.

Burnham, J. (2012). Developments in social GRRRAAACCEEESSS: Visible-invisible and voiced-unvoiced. In I. Krause (Ed.), *Culture and reflexivity in systemic psychotherapy: Mutual perspectives* (pp. 139–160). London: Karnac.

Carey, M., & Russell, S. (2002). Externalising: Commonly asked questions. *International Journal of Narrative Therapy & Community Work, 2002*(2), 76.

Clance, P. R., & Imes, S. A. (1978). The imposter phenomenon in high achieving women: Dynamics and therapeutic intervention. *Psychotherapy: Theory, Research & Practice, 15*(3), 241–247.

Cummins, I. (2018). The impact of austerity on mental health service provision: A UK perspective. *International Journal of Environmental Research and Public Health, 15*(6), 1145.

Delany, C., Miller, K. J., El-Ansary, D., Remedios, L., Hosseini, A., & McLeod, S. (2015). Replacing stressful challenges with positive coping strategies: A resilience program for clinical placement learning. *Advances in Health Sciences Education, 20*(5), 1303–1324.

Grice, T., Alcock, K., & Scior, K. (2018). Mental health disclosure amongst clinical psychologists in training: Perfectionism and pragmatism. *Clinical Psychology & Psychotherapy, 25*(5), 721–729.

Griffiths, L. (1998). Humour as resistance to professional dominance in community mental health teams. *Sociology of Health & Illness, 20*(6), 874–895.

Hannigan, B., Edwards, D., & Burnard, P. (2004). Stress and stress management in clinical psychology: Findings from a systematic review. *Journal of Mental Health, 13*(3), 235–245.

Harper, D., McGrath, L., Mundy, E., Curno, T., Thompson, S., Wood, K., . . . Buhagiar, J. (2015). Psychologists against austerity. *The Psychologist, 28*(3), 172.

Keville, S., Nel, P. W., Uprichard, S., McCarney, R., Jeffrey, S., Ford, D., & Leggett, S. (2009). Reaching the journey's end: Reflections on the final phase of a problem-based learning group. *Reflective Practice, 10*(5), 589–599.

Kinderman, P., Allsopp, K., & Cooke, A. (2017). Responses to the publication of the American Psychiatric Association's DSM-5. *Journal of Humanistic Psychology*, *57*(6), 625–649.

Kumary, A., & Baker, M. (2008). Stresses reported by UK trainee counselling psychologists. *Counselling Psychology Quarterly*, *21*(1), 19–28.

Lang, P., Little, M., & Cronen, V. (1990). The systemic professional: Domains of action and the question of neutrality. *Human Systems*, *1*(1), 34–49.

Lavender, A. (2003). Redressing the balance: The place, history and future of reflective practice in clinical training. *Clinical Psychology*, *27*, 11–15.

Lyons, A., Mason, B., Nutt, K., & Keville, S. (2019). Inside it was orange squash concentrate: Trainees' experiences of reflective practice groups within clinical psychology training. *Reflective Practice*, 1–15.

Mattheys, K. (2015). The coalition, austerity and mental health. *Disability & Society*, *30*(3), 475–478.

McElhinney, R. (2008). *Professional identity development: A grounded theory study of clinical psychology trainees*. (DClinPsy thesis), University of Edinburgh, Scotland, UK.

Morgan, H. C., Randall, J., Lyons, A. J., Oliver, S., Saffer, J., Scott, J. M., & Nolte, L. (2019). Pebbles in palms: Counter-practices against despair. *Psychotherapy and Politics International*, e1481.

Nel, P. W., Canade, R., Kelly, A., & Thomson, S. (2014). "Jumping on the bus": Reflections on introducing peer-assisted learning (PAL) in clinical psychology training. (DClinPsy thesis), University of Hertfordshire, Hatfield, UK.

Nel, P. W., Keville, S., Ford, D., McCarney, R., Jeffrey, S., Adams, S., & Uprichard, S. (2008). Close encounters of the uncertain kind: Reflections on doing problem-based learning (PBL) for the first time. *Reflective Practice*, *9*(2), 197–206.

Nel, P. W., Pezzolesi, C., & Stott, D. J. (2012). How did we learn best? A retrospective survey of clinical psychology training in the United Kingdom. *Journal of Clinical Psychology*, *68*(9), 1058–1073

Pakenham, K. I., & Stafford-Brown, J. (2012). Stress in clinical psychology trainees: Current research status and future directions. *Australian Psychologist*, *47*(3), 147–155.

Pica, M. (1998). The ambiguous nature of clinical training and its impact on the development of student clinicians. *Psychotherapy: Theory, Research, Practice, Training*, *35*(3), 361.

Randall, J. (2018). The personal politics of becoming a visibly tattooed psychologist: Participating in a chosen social grace of appearance. *Context*, *158*, 21–24.

Reynolds, V. (2010). Fluid and imperfect ally positioning: Some gifts of queer theory. *Context*, *111*, 13–17

Reynolds, V. (2019). The zone of fabulousness: Resisting "vicarious trauma" and "burnout" with connection, collective care and justice-doing in ways that centre the people we work alongside. *Context*, *164*, 36–39.

Shah, S., Wood, N., Nolte, L., & Goodbody, L. (2012). The experience of being a trainee clinical psychologist from a black and minority ethnic group: A qualitative study. *Clinical Psychology Forum*, *232*(April): 32–35.

Sheikh, A. I., Milne, D. L., & MacGregor, B. V. (2007). A model of personal professional development in the systematic training of clinical psychologists. *Clinical Psychology & Psychotherapy: An International Journal of Theory & Practice*, *14*(4), 278–287.

Smail, D. J. (2005). *Power, interest and psychology: Elements of a social materialist understanding of distress*. Ross-on-Wye: PCCS Books.

Stedmon, J., Wood, J., Curle, C., & Haslam, C. (2006). Development of PBL in the training of clinical psychologists. *Psychology Learning & Teaching*, *5*(1), 52–60.

Thomas, G. V., Turpin, G., & Meyer, C. (2002). Clinical research under threat. *The Psychologist*, *15*, 286–289.

Wade, A. (1997). Small acts of living: Everyday resistance to violence and other forms of oppression. *Contemporary Family Therapy*, *19*(1), 23–39.

Weingarten, K. (2000). Witnessing, wonder, and hope. *Family process*, *39*(4), 389–402.

Weingarten, K. (2010). Reasonable hope: Construct, clinical applications, and supports. *Family process*, *49*(1), 5–25.

White, M. (1997). *Narratives of therapists' lives*. Adelaide: Dulwich Centre Publications.

Woodward, N. S. (2014). *Experiences of personal and professional identities during clinical psychology doctoral training*. (Doctoral Dissertation). Retrieved from https://uhra.herts.ac.uk/bitstream/handle/2299/14778/12019314%20-%20Woodward%20Natasha%20-%20Final%20DClinPsy%20submission.pdf?sequence=1

Chapter 13

Sustaining selfhood and embracing 'selves' in psychology

Risks, vulnerabilities and sustaining relationships

Tanya Beetham and Kirstie Pope

This chapter is a joint reflection on sustaining 'selfhood' in psychology. It is a critical reflection on how our personal, 'professional' and political selves exist together and in relation to others. It explores the intersections of the different identities that can exist in learning and teaching contexts in psychology, focusing on student, teacher, client and therapist positions. It explores how taking risks and embracing vulnerabilities can provide hopeful opportunities to develop meaningful relationships in learning and teaching contexts in psychology. In jointly writing this chapter, we have had opportunities to learn more about each other, our relationship and the complexities, joys and vulnerabilities of what it means to embrace our 'selves'. We refer to 'selves' rather than 'self', as a way of acknowledging our multiple intersecting identities.

Reflections in this chapter are based on a student-teacher relationship in the context of a university psychology undergraduate degree programme. Kirstie is a student in an undergraduate psychology degree, and Tanya was her lecturer. In the spirit of embracing our multiple 'selves', we each occupy numerous positions as well as these. Amongst others, we are/have also been 'service users', clients in therapy, students, and, Tanya is also a therapist. We believe that *all* of these positions can be useful to explore and embrace if we are to form meaningful relationships in our training as psychologists, in client-therapist relationships and indeed, in student-teacher relationships. Embracing the multiple parts of our selves is necessary in order to sustain the self, and support others in doing so, in meaningful and whole-hearted ways. This can be defined as an intersectional approach –that our multiple identities are inseparable and that our identities and sense of belonging are shaped by our lived experiences of navigating structural, relational and process-based power relations (see Ahmed (2017) and Phoenix and Pattynama (2006) for further discussion).

Issues of power are complex, messy and inevitably woven through our relational and social lives, including in the very teacher-student relationship which we occupy. It is important to acknowledge the dilemma we faced when we began to explore our initial reflections on 'selfhood' in psychology. We explored how much of our 'selves' to uncover in a chapter about selfhood. How much to reveal? What risks can we take? What 'should' be censored? In our experience, these are fundamental questions that thread through learning, teaching and training roles and relationships. In order to jointly explore this, we adopted a relational epistemology (Brownlee & Berthelsen, 2008), meaning that knowledge is viewed as being produced in, and through, relationships. For example, the knowledge we have produced in this chapter is shaped by our joint reflections, and it is not a product of our individual stories and experiences only. Thus, knowledge production is both personal and political, as our individual lived experiences cannot be understood in isolation to the social, cultural and institutional contexts that we live in (Andrews, 2006; Wilkinson & Kitzinger, 2013). The personal, political and 'professional' are therefore inseparable. From this view, we challenge mainstream concepts of 'expertise' by addressing hierarchical power structures in which the 'teacher' is assumed to be the knower, positioning them in a place of 'epistemic privilege', whilst overlooking the knowledge and meaning-making of others (May, 2015). Epistemic privilege is a term used by Miranda Fricker (2007) to highlight that in certain contexts, the knowledge of those who are in positions of power, tends to obscure the knowledge that others offer. Thus, power relations play a part in shaping whose knowledge counts and in which contexts. These power relations are social, relational, nuanced and impactful, in learning and teaching contexts.

It is useful, if not necessary, to think deeply about the self. Psychology does not appear to be an area of work or study that we simply stumble into. Our histories, experiences, stories and hopes for our futures are not things we can easily separate. We have both occupied client/'service user' positions, as well as positions in psychology lecture theatres and classrooms. We have also come up against healthcare professionals who seem surprised that a psychology student or a psychologist could be seeking help from a person who could well have walked the same training path as they did. The 'us-them' boundary becomes complicated and unclear. Lives and identities intersect in complicated ways, leaving those of us who train in psychology, with some delicate conversations to unpack, and tricky terrain to navigate. Sustaining our 'selves' is therefore a sensitive task that also offers us some meaningful and enriching experiences.

Psychology carries a certain kind of disciplinary power (Burman, 2016; Rose, 1990). It tends to favour the 'objective', privileging positivist paradigms, and consequently de-authorising other ways of knowing. Particularly knowledge produced from voices and groups who might be marginalised by social inequalities or who have lived experiences that do not fit with the 'norm' (Fricker, 2007; May, 2015). At least traditionally, our discipline tends to value linear, non-contradictory narrative accounts of experiences, therefore smoothening out the tensions, contradictions and non-linear ways of telling stories of our 'selves' (Andrews, 2006). Whilst this might be considered an issue impacting only researchers, it also impacts those of us working in and studying psychology at a deeply structural level. Here, we consider how we tell stories of our 'selves' – who, and what is prioritised, and which parts of our 'selves' are consequently erased. The challenges and intricacies of how we construct and define our 'self' in different contexts, are crucial to explore. In early psychology training, and in neo-liberal institutions that value measurable outputs, psychology may diverge from the values we might seek to practise and embed in relationships. It is necessary to reflect on how 'objective' knowledge is privileged here, over lived experience. This approach to research outputs and outcomes does not necessarily align with values that embrace difference, diversity and complexity. These are issues we view as central to our profession.

If psychology disciplines us into single story thinking, it erases the multiplicity of being human – creating conditions for 'us'/'them' thinking. This presents particular challenges for classrooms that explore clinical or academic 'topics' that are also deeply personal. Occupying learning and teaching roles in psychology means that we enter into a context in which personal-professional boundaries become extended. Intersectional scholars (see for example Ahmed (2017)) have argued that a surface-level focus on sameness and difference, based on individual characteristics, runs the risk of making invisible structural inequalities. It is necessary, as psychologists, to attend to, and reflect on the socio-structural contexts in which we build and maintain relationships. Vivian May (2015) has argued that she is "sceptical of claims that we have fully disaffiliated from pathologising mindsets or wholly broken from past discriminatory practices" (p. 12). Further, she highlighted that

> the [self] is constantly against structures and systems which invite them to break apart, in order to align with and work within a homogenous, single-axis mindset and world. Therefore, selves, or parts of the 'self' are in opposition and cannot 'mesh' without 'erasure or distortion'.
>
> (p. 44)

This kind of erasure is a useful point of discussion – particularly in training and teaching settings where the 'professional' self tends to be privileged. Our experience is that this can be a risky journey to navigate for all who occupy these training and learning spaces. Our invisible vulnerabilities might be further erased if they sit in 'opposition' or struggle to 'mesh' with the professional self we are trained to privilege. Despite the 'hopeless' conclusion this leads us to, we have also found some 'hope-full' opportunities for dialogue. How can we embrace the challenge of learning collectively? Or to learn to un-learn this way of working? How can we challenge systems and structures that invite us to break apart? How do we learn to build ourselves, and each other, up and back together?

We begin to consider: if we come up against structures that invite us to break apart, how do we manage the vulnerabilities of taking risks within these structures? Vulnerabilities are often positioned as something we should protect ourselves (and others) from. Vulnerabilities are assumed to pose a risk. To require armour. From this view, if vulnerabilities pose a risk, vulnerabilities become shamed, silenced or problematised. When structures require us to break apart by refusing to accommodate the wholeness of our 'selves', we do indeed occupy risky spaces. Risky spaces, for some of us, can mean the 'self'/'other' are produced and conditions for othering are set. Maybe we *are* the other.

Classrooms are not immune from the kind of othering that can be produced by binary logics. Within the classroom it is almost assumed that those within it could not possibly have experienced any of the things they are learning about. This creates a difficult dynamic and a complex conflict as we begin to question whether to speak up or even silence ourselves through fear that our vulnerabilities and these othered parts of ourselves may be discovered. It can lead us to ask fundamental questions of belonging and selfhood. The perceived risk and fear of judgement functions to reinforce the belief that it is not 'acceptable' for those studying psychology to have their own stories of struggle. Being a student, it is difficult when a peer assumes you have previously worked with a specific 'disorder' or issue, and made it your specialism because you know so much about it. How do you explain to that person that you have not studied this 'topic' in depth at all? Rather, your knowledge is based on having spent many years in treatment for it? Similarly, from a teaching perspective, when teaching a 'topic' which is both academic, clinical, and intimately personal, how do the 'professional' and vulnerable parts of the 'personal' sit in dialogue with each other, when delivering a lecture which aims to teach a topic as if it is somehow 'out there' and not 'in here'? How is an acceptance of the self, and each other, modelled at a deep, vulnerable level, without embracing the risks that come with doing so?

Classroom, learning and teaching contexts can be sensitive relational spaces, and what feels vulnerable in one context, may not feel the same in another. What is 'speakable' in a large classroom or seminar group is not the same as what is speakable in a small reflection group, over lunchtime, in a peer relationship, or during a one to one tutorial. Yet student-teacher and peer relationships exist across all of these contexts, and opportunities to reflect on and explore our 'selves' exist in all of these spaces too. Notions of vulnerabilities and othering offers us opportunities to reflect on the contexts in which othering occurs and how vulnerabilities are produced. For example, the dynamics of our own relationship have shifted depending on the spaces we have occupied. For Tanya, her experiences teaching numerous, sometimes sizeable classrooms of undergraduate and graduate psychology students, means that sharing 'other' parts of herself, carries different kinds of risks and produces different kinds of vulnerabilities. Her own experience of eating disorder treatment and recovery undoubtedly shapes how she teaches about eating disorders. Yet it is not always explicitly acknowledged in lectures, but it is sometimes acknowledged and discussed in individual relationships. Certain settings and relationships exist in which we feel more able to allow our less 'acceptable' parts to be known – spaces in which there is less relational risk of judgement. There is something about shared common ground (e.g., personal experience of using services, accessing therapy or support in another way, or being in the 'client' seat, rather than therapist) – it is more than just being in the same profession or doing the same course, that allows individuals, irrespective of power or circumstantial differences, to connect.

We need to create spaces for vulnerabilities, not just in clinical contexts but extending to classrooms and training rooms too. It is a relational risk to share parts of our selves that have remained 'protected' before. We wonder what opportunities might arise if we challenge and resist the notion that vulnerabilities are *always* risky. Further, that *despite* risk, vulnerabilities can be embraced. Sara Ahmed (2017) argues that fragility and vulnerability are necessary to embrace if we are to challenge othering discourses and practises. She suggests building 'shelters' of shared vulnerabilities is a way of challenging the idea that vulnerabilities, and indeed emotions, are inherently risky and do not belong in shared spaces. She argues that carving creative and collective spaces for these shared vulnerabilities is a resistance against hierarchical structures – structures that can be harmful when we come up against them. We agree with Ahmed's arguments – however, this argument also poses some questions. What happens when we embrace vulnerabilities and 'risks' in a neoliberal socio-political culture that does not always value what – and who – is vulnerable?

Vulnerabilities can counter-intuitively be sites of relational depth and enrichment. Although complexities of power, judgement and difference thread through relationships, there is something powerful about creating spaces that enable risk and vulnerability in learning and teaching relationships and classroom spaces. Extending the boundaries of 'them'/'us' thinking is not only important, but it is meaningful and enriching, in academic and institutional contexts. The exposure of psychology classrooms and the vulnerabilities we embody, also offers opportunities for connection. Our experience is that there are many small and big ways in which meaningful relationships can be made and sustained through the very vulnerabilities that psychology might be built to discipline us out of.

Extending 'them'/ 'us' divisions is not only a way of challenging power relations but also a way of establishing a sense of collective care. Small relational shifts and acts of care can have big impacts, particularly in contexts where extending the boundaries of that relationship is 'risky'. Offering care and creating spaces of connection can be enriching in itself. However, in institutions where this kind of emotion-work is seen to challenge hierarchical boundaries (Koster, 2011) and more-so, may be risky, in that it extends 'them'/'us' divisions, it has a particular relational, personal and political meaning. Power threads through relationships, but care also threads through relationships that matter. Embracing the multiplicity and vulnerability of our 'selves' through relationships that mean something, and are full of meaning, can, in our experience, be enriching. We hope that we do not paint a rose-tinted picture. There is a structural reality of inequalities and hierarchies, which can limit what can feel relationally safe. However, a dialogue about embracing vulnerabilities and relational risk-taking in spaces where it is possible, may provide sites for care, relational depth and enrichment.

We conclude by suggesting that there is a messiness, complexity, and challenge in shared humanness. Jointly writing this reflection has offered us an opportunity to consider our shared, coexisting vulnerabilities and strengths, and the numerous relational risks we have ourselves taken. We have used an intersectional lens as a framework to support some of our reflections about how we sustain and care for our selves and each other. Through this framework, we have considered power as not just one way, but power as relational, and power relations as unavoidable. In writing this chapter, we have offered a reflection on student-teacher relationships, psychology classrooms and whole-hearted relationships which embrace multiple parts of the 'self'. Our chapter is intended as a reflection, rather than conclusion, and we embrace the tensions and contradictions inherent in themes of vulnerabilities, risk, relationships, and the self. We hope this reflection contributes to collective conversations about the ways in which embracing risk might enable growth, enrich experiences and facilitate meaningful relationships in teaching, learning and training spaces. Through engaging with notions of risk and vulnerabilities, we may contribute in a meaningful way to surviving psychology and sustaining our 'selves'.

References

Ahmed, S. (2017). *Living a feminist life*. London: Duke University Press.

Andrews, M. (2006). I. Breaking down barriers: Feminism, politics and psychology. *Feminism & Psychology, 16*(1), 13–17.

Brownlee, J., & Berthelsen, D. (2008). Developing relational epistemology through relational pedagogy: New ways of thinking about personal epistemology in teacher education. In M. S. Khine (Ed.), *Knowing, knowledge and beliefs* (pp. 405–422). Dordrecht: Springer Dordrecht.

Burman, E. (2016). Knowing Foucault, knowing you: "raced"/classed and gendered subjectivities in the pedagogical state. *Pedagogy, Culture & Society, 24*(1), 1–25.

Fricker, M. (2007). *Epistemic injustice: Power and the ethics of knowing*. New York: Oxford University Press.

Koster, S. (2011). The self-managed heart: Teaching gender and doing emotional labour in a higher education institution. *Pedagogy, Culture & Society, 19*(1), 61–77.

May, V. M. (2015). *Pursuing intersectionality, unsettling dominant imaginaries*. Oxon: Routledge.

Phoenix, A., & Pattynama, P. (2006). Intersectionality. *European Journal of Women's Studies, 13*(3), 187–192.

Rose, N. (1990). *Governing the soul: The shaping of the private self*. London: Routledge.

Wilkinson, S., & Kitzinger, C. (2013). Representing our own experience: Issues in "insider" research. *Psychology of Women Quarterly, 37*(2), 251–255.

The political

Selves and politics in practice

Part IV

The political

Selves and politics in practice

Chapter 14

Power in practice

Questioning psychiatric diagnosis

Sasha Priddy and Katie Sydney

Introduction

Diagnosis continues to hold a central position within the structure of mental health services as the dominant model for conceptualising psychological distress alongside troubled and troubling behaviour. The biomedical model, which underpins diagnosis, frames these experiences and behaviours as the result of an underlying biological pathology. In line with this, psychiatric diagnosis is seen by many professionals and service users as a pivotal component of somebody's treatment and can be an important factor in the way people make sense of the adversities they face.

The merits and faults of psychiatric diagnosis continue to be vehemently debated by those within the helping professions, service users, academics, and many others. Whilst some critical accounts of diagnosis have questioned the validity and reliability of discrete categories of functional mental health diagnoses (Kinderman, Read, Moncrieff, & Bentall, 2013; Pemberton & Wainwright, 2014), other accounts have emphasised the harmful nature of what they would deem to be damaging practices (Russo & Sweeney, 2016; Emmons, Manion, & Andrew, 2018). These debates have mostly focused upon 'functional' psychiatric diagnosis (e.g., schizophrenia), as opposed to neurodevelopmental diagnoses (e.g., autistic spectrum conditions), though the scope of the current critical discourse has encapsulated many aspects of diagnostic practices, rather than just the constructs themselves.

This chapter will consider what it is like to work within services dominated by psychiatric practises and explore a range of professional issues surrounding psychiatric diagnosis. We will then explore how individuals manage to develop personally and professionally in contexts where power imbalances are inherently linked to roles, entrenched in team cultures, or embedded in service design and implementation. We will consider how feelings of disempowerment can be common themes for prequalified individuals – themes that can foster feelings of self-doubt in the context of pressures to demonstrate 'brilliance' in order to progress along competitive professional paths.

Psychiatric diagnosis as a means of categorising distress

The Diagnostic and Statistical Manual of Mental Disorders (DSM; APA, 2013) is one of the dominant frameworks used by health professionals to classify and diagnose mental health difficulties (see also, the International Classification of Disorders; WHO, 2018). The theoretical underpinning of the DSM suggests that there are discrete psychiatric diagnoses that are comprised of 'symptoms', which co-occur and have a common aetiology. Within the biomedical model, this aetiology is presumed to be a physiological dysfunction located within the individual; with neurochemistry, brain structure and genetics touted as common causal candidates underlying presenting symptoms. To meet the criteria for mental disorder, the symptoms – which may include disturbance in cognition, emotion regulation or behaviour – must cause significant distress or impairment in functioning. Therefore, a reaction to a common stressor that is considered proportional in line with social norms does not constitute a mental disorder. Recent changes from DSM-IV to DSM-5 exemplify the concept of 'proportional' versus 'diagnosable' distress; for example, experiencing a recent bereavement became an exclusion factor in the diagnosis of major depression through the amendments released within DSM-5 (Pies, 2014).

The origins of the DSM can be traced back to the United States armed forces, with the American Psychiatric Association devising the framework to categorise psychological distress observed in those returning from military service. The DSM has since undergone five revisions, with the number of diagnoses increasing over time. The first compendium of the DSM included 102 broadly-construed diagnostic categories, which increased to 182 in the DSM-II, 265 disorders in the DSM-III, 292 in the DSM-III-R, 297 in the DSM-IV and 265 in the most recent DSM-5. For those who position themselves as accepting the distinction between 'well' and 'unwell', the expanding nature of the DSM has led to the concern that "the pool of normality is shrinking to a mere puddle" (Wykes & Callard, 2010, p. 302).

The empirical foundations upon which diagnostic frameworks have been built, appear to show further signs of erosion; whilst "reliability is the first test of validity for diagnosis" (Freedman et al., 2013, p. 1), 'kappa scores' have increasingly declined with each DSM revision. This reflects a decrease in the extent to which clinicians agree upon a diagnosis when presented with a given clinical picture. However, this pattern has not been observed with neurodevelopmental diagnoses (e.g., autistic spectrum condition), for which there have been improvements in inter-rater reliability up until the DSM-5 (Frances, 2012).

Thinking space

We invite you to reflect on what factors could account for changes in the quantity and reliability of diagnoses across the revisions of the DSM.

The offerings of diagnostic dialogue

Within the biomedical model, a psychiatric diagnosis can be used to guide decisions around treatment using professional guidelines that offer recommendations based on published research (i.e., National Institute for Clinical Excellence). Thus, proponents of diagnosis argue that it provides a structured framework that can objectively encapsulate symptoms and provide a language to communicate distress via categories of disorder.

Receiving a diagnosis can also be a gateway to accessing specialist services, such as eating disorder teams, which may require a diagnosis as a pre-requisite to accessing available resources. In addition to professional resources, diagnosis has also become a means by which individuals can seek out alternative sources of support, such as groups comprised of others with the same diagnosis or online resources. These communities can offer the opportunity for experiences of connection, normalisation and understanding within contexts where people may feel excluded, marginalised or misunderstood.

Based on these factors, it is understandable that a mental health diagnosis may also come with a sense of relief for many. Diagnosis can be seen to offer validation of an individual's lived experience and provide access to resources that continue to be ring-fenced by the necessity for distress to be justified by a 'diagnosable illness'. Governmental gateways to support are a pertinent example of this, where evidence of a recognised mental health diagnosis can provide vital support for an individual's state benefit application; which are increasingly difficult to obtain in the age of austerity (Watts, 2018).

Diagnosis has also been suggested to validate experiences of distress; this can be seen in the many anti-stigma campaigns that have adopted the idea that attributing distress to biomedical ideas will reduce public stigma. However, recent meta-analytic findings have shown that although biomedical origins of distress are increasingly more likely to be endorsed by the public, stigmatizing attitudes toward mental health difficulties appear to have *increased* in the decade between 1996 and 2006 (Schomerus et al., 2012).

Reflective activity: perspective-taking on psychiatric diagnosis

Based on your experience and understanding of the theoretical underpinnings, purpose and consequences of psychiatric diagnosis, spend some time considering your thoughts about the benefits and drawbacks of diagnostic practice; for example, you could structure this as a pro/cons table. You may want to experiment with undertaking this activity from a variety of viewpoints, for example:

- From your own personal and/or professional perspective;
- From the perspective of a service user within different services (e.g., community, inpatient);

- From the perspective of a family member, guardian, or carer;
- From the position of a mental health professional (e.g., psychiatrist, neuropsychologist, social worker, nursing staff).

You could also consider wider contextual viewpoints, such as those involved in commissioning or academic research. Once completed, to generate discussion and further explore your own and others' perspectives, you could meet with a fellow colleague to reflect on the similarities and differences between your ideas. Consider how your personal and professional backgrounds may have influenced areas in which your opinions seem more aligned or different.

What does it feel like to receive a diagnosis?

Any debate around the benefits and drawbacks of psychiatric diagnosis should prioritise the importance of how individuals experience and relate to receiving a diagnosis. A recent meta-analysis by Perkins and colleagues (2018) explored experiences of receiving a psychiatric diagnosis. Their results illustrated that diagnosis was sometimes experienced as a relief, a validation of suffering, an assurance that what the person was experiencing was 'normal', and that there would be hope for future recovery. The following quotes, taken from the research within the meta-analysis, demonstrate some of these themes:

> "*Having a name to put to that gave me something to attack. It gave me something to work with . . . a tangible framework of something I could manage*".
>
> (Perkins et al., 2018, p. 13)

> "*It was the beginning of being able to sort out a lifetime of feelings, events . . . my entire life. It was the chance for a new beginning*".
>
> (Ibid.)

Thinking space

Consider a time when you have experienced someone responding positively to a psychiatric diagnosis – try using the following questions as prompts to reflect upon their experience:

- What aspects of their diagnosis did they find helpful or meaningful?
- In what ways did a diagnosis contribute positively to their understanding, outlook or sense of empowerment?
- What factors might have contributed to this experience?
- What does this tell you about the factors that can influence someone's integration of a diagnosis into their identity or their relationships with others?

Other accounts shared within Perkin and colleagues' meta-analysis indicated that diagnosis could lead people to feel dehumanised, ashamed, isolated and "no longer seen as a person, but as a diagnosis" (Perkins et al., 2018, p. 13). This in turn, appeared to result in subsequent concerns about being mistreated and a sense of hopelessness for the future. Diagnosis was most likely to be experienced as meaningless or harmful when it was accompanied by no functional purpose, did not add any perceived value to one's situation, and could be considered a catalyst for the removal of an individual's support and/or resources. On the other hand, people were more likely to feel positive about their diagnosis when they felt that it accurately captured their difficulties, when it had been given after a thorough assessment, if it was explained to them in a way that they could understand and when it was perceived to facilitate access to useful services. Variations in experience were also identified according to the given diagnoses; with 'depression' being the most validating diagnosis to receive, and 'personality disorder' and 'schizophrenia' evoking accounts of more negative experiences. This was attributed to greater social stigma and less choice around intervention or treatment due to limited service provisions for these particular diagnoses. From these findings, it can be seen that the experience of receiving a diagnosis can change or challenge how people make sense of their circumstances.

Consider these ideas whilst reflecting upon Alex's account, shared next in the *In focus* box. In this account, Alex describes psychiatric diagnosis as playing a significant part in making sense of his distress.

In focus: Alex's[1] account of diagnosis

In 2016, I experienced a period in my life when my mental health began to deteriorate to the point where I could no longer recognise reality. Throughout my life I have experienced mental health difficulties to an extent but this period, which was later diagnosed as having been psychosis, stood apart from anything that I had experienced previously. It began from a period of intense stress and built up into what I can only describe as mania, with delusions of grandiose abilities – namely being psychic and being able to heal people psychologically. These delusions brought with them, a sense that my understanding of the world was evaporating, and a lingering sense of fear and confusion. I was certain that the builders I could hear working nearby were actually linked to my own health; that they were trying to repair me, and if they were not able to, then I would die. Many other similar themed delusions followed as I tried to understand what was happening to me. At the time I didn't realise these were delusions; I fully believed what I was experiencing was real, and quickly I became convinced that I was entangled in a battle between God and the Devil. For me two things were possible: either the world as I knew it was not real, that I had somehow broken through to a reality that was a constant war between heaven and hell, or simply that I had lost my mind. In that state, I leaned towards the former.

Swiftly my health deteriorated to the point where friends and family became involved and I woke one day in a hospital having no recollection of how I got there. I later learnt that the doctors were sure I had taken drugs of some sort and were waiting for those to exit my system. This didn't happen; there had been no drugs. Instead I was diagnosed with psychosis and spent a short period in this environment before feigning my way out by pretending to be okay. Delusions had led me to feel unsafe in the hospital but I now had a meaning behind my experiences and medication, which I hoped would take effect and bring me back to normality. It took a few months before my psychotic symptoms disappeared, but now, I was armed with the knowledge that I was experiencing psychosis, that what I thought had been real was not real but in my head. Although at times that was hard to appreciate and I lingered between uncertainty in knowing what was real and what wasn't, I could keep myself relatively grounded by remembering the diagnosis and challenging the experiences I was having.

By the time I was offered any practical help, the symptoms had passed and things were more geared towards preventing relapse. I was under the care of a psychiatrist who by their own admission did not know much about psychosis. He erred on the side of caution with every decision based on the diagnosis and not on my current state. His words were that I should stay on medication for five years, regardless of what was happening in my life. He even stated that it would definitely come back within the five years. The stressors that had likely caused the psychosis in the first place were long gone. I felt healthier and happier than I previously did but all this was disregarded based on the diagnosis. I was confused by his stance and fearful that based on his words I had something that would affect me on and off for the remainder of my life. To clarify, I approached an independent psychiatrist whose view varied from the psychiatrist who looked after my care. They felt that based on my current state, it was highly possible that I would be unlikely to relapse, though of course she reiterated that nothing was certain. But it was less devastating than the news I had been given before.

I then received a follow up letter from the independent psychiatrist where she diagnosed my experience as bipolar disorder with psychotic symptoms. This diagnosis came as a surprise. There had been no mention of this during our meeting and seemed to contradict what she had said. If it was bipolar then there could easily be another similar experience. This diagnosis, I felt was wrong. I had no other symptoms of bipolar, the only high I experienced was during the psychosis, never before or since, and I had experienced no lows typical of bipolar either. I couldn't understand her reasoning behind the diagnosis and so I withheld it from my treatment team as I felt it would only complicate matters.

Ultimately, I felt that my psychosis diagnosis was critical for me. I genuinely felt that reality had disintegrated around me and I couldn't comprehend what was happening to me. That diagnosis was a relief and allowed me to challenge thoughts, which I hadn't been able to do previously. For my own wellbeing it was essential; it allowed me to understand my experience, to step outside it, rather than be dragged along by it. However, my diagnosis had little relevance outside of my own wellbeing. I was offered too little help by mental health teams, and too late. At first, they simply seemed to be monitoring whether I was a risk to myself or others, rather than helping me get better. After I moved house and found myself under the care of another team, it took a substantial period of time to get any support from them. I dealt with the psychosis with friends and family, not professional help. I would have hoped a diagnosis would allow a treatment team to intervene in effective ways but that was not my experience of it. Once I had stabilised, they put in place treatment plans to prevent relapse but during the episode itself I had been left to my own devices. Had it not been for those around me I would have struggled with my experiences but thankfully I had support. Diagnosis therefore felt a bit irrelevant in the grand scheme of things, useful for me to understand my experience, but of no use, and in ways even counterproductive in obtaining support from professionals who viewed me by the label rather than by my current circumstances.

Widening our perspective: social inequality and 'othering'

Despite biomedical ideas largely governing the current paradigm of care, clinicians, academics and activists are increasingly emphasising how crucial social context is, to issues relating to mental health and wellbeing. The largest division of the British Psychological Society, the Division of Clinical Psychology (DCP), for example, declared the need for a paradigm shift towards understanding distress in terms of the 'psychosocial' and released a range of documents championing alternatives to the dominance of the biomedical model (DCP, 2013, 2015).

In 2010, the DCP's "Understanding Bipolar Disorder" document suggested that "services should not insist that all service users see their problems as an illness" (p. 8). This invitation to accept alternative accounts of distress can be seen partially as a response to the increasing evidence that identifies early childhood trauma and adverse environmental contexts as 'risk factors' for poor psychological wellbeing in later life (see Johnstone et al., 2018). A recent meta-analysis identified discrimination, employment status, low income, poor quality housing, familial relationships, neighbourhood safety and community violence as key social determinants of psychological distress (Alegría, NeMoyer, Bagué, Wang, & Alvarez, 2018). Furthermore, the impact of social inequalities on mental health have been found to multiply across the lifespan (Allen, Balfour, Bell, & Marmot,

2014). Findings such as these have made it impossible to deny the importance of social contexts. Thus, the increasing amount of research evidencing the influence of relational and contextual factors clearly points to the undeniable need for models that do not dismiss such societal factors through attributing distress to underlying pathologies within individuals. These developments have led many psychologists to strongly advocate for an alternative position to understanding distress, whereby we move from asking "what is wrong with you?" to "what has happened to you?" (Johnstone et al., 2018).

As noted earlier in this chapter, Alex's account detailed how psychiatric diagnosis can be beneficial and helpful – despite some challenges from others. Now we turn to Katie's account of receiving the diagnosis of 'borderline personality disorder' (BPD).

In focus: Katie's account of psychiatric diagnoses

BPD used to make sense to me as an explanation for the intense distress I felt. I initially wanted to be diagnosed because I naively thought it would allow me to access the treatment I needed to get better. I had not encountered any critical analysis of psychiatric diagnosis in the first year of my degree and took diagnosis to be fact, but the way I was treated in 'the system' radically changed my views. BPD is now a label that I reject, because I think it is damaging and offensive to label people who have survived difficult circumstances as having 'disordered' personalities.

I found that even when I had a diagnosis of depression there were coercive elements to my treatment but once I had a BPD diagnosis, I had no control at all. Any attempt to assert my own needs or contradict professional opinion was considered a symptom of my diagnosis. The final straw was when a consultant psychiatrist who I had never met wrote a letter to my GP saying that I was self-harming for attention. Having this on my medical records made me feel hopeless as I knew that my views on the matter would never be held with as much value and truth as hers, despite her never having even spoken to me (a fact that was omitted from the letter). When I called her and politely pointed out the danger of labelling someone with suicidal ideation as attention seeking, I was told I was hostile, and the call was terminated. I hit rock bottom and came to the uncomfortable realisation that the people who were meant to help me were making me worse and I disengaged from services.

Around this time, I watched Jacqui Dillon's talk "The Psychological is Political" (2017), in which she speaks about how she finds it offensive to label trauma survivors as personality disordered. This was a major epiphany for me. I began to see my own difficulties not as the consequence of a malevolent illness entity named BPD, but as understandable reactions to my environment – including the way I was treated by mental health services. Escaping the diagnosis' imposition on my identity has done more for my wellbeing than any medication or therapy I was ever offered. Almost two years on I have a quality of life I never thought would be possible, although I still have dark times.

I have since completed my undergraduate placement year in the psychology department of a psychiatric hospital, which had a 'personality disorder' service. It may seem contradictory to some to still want to work in mental health services having had such bad experiences, but my drive is to make things better for people like me. I started the placement determined to hide my experiences for fear of being seen as incompetent. It is still something I worry about, but I don't want to conceal where I come from because I think it can be a strength. My experience has coloured the kind of psychologist I want to be – one who works with service users to make their own choices and create their own narratives, rather than imposing one on them.

Disputing 'reasonable' explanations of distress: elucidating the smokescreen for a society that is 'unreasonable'

The concept of underlying biomedical disorders has also allowed the diagnostic categories devised in Western societies to be imposed cross-culturally. This imposition has undermined the meaning and explanations of distress offered within other cultures, whilst also attempting to interpret and categorise behaviour according to a Eurocentric norm. In discussing the ethnocentric biases of psychiatric diagnosis, Fernando (1991) states that:

> In considering diagnosis, two facts should be borne in mind: first, psychiatry is ethnocentric and carries the ideologies of Western culture, including racism; secondly, the practice of psychiatry, including its ways of diagnosing are influenced by the social ethos and the political system in which it lives and works.
>
> Fernando (1991, p. 61)

Research on the influence of ethnicity on diagnostic practices illustrates that cultural biases are embedded within practises and dominates perceptions of psychological distress and psychiatric disorder. For example, black individuals are three to four times more likely to be diagnosed with a psychotic disorder than white counterparts (Schwartz & Blankenship, 2014) and are subsequently more likely to be admitted to psychiatric hospital under the Mental Health Act (Mann et al., 2014), whilst also being at an increased risk of experiencing negative, harmful and adversarial 'care' (Morgan, Mallett, Hutchinson, & Leff, 2004). Neighbors and colleagues (1989,

2003) attempted to shed light on the mechanism underlying these biases, concluding that clinicians' stereotypes and lack of sensitivity to cultural differences influence diagnostic decision-making. The embedded prejudices at play within the diagnostic framework and their implementation has led to the suggestion that structural and social inequalities have been reframed within psychiatric discourse as medical disorders (Thornton, 2010), which further precludes social and political oppression. Thus, adding additional weight to the proposition and recognition that diagnosis is not, and cannot be, a 'benign' administrative process.

The social context can be seen to be further dismissed through the subjective bias imposed by professionals via assumptions made about individuals' gender, sexuality and class. For example, an individual experiencing significant distress might cope with that distress through self-harming. If that individual is a woman, they may be more likely to be given a diagnosis of 'borderline personality disorder' (BPD); this is illustrated in statistics that demonstrate that women are three times more likely to be given this diagnosis than men (APA, 2000). To account for gender differences within psychiatric diagnosis, a number of explanations have been documented and evidenced, including higher levels of betrayal trauma in women (Kaehler & Freyd, 2009), attribution bias in clinicians (Becker & Lamb, 1994), and biased diagnostic criteria (Bjorklund, 2006). The association between experiences of sexual trauma and later diagnoses of BPD has been well established; around 70% of individuals diagnosed with BPD have been found to report experiences of sexual abuse (Castillo, 2000). This has led to criticisms that diagnosis serves to conceal external influences of power through encouraging clinicians, services and clients to make internal causal attributions of women's distress (Shaw & Proctor, 2005). This process of continually medicalising responses to trauma only perpetuates societal violence and oppression, through solely 'treating' the individual, rather than the societal expressions of power which have led to their difficulties. This is exemplified within the following quote from Suzi, who was diagnosed with BPD: "I cannot understand how the vast majority of perpetrators of sexual violence walk free in society; whilst people who struggle to survive its after effects are told they have disordered personalities"(Shaw & Proctor, 2004, p. 12).

Governmental decisions to impose austerity measures within the UK also draws attention to the process of obscuring societal responsibility for individual wellbeing. Barr, Kinderman, and Whitehead (2015) investigated the impact of austerity and welfare reforms on rates of psychological distress between 2004 and 2013 in England. They reported an upward trend in the prevalence of mental health difficulties throughout this period, which was substantially greater than previous periods. Moreover, this increase was seen to be greatest within those from the lowest socioeconomic groups. This evidence lends to the notion that society is perpetually pathologising poverty (Hansen, Bourgois, & Drucker, 2014). Smail (2005) succinctly explained this process, and its consequences: "[T]he social havoc wreaked by unfettered economic greed comes to be interiorised as the personal weakness and irresponsibility of those principally affected"(Smail, 2005, p. 61).

Based on the ideas presented above, it seems clear that our professional practice in relation to diagnosis may be heavily determined by an arguably complex interaction of choice, power, context and interests. This intricate and confusing process is likely to also underpin our personal relationship to the diagnoses which have been applied to us, as individuals using services. What follows, is Sasha's account of psychiatric diagnosis, capturing a winding, nonlinear relationship to diagnosis – which is a nuanced, changeable and dynamic.

In focus: Sasha's account of psychiatric diagnosis

As an author of this chapter, I felt it important to revisit my own relationship to receiving a mental health diagnosis. My first experience of this was during my teenage years, whilst I was a 'service user' under Child and Adolescent Mental Health Services (CAMHS). Looking back at my medical record from this time paints a disparaging picture; the first diagnosis I was given was panic disorder, followed by anorexia nervosa a few years later. Receiving these diagnoses has undoubtedly influenced my own practice, beliefs and values; in ways which would not have occurred without having been on the 'other side' of the mental health system. My experience has taught me that receiving a diagnosis is not just about the label; a diagnosis reflects power, relationships, societal values, and much more. Furthermore, the process in which a diagnosis is communicated and 'used' by professionals (e.g. to restrict or increase the choices available to a person) will inevitably impact on their relationship to the label they are given.

My diagnosis of anorexia nervosa was not communicated to me in person; it was articulated within letters between my GP, CAMHS and an eating disorders team. In the context of my difficulties at this time, reading these letters created further feelings of powerlessness over my environment. Whilst at the same time, I was relieved that my embodied communication of distress had been undoubtedly recognised. Following these diagnoses, I attended numerous appointments within mental health services. During these appointments, I recognised how further difficulties can arise when the professionals around you are focused on reducing 'symptoms' which have operated as coping strategies for many years. It was this experience which led me to believe that diagnoses frequently serve to mask underlying difficulties; leading professionals, who may have the best intentions, to focus their efforts on facilitating 'change' in superficial (and potentially damaging) ways.

My difficulty at this time was not my weight, nor was it my belief that I was fat, or my anxiety about attending school. My difficulties extended beyond me, to my immediate environment and my experiences of societally held beliefs. It was related to my relationships; those that were absent, those that were painful and those that communicated to me what I 'should' be. From this, it follows that gaining weight and challenging my beliefs did not facilitate positive change – it was the process of fostering safe, consistent and caring relationships with others, which enabled me to develop a better relationship to my own sense of self.

Whilst the diagnosis I received felt unrelated to the needs which it expressed, I can retrospectively value the sense of validation which it provided. On a practical level, it enabled me to access services which may have been unavailable to me. On a personal level, a diagnosis communicated that others had witnessed my distress as tangible. However, acknowledging distress as 'seen' is not enough. It was only when my emotional pain was given a voice, and 'heard' by others, that a healing relationship could truly begin. For me, diagnosis silenced and distorted this voice in order to create a more palatable narrative for those around me.

Power in practice: even a cat may look at a king

On the journey to qualification, psychologists are likely to sit at different positions along the continuum of diagnostic debate – from those more aligned to working within the dominant conventions of psychiatric diagnosis, to those participating in, yet challenging diagnostic practices, to those who choose to resist/protest against psychiatric diagnoses (Randall-James & Coles, 2018; Randall, Gunn, & Coles, in press). This position is also likely to change throughout their personal and professional development. Regardless of this, aspiring clinical psychologists will inevitably encounter the ripples of unresolved conflict from debates concerning the plurality of ways to conceptualise human distress.

Such debates may activate vulnerabilities and worries about voicing one's views on contested issues, particularly when it is different from the prevailing view of their supervisors or colleagues. Throughout the research in this area, prequalified individuals appear to have clear reservations about challenging diagnostic thinking, as illustrated below:

> "Clinical psychology is so competitive, you think, no, you know. . . . You really do feel like you are very replaceable".
>
> (Randall, 2015, p. 21)

> "It feels almost as if you are questioning your supervisor's experience, or questioning their knowledge. I guess, in something competitive like training in clinical psychology, these people may be potentially writing you off."
>
> (Ibid., p. 20)

Within these quotes, the notion that challenging diagnostic practice can feel threatening due to concerns around the expendability of prequalified positions is clearly illustrated. It appears that pre-qualified individuals often find themselves experiencing a sense of powerlessness within a hierarchical structure, which subsequently results in a silencing of personal values in order to protect oneself.

The degree of uncertainty which pre-qualified individuals experience when navigating the contested grounds of psychiatric practices is likely to vacillate throughout their training. Jones and Thompson (2017) identified the undulating nature of 'imposter syndrome', whereby trainees would fluctuate from lacking confidence in their ability, to rating themselves highly, across each of their placements. From this it can be seen how contextual and relational factors may lead prequalified individuals to further question their professional identity, and at times, diminish their self-belief in the validity of their position on topics that conjure passionate debate, such as diagnosis.

Balancing the scales of 'power' and 'truth': finding one's own voice

From this, we would propose that two primary factors appear to exert influence upon the likelihood that our opinions will be voiced. Firstly, our perceived power in relation to our context; predominantly created by powerful others around us. Secondly, the stability of perceived 'truths'; from the perspective of the individual and others. For example, an individual who feels questioning of, but 'open' to the concept of BPD may perceive this diagnosis as a relatively unstable 'truth'. Simultaneously, they may assess the stability of this 'truth' for those around them; in relation to their own position. *Figure 14.1* illustrates how these two processes influence the anticipated consequences of voicing one's perspective, which in turn contributes to a confidence to 'speak out'. Using this understanding, we can consider how we can negotiate our position; through paying attention to shifts in contextual power, or seeking to develop our own understanding of a perceived truth. For example, a trainee may not feel able to voice their opinion on diagnosis within a multidisciplinary team (MDT) professionals' meeting. However, by building relationships and contributing to the team, they may begin to feel more empowered, whilst also developing an understanding of the range of narratives the team holds to be 'true'. They may start to question their own 'truths' within this context, or observe evidence to support their own perspective. Alternatively, the trainee may seek to exit this dynamic by entering a 'questioning' or 'curious' stance – which in turn enables ideas to be voiced, without necessarily challenging the sources of power directly, or contesting the dominant 'truth' held within such contexts.

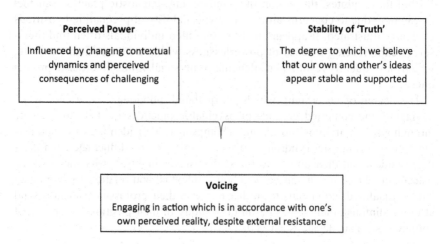

Figure 14.1 The scales of finding one's voice

Thinking space

Consider some of the challenges that you have faced in clinical practice or in lectures. Use the questions below to explore these experiences and as an aid to develop your understanding of the processes at play:

• Have you experienced times in which you held back from contributing to discussions around diagnosis and formulation, when you feel that you could have offered something useful?
• What is it that you were holding back from addressing? And what factors led to you not contributing at that time?
• Maybe you have noticed other times in which a similar situation has occurred, and if so, what things would need to change in order for you to feel able to contribute, potentially going against more dominant voices within your team?
• Perhaps there are others who feel similarly within your team – in what ways do you think you could support not only yourself, but others, to feel free to contribute in such a way?

Positions of professional questioning: playing the 'diagnostic game'

There are many factors at play which encourage professionals to maintain the most commonly held narrative within the services in which they are positioned.

However, for those who may not personally hold these ideas as being consistent with their own, strategies can be implemented to sustain oneself within challenging professional contexts. In Randall-James and Coles (2018), individuals appeared to engage in what was construed as 'playing the diagnostic game', in order to manage the anxiety of speaking out and maintain one's professional standing. This approach involved subtly challenging diagnostic processes by negotiating meanings with colleagues or adapting small practices within the broader system, or indeed using diagnosis as and when deemed necessary by the clinician. For some then, 'playing the diagnostic game' could entail a degree of inauthentic action in order to maintain congenial relationships and arguably, retain a sense of power. As one participant in their study suggested: "Diagnoses give a certain, or perceived, sense of power; to be able to use. . . These terms, they give power to the psychologists themselves" (Randall, 2015, p. 73).

It is understandable that prequalified individuals would immerse themselves in the contexts available to them, and that given the dominance of service models designed around psychiatric disorders, early-career experiences are most likely to be shaped by these ideas and practices. For those who go on to engage more critically, a complex web of relationships and power means these pre-qualified individuals will face difficult decisions in terms of their own engagement with particular practices and discourses, which may not fit with the clinical psychologist they wish to become. This dilemma of navigating such contexts is illustrated by this quote:

"As a trainee I am also very aware that my practice is assessed. I therefore tend not to be too outspoken about views I express on clinical placement" (Randall, 2015, p. 22).

Similar tensions are also experienced by those receiving a diagnosis. For example, individuals may reject their diagnosis at a personal level, yet feel obligated to use them within systems and services that continue to use a diagnostic model. Indeed, for some, there can be significant costs to selfhood when believing one has been misdiagnosed. Disowning these diagnostic labels (i.e., diagnostic dissent), can facilitate the reassertion of one's agency:

Diagnostic dissent can also be a means by which individuals retain experiential sovereignty over their selfhood, even if others have otherwise assumed control of their corporality through institutionalization or coercive treatments. Through diagnostic dissent, individuals assert their self-experience in contrast to what they believe is an erroneous label, an act that ultimately reaffirms their sense of personal agency.

Forgione (2019, p. 85)

Challenges to challenging diagnostic practice: can the master's tools ever dismantle the master's house?

Some professionals remain sceptical about the effectiveness of choosing to question or challenge diagnostic practice through small acts of dialogical resistance, such as changing the ways in which we describe experiences of distress. Boyle (2013) argues that concepts that place themselves in a middle ground via attempting to gradually move thoughts away from the psychiatric model, eventually become integrated into the existing medical model. This can be seen in concepts intended to empower individuals such as 'recovery' and 'peer support', which have arguably become diluted by their integration into the current framework of mental health services. For example, Burstow (2013) argues that by using psychiatric language in lay discourse, we perpetuate its symbolic power. Therefore, through the use of 'psychiatry-resistant' or 'psychiatry-free' language, we can use the power available to us to contribute towards wider change. An example of this is how the concept of recovery has arguably become synonymous with the intention to thrust people back to employment and limit their support (Beresford & Russo, 2016). At the same time, 'peer support' has arguably been turned into a source of voluntary or low paid labour that devalues the knowledge of experts by experience (Beresford & Russo, 2016). The concept of recovery then, becomes an additional smokescreen that continues to invalidate experience and reframe social injustice as problems of health (e.g., experiences of poverty, trauma, limited opportunities). Thus, Boyle (2013) argues that ultimately, middle ground approaches continue to turn the focus away from societal issues and perpetuate the idea that the cause of human distress is located within the individual.

Ourselves and others in context: questioning our own practice

In using our own accounts of psychiatric diagnoses, we hope to have demonstrated the importance of recognising our relationship to diagnostic practices as not being about 'others' – these are issues pertinent to ourselves, as much as they are to our colleagues and clients. Furthermore, when considering the merits and faults of psychiatric practices, we cannot limit such an exploration to just conceptualisations of distress using psychiatric diagnoses of disorder. We must address our own approaches within clinical psychology, as these may also fall foul to the flaws of pathologising processes. Whilst one prominent criticism of diagnosis is the embedded internal attribution for the causes of distress, the choreographed therapeutics of the clinic and therapy room also have the potential to enact similar short-sighted practices.

The frameworks in which we work as psychologists in conventional settings mean that the *consequences* of distress are brought by the individual into therapy; thus, the focus of change remains an embodied and decontextualized representation of the external world. Indeed, Smail reminds us that an individual's distress is "not so much their own mistakes, inadequacies and illnesses, as the powers and influences that bore down upon them from the world beyond their skin" (Smail, 1996/2018, p. 12), thus the therapy space should reflect this through an "analysis not of their 'psyches' but of the predicaments that cause them distress" (Ibid., p. 13). It is imperative then, that in order for clinical psychology to avoid replication of a framework that pathologises understandable reactions to inequality, trauma, prejudice and other forms of oppressive powers, we must seek to look beyond the 'illusionary promises' of the therapy room and attempt to make "the world a more comfortable place for people to live in" (Smail, 2011, p. 238).

We cannot, and should not, omit ourselves from these discussions; finding our voice is necessary to prevent silent collusion with unhelpful practices, including when in pre-qualified positions. In doing this, it seems essential that we seek to respect the meaning that is most helpful for the individual when understanding their difficulties, whilst simultaneously looking outside of the clinical restraints, which can blind us to the roots of human distress. In questioning diagnosis, we must question ourselves and our context – in order to acknowledge the suffering caused by social injustice and offer hope to those whose voices remain unheard.

Acknowledgements

We would like to thank Luke Childs, Aisling McFadden and James Randall for their reflections and support in the writing of this chapter.

Note

1 Pseudonym (chosen by the contributor).

References

Alegría, M., NeMoyer, A., Bagué, I. F., Wang, Y., & Alvarez, K. (2018). Social determinants of mental health: Where we are and where we need to go. *Current Psychiatry Reports, 20*(11), 95–108.

Allen, J., Balfour, R., Bell, R., & Marmot, M. (2014). Social determinants of mental health. *International Review Psychiatry, 26*(4), 392–407.

American Psychiatric Association. (2000). *Diagnostic and statistical manual of mental disorders* (4th ed., text rev.). Washington, DC: American Psychiatric Publishing, Inc.

American Psychiatric Association (2013). *Diagnostic and statistical manual of mental disorders (DSM-5)*. Washington, DC: American Psychiatric Pub.

Barr, B., Kinderman, P., & Whitehead, M. (2015). Trends in mental health inequalities in England during a period of recession, austerity and welfare reform 2004 to 2013. *Social Science & Medicine, 147*, 324–331.

Becker, D., & Lamb, S. (1994). Sex bias in the diagnosis of borderline personality disorder 252 and posttraumatic stress disorder. *Professional Psychology: Research and Practice, 25*(1), 55–61.

Beresford, P., & Russo, J. (2016). Supporting the sustainability of mad studies and preventing its co-option. *Disability & Society, 31*(2), 270–274.

Bjorklund, P. (2006). No man's land: Gender bias and social constructivism in the diagnosis of borderline personality disorder. *Issues in Mental Health Nursing, 27*(1), 3–23.

Boyle, M. (2013). The persistence of medicalisation: Is the presentation of alternatives part of the problem. In S. Coles, S. Keenan, & B. Diamond (Eds.), *Madness contested: Power and practice* (pp. 3–22). Monmouth: PCCS Books.

Burstow, B. (2013). A rose by any other name: Naming and the battle against psychiatry. In B. LeFrançois, R. Menzies, & G. Reaume (Eds.), *Mad matters: A critical reader in Canadian mad studies* (pp. 79–90). Toronto: Canadian Scholars' Press.

Castillo, H. (2000). You don't know what it's like. *Mental Health Care, 4*(2): 53–58.

Dillon, J. (2017, June). *The psychological is political.* Retrieved from www.jacquidillon. org/2723/media/film/the-psychological-is-political

Division of Clinical Psychology. (2010). *Understanding Bipolar Disorder: Why some people experience extreme mood states and what can help.* Leicester: British Psychological Society.

Division of Clinical Psychology. (2013). *Classification of behaviour and experience in relation to functional psychiatric diagnoses: Time for a paradigm shift: A Position Statement.* Leicester: British Psychological Society.

Division of Clinical Psychology. (2015). *Guidelines on language in relation to functional psychiatric diagnosis.* Leicester: British Psychological Society.

Emmons, R. S., Manion, K., & Andrew, L. B. (2018). Systematic abuse and misuse of psychiatry in the medical regulatory-therapeutic complex. *Journal of American Physicians and Surgeons, 23*(4), 110–115.

Fernando, S. (1991). *Mental health, race & culture.* London: MIND.

Forgione, F. A. (2019). Diagnostic dissent: Experiences of perceived misdiagnosis and stigma in persons diagnosed with Schizophrenia. *Journal of Humanistic Psychology, 59*(1), 69–98.

Frances, A. J. (2012). *Newsflash from APA meeting: DSM 5 has flunked its reliability tests.* Retrieved from www.psychologytoday.com/gb/blog/dsm5-in-distress/201205/newsflash-apa-meeting-dsm-5-has-flunked-its-reliability-tests

Freedman, R., Lewis, D., Michels, R., Pine, S., Schultz, S., Tamminga, C., . . . Yager, J. (2013). The initial field trials of DSM-5: New blooms and old thorns. *American Journal of Psychiatry, 170*(1), 1–5.

Hansen, H., Bourgois, P., & Drucker, E. (2014). Pathologizing poverty: New forms of diagnosis, disability, and structural stigma under welfare reform. *Social Science & Medicine (1982), 103*, 76–83.

Johnstone, L., Boyle, M., Cromby, J., Dillon, J., Harper, D., Kinderman, P., Longden, E., Pilgrim, D., & Read, J. (2018). *The power threat meaning framework: Overview.* Leicester: British Psychological Society.

Jones, R. S., & Thompson, D. E. (2017). Stress and well-being in trainee clinical psychologists: A qualitative analysis. *Medical Research Archives, 5*(8), 1–19.

Kaehler, L. A., & Freyd, J. J. (2009). Borderline personality characteristics: A betrayal trauma approach. *Psychological Trauma: Theory, Research, Practice, and Policy, 1*(4), 261–268.

Kinderman, P., Read, J., Moncrieff, J., & Bentall, R. P. (2013). Drop the language of disorder. *Evidence Based Mental Health, 16*(1), 2–3.

Mann, F., Fisher, H. L., Major, B., Lawrence, J., Tapfumaneyi, A., Joyce, J., . . . Johnson, S. (2014). Ethnic variations in compulsory detention and hospital admission for psychosis across four UK early intervention services. *BMC Psychiatry, 14*(1), 256–268.

Morgan, C., Mallett, R., Hutchinson, G., & Leff, J. (2004). Negative pathways to psychiatric care and ethnicity: The bridge between social science and psychiatry. *Social Science and Medicine, 58*, 739–752.

Neighbors, H. W., Jackson, J. S., Campbell, L., & Williams, D. (1989). The influence of racial factors on psychiatric diagnosis: A review and suggestions for research. *Community Mental Health Journal, 25*(4), 301–311.

Neighbors, H. W., Trierweiler, S. J., Ford, B. C., & Muroff, J. R. (2003). Racial differences in DSM diagnosis using a semi-structured instrument: The importance of clinical judgment in the diagnosis of African Americans. *Journal of Health and Social Behavior, 44*(3), 237–256.

Pemberton, R., & Wainwright, T. (2014). The end of mental illness thinking? *International Journal of Clinical and Health Psychology, 14*(3), 216–220.

Perkins, A., Ridler, J., Browes, D., Peryer, G., Notley, C., & Hackmann, C. (2018). Experiencing mental health diagnosis: A systematic review of service user, clinician, and carer perspectives across clinical settings. *The Lancet Psychiatry, 5*(9), 747–764.

Pies, R. W. (2014). The bereavement exclusion and DSM-5: An update and commentary. *Innovations in clinical neuroscience, 11*(7–8), 19–22.

Randall, J. (2015). *Swimming against the psychiatric tide.* Unpublished manuscript.

Randall, J., Gunn, S., & Coles, S. (in press). New ideas and new times for psychiatric diagnoses: Taking a position within powerful systems. In *New ideas for new times: A handbook of innovative community and clinical psychologies.* London: Palgrave.

Randall-James, J., & Coles, S. (2018). Questioning diagnoses in clinical practice: A thematic analysis of clinical psychologists' accounts of working beyond diagnosis in the United Kingdom. *Journal of Mental Health, 27*(5), 450–456.

Russo, J., & Sweeney, A. (Eds.). (2016). *Searching for a rose garden: Challenging psychiatry, fostering mad studies.* Monmouth: PCCS Books.

Schomerus, G., Schwahn, C., Holzinger, A., Corrigan, P. W., Grabe, H. J., Carta, M. G., & Angermeyer, M. C. (2012). Evolution of public attitudes about mental illness: A systematic review and meta-analysis. *Acta Psychiatrica Scandinavica, 125*, 440–452.

Schwartz, R. C., & Blankenship, D. M. (2014). Racial disparities in psychotic disorder diagnosis: A review of empirical literature. *World Journal of Psychiatry, 4*(4), 133–140.

Shaw, C., & Proctor, G. (2004). Suzi's story. *Asylum (Special Edition: Women at the Margins), 14*(3), 11–13.

Shaw, C., & Proctor, G. (2005). I. Women at the margins: A critique of the diagnosis of borderline personality disorder. *Feminism & Psychology, 15*(4), 483–490.

Smail, D. (2005). *Power, interest and psychology: Elements of a social materialist understanding of distress.* Monmouth: PCCS Books.

Smail, D. (2011). Psychotherapy: Illusion with no future? In M. Rapley, J. Moncrieff, & J. Dillon (Eds.), *De-medicalizing misery: Psychiatry, psychology and the human condition* (pp. 226–238). London: Palgrave MacMillan.

Smail, D. (2018). *How to survive without psychotherapy.* London: Routledge. (Original work published 1996).

Thornton, D. J. (2010). Race, risk, and pathology in psychiatric culture: Disease awareness campaigns as governmental rhetoric. *Critical Studies in Media Communication, 27*(4), 31–335.

Watts, J. (2018). *Supporting claimants: A practical guide by Jay Watts* (originally published in Asylum magazine). Retrieved from http://asylummagazine.org/2018/08/supporting-claimants-a-practical-guide-by-jay-watts/

World Health Organization. (2018). *International statistical classification of diseases and related health problems* (11th Revision). Retrieved from www.who.int/classifications/icd/en/

Wykes, T., & Callard, F. (2010). Diagnosis, diagnosis, diagnosis: Towards DSM-5. *Journal of Mental Health, 19*(4), 301–304.

Chapter 15

Power in context

Working within different organisational cultures and settings

Annabel Head, Jacqui Scott and
Danielle Chadderton

Your path towards clinical training will no doubt have been unique and distinctive so far. We feel lucky to write for this book, which celebrates the myriad of different journeys that trainees take on the way to qualifying. However, these journeys are not without their difficulties. You may have worked in one job before gaining that sought-after place, or – more likely – you may find yourself moving between very different and varied work contexts to gain experience. We believe that power is integral to this process. This chapter is divided into two parts, each of which addresses a different aspect of power. Firstly, how, as aspiring trainees, we can find ourselves negatively influenced by power as we strive to get into the career; then secondly and conversely, what we can do with the power we ourselves hold to influence these contexts.

Power

What do we mean by power? We see power as a relational concept – i.e., it occurs when there is a difference between two or more people, groups or other structures (Guinote, 2016). Power is theorised to influence us in both obvious and imperceptible ways, through individuals and groups exerting dominance over one another (Smail, 2005a; White, 2002). Recently, psychologists have attempted to define some of the types of power which may impact negatively on people's lives, including economic power, such as access to housing and security, and powerful legal systems such as the Mental Health Act (Johnstone et al., 2018).

Part one: what are the challenges?

This first section will look at some of the challenges of working in different contexts. Case studies will illustrate some dilemmas faced on the road to qualification; we will also address some ideas of how to reflect on your own experiences.

In focus: working in the private sector

"Some years after graduating, I worked in a private hospital as a mental health support worker. I found non-psychologist friends I had graduated with overtook me financially. When invited out to dinner I made sure I chose the cheapest option on the menu, and I accepted lots of overtime shifts to afford my rent. While the experience I gained in the service was invaluable for some of the things I learnt, I became aware that I felt quite powerless. I felt upset – as an enthusiastic psychology graduate, I took on lots of opportunities to gain more experience, such as co-facilitating groups, but these were often beyond the scope – and pay scale – of the job description. Cynicism crept in – I felt like my job was taking advantage of my enthusiasm without the pay packet! It felt like there were all sorts of barriers up against my getting onto training. I knew a master's degree might help my chances, but I couldn't afford to take this path. Even though I am lucky to be privileged enough that I'm sure family would have supported me financially, I felt angry that money seemed to be so influential in one's path to training. I felt stuck, and quite hopeless about my chances of getting a coveted assistant psychologist post".

Laura (pseudonym)

Does Laura's story resonate at all with your own experiences? There are a range of challenges that people face in their careers in clinical psychology, and perhaps some of these are felt most acutely early on, when pressure to 'gain more experience' means we feel at the mercy of those with more power and seniority. We have been aware that this kind of experience can be felt equally in public sector contexts, with a prevalence of honorary contracts, as well as the private sector experience that Laura describes. The following sections introduce some theory to understanding specifically some of the issues around power in the workplace.

Being within a team

Within teams, we find ourselves involved in a range of relationships, directly and in-directly, as others build relationships around us – forming a complex web of interconnected people. One idea from systemic theory, *positioning* (Davies & Harré, 1990), can be helpful in discussing this concept. In families or other systems, we can talk about people having roles (for example, in Western cultures, there has traditionally been a discourse of 'Mum as the carer'). Ideas about positioning take the idea of roles one step further, to add a further dynamic component. This approach emphasises that positions are discursive – i.e., they exist in, and because of, language and conversations (Davies & Harré, 1990). There are some positions that we are able to take for ourselves; and others that are given to us. How is clinical psychology seen in your team? Some research has shown that clinical psychologists can be seen as 'aloof' in their teams (Osborne-Davis, 1996; as cited in McBrien & Candy, 2012), which no doubt impacts on team dynamics. Across this complex web, there is inevitably the influence of power. Who is more powerful, and who is less? Is this because of their professional role, length of time with the team, individual characteristics – or a combination of all these factors, and/or something else?

Reflective activity: mapping relationships in your team

This exercise draws on ideas from systemic theory positioning (Davies & Harré, 1990), as well as systemic practice of 'sculpting'. In a family sculpt, a family member is invited to choose items to represent different family members (for example, buttons). They can then move the buttons around to demonstrate ideas and relationships such as "who is closest to who?" "what do other people in the family do when Dad and Mum argue?" and so on.

We invite you to use these ideas to 'sculpt' your team – you can use small items to represent different team members, or write their names on pieces of paper. You may want to try this in supervision, or as an exercise on your own.

Move your pieces around to create a map of the service/team you are in, by placing people near to others who they seem close to. This could be both personal and professional closeness. What sense can you make of the relationships? For example, do the nurses and psychiatrists seem aligned with each other, but far away from the therapists? Do admin staff seem close to the caseworkers who are in the office more of the time, and less close to those who go out on a lot of visits? How do issues and struggles of power help make sense of the relationships that you have noted in your team?

Your map can be in a constant state of flux – is there anyone who moves about between groups? It can be used as a snapshot in time, or to map a change – for example, what changes when one of the team gets a promotion to a new post; how does this affect the dynamics?

Does doing this exercise give you any ideas about why some things have been difficult in your team? Does it make you think about yourself, and who you are positioned near – is this your choice? Or have you been positioned there by others? Why might that be? What opportunities might there be to move position? What impact might this have on the other positions? Do you think this would change the position of others, as a result of your re-positioning?

Working where there is conflict

Many clinical psychologists work in multidisciplinary teams (MDTs) and with multiple agencies outside of their own organisations. Within your own teams, it is likely that there are a number of different professional and personal perspectives which contribute to team decisions and ways of working. Identifying with the team and its goals is vital to delivering integrated care; however, maintaining a sense of individuality as a practitioner at any level is equally important to preserving the benefits of MDT working. The Division of Clinical Psychology document "Working in Teams" (2001) states that "one core rationale of multidisciplinary teams is that they should encompass a range of knowledge, skills and experience which reflects the complex needs presented by clients" (P. 57). Therefore, a key benefit of this way of working is lost if we do not feel able to contribute our specific professional or personal perspectives on important issues.

Unfortunately, it can be very easy to avoid doing this in the interest of maintaining relationships within the team and avoiding conflict. Professionalism and respect for the expertise of other colleagues may make it seem that a 'cohesive' team only works when everyone agrees with each other. This can maintain a working environment where dominant ideas and ideologies go unchallenged; at best restricting reflection and growth, and at worst allowing and normalising unsafe and inappropriate practices. One example of this is the case of Winterbourne View (a hospital for adults with learning disabilities in the UK) where abusive practices began and continued because poor practice became the norm, and staff did not speak up in the culture of cruel treatment that prevailed (Hill, 2012). A discussion paper from the Mental Health Commission (2006) on MDT working describes conflict as 'inevitable' in teams, suggesting that the importance lies in whether the conflict leads to "non-productive escalation" or "quality final products'" (p. 46). More simply: is the conflict going to lead to more arguments, or to something constructive, in line with the aims and values of the team?

Thinking space

Think about a time where your perspective has differed from the dominant view in a team. How have you approached the situation? Is there anything you could have done differently? What might help you feel more able to challenge things in the future?

One common example of conflict within teams is where difference of opinion lies in a preferred model or professional viewpoint. Gelsthorpe (1999) addresses the tensions that exist between working in a team and maintaining your individual perspective. He emphasises that while a psychological perspective may be seen as an unpopular alternative when compared to the more dominant medical model, in a multi-disciplinary setting we are "paid to disagree and have to find appropriate ways of doing so" (p. 16). For example, as a support worker or newer member of a team, you may find it difficult to challenge or question decisions by team members who seem to be in more powerful positions than you. This could be a manager, a psychiatrist, a psychologist, or anyone who you feel has more experience or influence than you. All the while, it may be that in your role, you have spent more time with a client than anyone else in the team, or have a unique perspective based on your background that means you have seen something that others might have missed. By respectfully contributing your viewpoint (whether in a meeting or directly to a colleague), you are fulfilling your role as part of a group of diverse professionals who all want the best for the people under their care.

In focus: working in academia

"Prior to gaining a place on the clinical doctorate I had a number of roles in health and social care agencies and in academic institutions, culminating in roles as a PhD student and subsequently postdoctoral research assistant/fellow positions. These posts have involved working in different teams, structures and organisations, with different levels of power and influence.

Reflecting on these experiences, I can see the influence of power throughout. In my experience, a research environment can be hierarchical, highly competitive and fast-paced, and learning to navigate this can be a challenging experience. As a student and early career researcher, it can be difficult to challenge someone in a position of power in relation to you (e.g., supervisor, line manager), as your working life can be heavily influenced by the relationship you have with them. You are reliant on them to create a safe, contained space for supervision and often depend on them in order to secure opportunities for career progression (e.g., references, recommendations to colleagues).

It can be hard to challenge these power structures, especially if they seem 'set-in-stone'. However, taking the risk to challenge them can pay dividends. For example, as a relief support worker I was not paid to attend team meetings that occurred outside of the hours that the relief-staff worked. However, I was able to negotiate with management to claim the time back in the working week. This allowed me to gain experience of contributing to multidisciplinary team meetings and, as the only person with a background in psychology, make suggestions based on psychological theory".

Gemma (pseudonym)

Facing discrimination

> "Power is generated within and through social institutions. The institutions of power operate independently of particular individuals and at various distances from them, affecting them via almost unimaginably complex lines of influence"
>
> (Smail, 2005b, p. 10)

When we refer to power in our working environments, we find it imperative to acknowledge issues of oppression and experiences of discrimination, even if we are to admit that this topic warrants a much larger space. In writing this short section we wish to draw attention to the issues of power in society; clinical psychology as a profession is not immune to these issues, and in fact may often replicate them. Within clinical psychology, there are few theories that consider the influence of societal powers as central, although there are exceptions, such as the Power Threat Meaning Framework (Johnstone et al., 2018), and power-mapping (Hagan & Smail, 1997). We note that inequalities can serve both to disadvantage service users who identify with oppressed and marginalised groups, as well as to create experiences of difference amongst our own colleagues.

The profession we aspire to work in lacks diversity and representation among many facets of Burnham's social differences (1992), including age, ability, sexuality, race, class, culture, and so on (e.g. BPS, 2016; Turpin & Coleman, 2010). Trainees (and staff) who identify, or are identified, as members of minority groups face cumulative and commonplace discrimination, either intentional or unintentional (e.g. Sue et al., 2007). For example, research into Black, Asian and minority ethnic (BAME) trainees' and qualified psychologists' experiences (e.g. Odusanya, Winter, Nolte, & Shah, 2018; Shah, Wood, Nolte, & Goodbody, 2012) has included findings relating to:

- Feeling visibly different, at times like an outsider, isolated and marginalised;
- Feeling added pressure to 'prove their worth';
- Experiencing an expectant and imposed burden of raising issues of race and culture fall on minority-group members; and
- Feeling that peers and supervisors often avoid topics of race and culture.

Such research leads to questions around how experiences of discrimination are addressed within training contexts and beyond. The "range of entrenched daily practices and active denial of institutional racism in clinical practice, in services, in training institutions, and more widely in the profession, accompanied by acute discomfort [experienced] by colleagues [demonstrates how] Whiteness and related privileges are scaffolded, reproduced and reinforced within clinical psychology" (Wood & Patel, 2017, p. 287).

When faced with issues around discrimination, of *any* difference or differences, we heed the words of Wood and Patel, and acknowledge "the need to take risks, to get it wrong [and] to say the unspeakable" (2017, p. 293).

Part two: what can we do with the power we have?

Having discussed issues of ourselves as professionals being in less powerful positions, we now turn to acknowledging and examining our relatively (and often very) privileged positions in regards to the power we have over the lives of people who use the services we work within. We will offer ideas for how clinical psychologists (and those on the journey in the profession) can use their relative power at different levels; from day to day practice up to influencing practice at the widest levels.

In focus: the impact of power when working in the third sector

"During training, I undertook several activities that involved working within or alongside the third sector, including a specialist placement and research projects. These organisations varied from small community groups, working on a month-to-month basis, to a multi-million-pound per year organisation, complete with a fundraising department and royal patronage. As a trainee, I was interested in how these experiences compared to that of working in the NHS, in terms of the psychological work that is available, and in terms of who holds the power to determine what work is possible.

For me, there are various pros and cons to third sector work. The main dilemma I personally came across is when there is a feeling that charities are picking up work where the statutory services are falling short; with potential implications that public sector cutbacks, at best, have a reduced visible impact, and at worst, are legitimised. On the other hand, the third sector provides some services that are unlikely to ever be publicly funded, or have been so seriously underfunded that there is now a humanitarian need (consider services for the homeless, refugees, food banks, etc.).

In reality, what I experienced was that such organisations, due to having no statutory ties, can often much better meet the needs of such groups, for example, due to the stigma of accessing services, and/or due to the ability to tap into, or be entirely driven by, local knowledges.

Services work at their best, however, when working collaboratively, by linking public responsibilities with a local community level awareness and response. For example, a local support group for people living with HIV that has links with a health clinic enables a non-stigmatising and humanising experience, whilst having the back-up of medical care and expertise if required. Unfortunately, funding became so low for this service that one of two local 'branches' had to close, leaving many people struggling without local community support. Similarly, the youth project for young refugees and migrants that I worked alongside during my research also had to close due to a lack of funds. This leads me to realise that, ultimately, power is money. In the statutory sector, cuts are difficult, result in strains and stress on staff, and sometimes a reduced service. In the third sector, it means an end to the service. Most painful for me is the perception that some types of projects (or groups of people) seem to receive more public donations and successful funding bids than others; often on the basis that the most excluded, oppressed or stigmatised groups, and the smallest, most localised, independent (and often valuable) projects, are least likely to receive support and funding".

Jacqui

Reflective activity: your role as a 'helper'

David Smail (1938–2014) was a clinical psychologist who believed that psychological distress was directly linked to social circumstances rather than some internal deficit or process within the 'patient'. He argued that, as psychologists, we have to be aware of how economics and financial interest influence the constructs of 'mental health problems'. In relation to this, we invite you to consider the following quotation, about how *anyone* can develop psychological distress:

"[You] may become aware that the particular world you occupy departs in some respect from the ideals and values of the wider society, or that you personally do not match up to what seems to be valued. . . . If you fail, as you are bound to do, in [many different] respects, you will find whole armies of professionals ready to iron out the bumps: psychiatrists, psychologists. . . . In the vast majority of cases the professionals share a common aim – to fit you better into society, not to alter our social institutions so that they will make more comfortable room for you"

(Smail, 2001, p. 24)

Figure 15.1 An illustration of power in context: Your role as a 'helper'

How does this quote make you think about your role as a helper? Do you agree, that your profession seems to be trying to get people to fit into a society that seems to reject some aspect of them? Does it make you question what else we could be doing as psychologists instead? Figure 15.1 shows Ben Ellsworth's creative response to such questions (with thanks to Ben for creating this artwork for *Surviving Clinical Psychology*).

Enacting power in our everyday work

The way many services are set up places the users of the service in a less powerful position from the outset. Practices such as inviting people to come to meet us in our service building, or requiring people to fill out routine outcome measures, can be disempowering acts. The whole system of assigning psychiatric diagnoses, and needing one of these to access services, has been argued to be an even more fundamentally disempowering practice (Johnstone et al., 2018). There are some small ways, however, that we can take steps to readdress some of these imbalances.

Readdressing power at the assessment

When we invite people to an assessment, we often have constraints from the services we work in – we need to collect information on particular aspects of someone's life, for example "what medication are you taking?" and "what other services are involved?" Even with the best of intentions from individual clinicians, these routines can place the clinician as 'expert' and the other as 'investigated'. As a counter-practice to these traditions, Madsen (2007) suggests the therapist can actively position themselves alongside the client, as co-investigators of the externalised 'problem'. He suggests doing this through asking questions from a narrative perspective, such as "how do you explain the problem? How does the problem interfere with your preferred life? What is the history of the relationship between the problem and you? When have you been stronger in the history of that relationship?" (Madsen, 2007, p. 54).

How we contact clients

The Academy of Medical Royal Colleges (2018) has recently published '*Please write to me*', a guidance on how and why clinicians should write their letters directly to the client, rather than another person such as the referrer or their GP. Have you ever received a letter about yourself that was written to someone else, in which you had only been copied into? For example, a letter about a medical check-up? How did it make you feel – in control and powerful, or something else? In the service you work in, is writing directly to clients common practice? If not, how do you think you could go about starting conversations in your team about changing this practice?

Using supervision

Many readers will have experience using cognitive behavioural therapy (CBT); this model has a focus on a collaborative stance, which is important for giving individuals opportunities to make choices and for reclaiming power within services that would traditionally have replicated their disempowerment. For example, it is important to remind clients that they have a choice over whether to engage with therapy or not, which can help them to feel in control, and on a more equal level to clinicians (Beck, 2011). We also, ourselves, have opportunities to reflect on our positions and power within the therapeutic context. Making use of supervision, to reflect on and understand our own reactions – like in the example below – can help us to stay mindful of times when we might be acting in ways which inadvertently try to take power back in our work, for our own reasons – rather than for the individuals we see (Beck, 2011).

In focus: learning from times we have disempowered others, to empower ourselves

Dave worked as an assistant psychologist in a mental health hospital. He regularly took patients from the ward to a group in the therapy room downstairs. One day, one of the patients reported feeling particularly low, and was slow in coming to the door. Dave was fed-up of her 'dawdling' and told her she was too late and he would not let her through. She became upset with him, and told him he was "on a power-trip." These words really affected Dave and he took the incident to supervision. Talking it through, he realised that he had felt 'not in control' in the situation, which had brought up some of his anxieties about 'not being good at my job.' He realised that he had taken back power to counteract his own feelings of inadequacy at the time; he used this incident to become more self-reflexive about what he was enacting moment-to-moment with the people on the ward.

Taking risks

It can be daunting to speak up to power. As suggested in Gemma's story above though, taking risks can pay off. Barry Mason (2005) discusses the importance of 'relational risk-taking' and suggests that, contrary to common belief, we do not have to wait for a sense of 'trust' in a relationship before taking a risk with something new or different. In fact, he proposes that there is a cycling pattern between trust and risk – taking a risk helps build trust, and then a sense of trust helps us take further risks, and so on. This can be seen as an invitation to try taking risks, both in our work clinically and also with our colleagues (Mason, 2005). For example, I (Annabel) and James Randall took inspiration from these ideas during training, and facilitated a reflective exercise for a staff team who were struggling with changes to their service (Randall-James & Head, 2018). Though it at times felt 'risky' to facilitate this, we found that using our position as 'outsiders' enabled us to make space for conversations that otherwise may not have been easy to have (ibid.).

Being a leader

There are strong narratives in our profession about leadership. This can be seen as a conscious acknowledgement of our positions of power, and how we can use these positions to try to positively influence the services we work in. We have opportunities to exercise our leadership skills at all levels of the profession, as leadership is not just about who is at the top, but about influencing systems at multiple levels – everyone is valuable and can play a leadership role.

We can demonstrate leadership in many ways, including:

- Supporting others to develop their skills through teaching or consultation;
- Using our knowledge of psychological theory to understand the interpersonal dynamics – meaning clinical psychologists have a role in managing teams;
- Sharing our psychology knowledge with non-psychologist colleagues, at all levels, and helping services to be designed and function in line with these – for example, using knowledge about response to trauma to influence how we set up a community team for people who may have lived experience of trauma;
- Conducting research to add to an evidence base, and/or critiquing existing evidence to shape our (and others') clinical practice.

There are probably some leadership activities that you have already undertaken recently without even knowing! For example, there are expectations that trainees are able to build relationships with colleagues; critically use the evidence base to inform practice; and be aware of issues of diversity and difference. Do these sound like things you might already be doing, or nearly doing? If not, can you identify things that you could do to work towards exercising your skills and awareness in these areas? For further ideas about leadership at different stages of your career, please see the *Clinical Psychology Leadership Development Framework* (DCP, 2010).

Influencing at the widest levels

Clinical psychologists can use their skills to influence at policy and political levels. Numerous theories point toward the social need for change at these higher levels, to address the increasing extent of distress and mental health that has been linked with social inequalities (e.g. Marmot, 2010, 2015). For example, systemic ecological models describe how top-down enactments of power from social policies have repercussions within communities and in individual lives (Bronfenbrenner, 1979; Nelson & Prilleltensky, 2010). Likewise, critical community psychology suggests that difficulties experienced by individuals can be created by the conditions and contexts of experience. This includes social, political, historical and local contexts; contexts that can infringe individual autonomy with the result of disempowerment (Orford, 2008).

Over recent years, models for the provision of psychological therapies to "treat" mental health on the population level have been driven by a top-down government agenda. The mental health strategy has arguably been delivered in the context of overall market-driven changes in NHS services, leading to increased privatisation and competition between providers (Allsop & Baggott, 2004). In addition, austerity, cuts to welfare, and ongoing changes to the benefits system, have been found to result in furthering the impact of health inequalities (e.g. Barr, Kinderman, & Whitehead, 2015).

Meanwhile, there has been streamlining of psychological support and therapies, primarily via the Improving Access to Psychological Therapies model (see Clark et al., 2009). This approach has been widely debated (e.g. Watts, 2016; Peacock-Brennan, 2016), receiving criticism that it tends to reinforce a societal discourse around mental health as an individualised and individually-treatable problem: a problem residing within the individual, or within 'problem' communities.

Thinking space

Consider the individuals and groups of people who you work with in your professional life:

- What sort of things influence the need for services – are these individual, community, social influences, or a combination of these or other things?
- What level does your intervention address?
- What other things need to change in order to facilitate the wellbeing of these individuals and communities?
- Do you think there is a role for psychology beyond individual-level intervention?

Policies on the one hand, have the power to disadvantage, but on the other hand, they may empower and create opportunities for people to elicit change in their own lives. What skills can psychologists develop to enable effective influence on the policy level? See below a case study of psychologists working at the World Health Organisation (WHO), whose work demonstrates a range of skills at this level.

In focus: working at the World Health Organisation (WHO)

"The World Health Organisation, an agency of the United Nations (UN), aims to take an international approach to addressing health and mental health issues across the world. We work in the Department of Mental Health and Substance Abuse.

One of the activities within the department is to increase access to psychological interventions. This is done through the development of scalable psychological interventions (e.g., brief evidence-based interventions), which can be delivered by non-specialised staff or other approaches which can increase accessibility (e.g. digital technology).

The interventions undergo systematic cultural adaption specific to the context. The effectiveness of these interventions is tested through research, and our team's work includes supporting the scale-up of these interventions in services, following positive results. Skills from training and practicing as a clinical psychologist are essential to our work.

When developing interventions, cycles of assessment, formulation and evaluation are utilised to ensure the intervention is culturally relevant and effective. We work closely with prospective clients and health workers to learn about, develop a shared understanding of, and consider solutions to barriers for accessing and providing treatment. A number of core competencies support this process. A 'reflective-scientist-practitioner' approach is taken to ensure adaptations are grounded in evidence and active therapeutic components are not lost. Working with difference and diversity to understand constructs of mental health and power is essential when collaborating with local staff. Effectively working with systems, such as Ministries of Health, local organisations and other UN colleagues, allows successful implementation. Leadership and consultation skills are used to coordinate the overall development and evaluation processes. Supervision and training skills are needed to support local staff in the initial and subsequent cascaded roll-out of the intervention".

Dr Jennifer Hall & Dr Aiysha Malik,
Consultant Psychologists, WHO

Here, we introduce a small selection of examples of contributions that psychologists have made to policy. Further discussion and, more specifically, ideas for developing self-reflection on your own relationship to standing alongside others and supporting social change.

- Psychologists contribute to societal understandings of distress and mental health, to influence discourses that have historically tended to individualise distress, with the intention to create a more socially and psychologically-minded population. This is done through small actions on social media, as well as publication of research findings and ideas in mainstream media. (e.g. Head & Bond, 2018; Watts, 2016, 2018a)
- Psychologists can start lobbies that both raise awareness, draw in others to speak out on issues, and that ultimately contribute to a social movement towards more helpful political approaches towards wellbeing and mental health.
- Psychologists can stand alongside and support community-led initiatives, and push for social resources that support user-led campaigns (e.g., the

benefits system and impartial advice). After all, "the knowledge on what is happening is held by disabled activists so connect with and offer yourself as an ally to national groups, such as Disabled People Against Cuts, Mental Health Resistance Network, Black Triangle, Recovery in the Bin and Win-Visible" (Watts, 2018b).

The skills we hold make us as psychologists some of the best equipped professionals in understanding systems-level change. These levels ultimately bear the most weight on lived experiences, and thus affect many of those who access, and those who struggle to access, the services we run.

Where there is a tendency towards division and discord, within and across professions, therapist and activist Vikki Reynolds calls for us to be drawn together in solidarity: "we do the work on the shoulders of others, and we shoulder each other up" (Reynolds, 2011, p. 32). She argues that rather than seeing "burnout" as a problem within an individual who has 'not been able to cope', it should be seen instead as our emotional pain at witnessing the injustices that we encounter in our work with clients. We may often find ourselves working with clients who have current or past negative experiences of power from the structures of society; for example, having been found as 'fit for work' by a benefits advisor, or refused housing as there were not enough properties on the books for their needs. Coming up against these power frameworks can leave us feeling powerless and hopeless. However, our joint ethics, held with different professionals (i.e. the values that we hold dear and that brought us into this work to begin with) can keep us connected to others (Morgan et al., 2019). It can help us to keep working towards our collective goals of improving the experiences of those who come into our services and working towards a better world.

Conclusion

Power is a complex and sometimes divisive issue in the profession, and across the wider mental health world. We do not claim to be able to do justice to such a wide-ranging, longstanding and embedded issue in this short chapter. However, it is important to acknowledge that on the route to training, we can hold a 'both-and' position of sometimes feeling powerless, and also of holding much power ourselves. It is vitally important that we continue to have conversations about power at all stages of our progress in the career-path, and we hope this chapter has helped you to explore these ideas.

Acknowledgements

A huge thank you to Kirsty Killick for her very significant work towards shaping this chapter.

References

Academy of Medical Royal Colleges. (2018). *Please write to me guidance.* London, UK: Academy of Medical Royal Colleges.

Allsop, J., & Baggott, R. (2004). The NHS in England: From modernisation to marketisation? *Social Policy Review, 29*–44.

Barr, B., Kinderman, P., & Whitehead, M. (2015). Trends in mental health inequalities in England during a period of recession, austerity and welfare reform 2004 to 2013. *Social Science & Medicine, 147,* 324–331.

Beck, J. S. (2011). *Cognitive therapy for challenging problems: What to do when the basics don't work.* New York, USA: Guilford Press.

BPS (2016). Achieving representation in psychology: A BPS response. *The Psychologist, 29,* 246–255.

Bronfenbrenner, U. (1979). *The ecology of human development.* Cambridge, MA: Harvard University Press.

Burnham, J. (1992). Approach-method-technique: Making distinctions and creating connections. *Human Systems, 3*(1), 3–26.

Clark, D. M., Layard, R., Smithies, R., Richards, D. A., Suckling, R., & Wright, B. (2009). Improving access to psychological therapy: Initial evaluation of two UK demonstration sites. *Behaviour Research and Therapy, 47*(11), 910–920.

Davies, B., & Harré, R. (1990). Positioning: The discursive production of selves. *Journal for the Theory of Social Behaviour, 20*(1), 43–63.

Division of Clinical Psychology. (2001). *Working in teams.* Leicester, UK: British Psychological Society.

Division of Clinical Psychology. (2010). *Clinical psychologist leadership development framework.* Leicester, UK: British Psychological Society.

Gelsthorpe, S. (1999). Psychiatry: We are all paid to disagree–Using the bad feelings positively. *Clinical Psychology Forum, 127*(5), 16–19.

Guinote, A. (2016, June 7). *What is power and how does it affect people?* [Blog post]. Retrieved March 24, 2019, from www1.bps.org.uk/networks-and-communities/member-microsite/social-psychology-section/blog/what-power-and-how-does-it-affect-people

Hagan, T., & Smail, D. (1997). Power-mapping–I. Background and basic methodology. *Journal of Community & Applied Social Psychology, 7*(4), 257–267.

Head, A., & Bond, J. (2018, May 20). We need to address the socioeconomic causes of mental health issues if we really want to tackle the problem. *The Independent.* Retrieved March 24, 2019, from www.independent.co.uk/voices/mental-health-help-how-change-awareness-causes-treat-a8357741.html

Hill, A. (2012, October 26). Winterbourne view care home staff jailed for abusing residents. *The Guardian.* Retrieved March 24, 2019, from www.theguardian.com/society/2012/oct/26/winterbourne-view-care-staff-jailed

Johnstone, L., Boyle, M., Cromby, J., Dillon, J., Harper, D., Kinderman, P., Longden, E., Pilgrim, D., & Read, J. (2018). *The power threat meaning framework: overview.* Leicester, UK: British Psychological Society.

Madsen, W. (2007). Working with traditional structures to support a collaborative clinical practice. *International Journal of Narrative Therapy & Community Work, 2007*(2), 51–61.

Marmot, M. (2010). Fair society, healthy lives. *The Marmot Review.* UCL Institute for Health Equity. Retrieved March 24, 2019, from www.instituteofhealthequity.org/projects

Marmot, M. (2015). *The Health Gap: The challenge of an unequal world*. London, UK: Bloomsbury Publishing.

Mason, B. (2005). Relational risk-taking and the therapeutic relationship. In C. Flaskas, A. Perlesz, & B. Mason (Eds.), *The space between: Experience, context and process in the therapeutic relationship* (pp. 157–170). London, UK: Karnac.

McBrien, J., & Candy, S. (2012). Working with organisations or: Why won't they follow my advice? In E. Emerson et al. (Eds.), *Clinical psychology and people with intellectual disabilities* (pp. 161–180). Chichester, UK: Wiley-Blackwell.

Mental Health Commission. (2006, January). *Multidisciplinary team working: From theory to practice*. Retrieved March 24, 2019, from www.mhcirl.ie/file/discusspapmultiteam.pdf

Morgan, H. C., Randall, J., Lyons, A. J., Oliver, S., Saffer, J., Scott, J. M., & Nolte, L. (2019). Pebbles in palms: Counter-practices against despair. *Psychotherapy and Politics International, 17*. doi:10.1002/ppi.1481

Nelson, G., & Prilleltensky, I. (2010). Ecology, prevention and promotion. In G. Nelson & I. Prilleltensky (Eds.), *Community psychology: In pursuit of liberation and well-being* (2nd ed.). Basingstoke, UK: Palgrave Macmillan.

Odusanya, S., Winter, D., Nolte, L., & Shah, S. (2018). The experience of being a qualified female BME clinical psychologist in a national health service: An interpretative phenomenological and repertory grid analysis. *Journal of Constructivist Psychology, 31*(3), 273–291.

Orford, J. (2008). *Community psychology: Challenges, controversies and emerging consensus*. Hoboken, NJ: John Wiley & Sons.

Peacock-Brennan, S. (2016). *A genealogical investigation of the conditions of possibility for the emergence of Improving Access to Psychological Therapies (IAPT) Services*. (Doctoral dissertation), University of East London, London, UK.

Randall-James, J., & Head, A. (2018). Taking conversations forward: A systemic exercise for teams threatened by service restructures. *Journal of Family Therapy, 40*(3), 447–458.

Reynolds, V. (2011). Resisting burnout with justice-doing. *International Journal of Narrative Therapy & Community Work*, (4), 27–45.

Shah, S., Wood, N., Nolte, L., & Goodbody, L. (2012). The experience of being a trainee clinical psychologist from a black and minority ethnic group: A qualitative study. *Clinical Psychology Forum, 232*(4): 32–35.

Smail, D. J. (2001). *Why therapy doesn't work; and what we should do about it*. Edinburgh, UK: Constable Robinson.

Smail, D. J. (2005a). *Power, interest and psychology: Elements of a social materialist understanding of distress*. Monmouth, UK: PCCS Books.

Smail, D. J. (2005b). *Power, responsibility and freedom: An internet publication*. Retrieved March 24, 2019, from https://the-eye.eu/public/WorldTracker.org/Sociology/David%20Smail%20-%20Power%2C%20Responsibility%20and%20Freedom%20-%20Internet%20Publication%20%282005%29.pdf

Sue, D. W., Capodilupo, C. M., Torino, G. C., Bucceri, J. M., Holder, A., Nadal, K. L., & Esquilin, M. (2007). Racial microaggressions in everyday life: Implications for clinical practice. *American psychologist, 62*(4), 271–284.

Turpin, G., & Coleman, G. (2010). Clinical psychology and diversity: Progress and continuing challenges. *Psychology Learning & Teaching, 9*(2), 17–27.

Watts, J. (2016). *Social media doesn't make teenagers self-harm, neoliberalism does.* Retrieved March 24, 2019, from www.independent.co.uk/voices/self-harm-social-media-teenagers-nspcc-neoliberalism-does-a7465691.html

Watts, J. (2018a). *Mental health labels can save lives: But they can also destroy them.* Retrieved March 24, 2019, from www.theguardian.com/commentisfree/2018/apr/24/mental-health-labels-diagnosis-study-psychiatrists

Watts, J. (2018b). Supporting claimants: A practical guide by Jay Watts. *Asylum Magazine.* Retrieved March 24, 2019, from http://asylummagazine.org/2018/08/supporting-claimants-a-practical-guide-by-jay-watts/

White, M. (2002). Addressing personal failure. *International Journal of Narrative Therapy & Community Work, 2002*(3), 33–76.

Wood, N., & Patel, N. (2017). On addressing "Whiteness" during clinical psychology training. *South African Journal of Psychology, 47*(3), 280–291.

Chapter 16

It's not just about therapy

Our 'selves' in our communities

Stephen Weatherhead, Ben Campbell,
Cormac Duffy, Anna Duxbury,
Hannah Iveson and Mary O'Reilly

The role of a psychologist begins with listening and truly hearing the individual and collective stories that led a person to where they (and we) are today. With this in mind, we begin this chapter with an invitation to truly hear Mary's story:

There is a file on my computer recording my engagement in twenty years of mental health activism. This file was initially entitled Mental Health. But I have been driven to rename it. It is now entitled The War. I do not use the term lightly. I have long attempted to engage respectfully in reform of a system that has degraded into instrumental abuse. Over the past ten years I have witnessed the decimation of mental health services.

The headlong, lemming-like drive to Foundation Status with its deeply flawed and utterly unprofessional version of business modelling destroyed so much. User/carer involvement, once supported by some authentic well-intentioned commitment by services to inclusive, consultative, humane care, became no more than an instrumental, tokenistic, tick-box exercise. Mental health executives and managers tweet, text and self-promote on social media while dangerous, neglectful, edgy, understaffed services provide little other treatment or support than medication and custody. Funds are squandered on trophy buildings within which regimes of commodified, instrumental care continue to be administered by a mental health nursing profession dedicated to nothing more than medicating, feeding, custody and paperwork. Services have been subjected to systemic brutalisation.

During the past year, as a result of major depression and two suicide attempts, I have been a patient on two different psychiatric wards for two separate ten week periods. My first hospitalisation was in Adult Services. The second was in Elderly Services. My route to both was via General Hospital A&E – the only mental health crisis service available.

On the first occasion, prior to accessing Adult Services, I spent ten days on a general ward. I was the psych case in the corner bed: ignored but talked about by most staff and recipient of the odd humane gesture from the few not yet desensitised by the system. Four of the beds on this eight-bedded female ward were occupied by dementia patients in states of terrible confusion and distress. Day and night, they called for nursing attention and assistance. This attention was random and seldom, if ever, immediate. On many occasions these women left their beds and wandered out of the ward unsupervised and undressed. During the night it was also a regular occurrence for male dementia patients from an adjacent ward to find their distracted way into our ward. Buzzers to summon staff to such incidents were rarely responded to.

The level of night-time noise created by the anguished cries of distressed patients and the raucous voices of nursing staff made sleep a virtual impossibility. Nightly chaos and neglect was replaced at daybreak with the arrival of a day shift of Health Care Assistants (HCAs) who could only be likened to a flock of feral marauding macaws. Their loud, garrulous presence was accompanied by the static torture of pop music blaring from their tiny transistor radio. They went about their business of caring i.e., bed making and ward cleaning, with all the delicacy and empathy of a butcher processing sausages while exchanging loud vacuous gossip over and around their victims.

After ten days in this hellish setting, a bed was found for me on a female ward in a local newly built £25 million Mental Health Hospital boasting in-patient single rooms throughout and en-suite bathrooms. This trophy building offers, in reality, nothing more than the medical model of psychiatric care in a costly setting. The propaganda created around it gushes with grandiosity – 'perfect care' and the 'pursuit of excellence' – 'state of the art care' – 'specialist service' – 'continuous improvement' – 'dignity' – 'respect' – 'enthusiasm' – zero tolerance approach to suicide, and so on.

My first experience of state of the art care and specialist service was on the day following my admission. Still in an extremely distressed state, I was summoned to meet with a glib, polished specimen of psychiatric consultancy. Within minutes of our first meeting and having expressed neither interest nor curiosity in my condition or personal history, other than with reference to previously prescribed drugs, he pronounced ECT as his treatment of choice. Aware of the worrying increase in the use of ECT on older females (data from a group of NHS trusts in England between 2011 and 2015, found that, on average, two thirds of recipients of ECT were women, and 56% were people aged over 60. The 2016–17 annual dataset released by the Royal College of Psychiatrists reveals that 67% of patients receiving acute courses of ECT were female, as were 74% of those receiving ECT to prevent relapses – so-called "maintenance ECT"),[1] I was also aware of my vulnerability in the coercive environment of a psychiatric ward. The possibility of enforcement of a treatment that invariably causes brain damage, memory loss, and cognitive malfunction increased my already traumatised state but also determined me to evidence mental capacity. I refused to see this consultant again and requested another psychiatrist.

There was no programme of recovery, rehabilitation or activity in this specialist mental health service. Harassed nursing assistants occasionally organised a bingo or karaoke session or opened, for short periods, a disorganised and seldom used activity room to oversee patients colouring in – state of the art therapy. The ward did not have an occupational therapist and psychological provision was limited to one hour per week for those fortunate enough to access it at all.

The building is provisioned with expensive state of the art gym equipment that cannot be accessed regularly as staff are untrained in its use and are dependent on a local charity to provide supervision. The underfloor heating in my single en-suite Room did not work for most of my ten week stay, the shower regularly provided only cold water. During weeks of fruitless requests for an extra blanket, I resorted to covering my bed with a dressing gown and coat for warmth. For the majority of my stay my bedroom window, which overlooked a public pathway had only one inadequate, gaping curtain. My request for the missing second curtain was routinely ignored. The community dining room did not provide adequate seating or table space to accommodate all eighteen patients and was also the cramped public setting in which detained patients were obliged to receive visitors. A thoroughfare for continual distressed trafficking back and forth through its glass doors to the outside garden, it was also a setting for the public enactment of frustration and despair by many patients.

Having succeeded in dismissing the advocate of ECT, I was assigned another psychiatrist. She prescribed medication, the side effects of which were migraine, visual disturbance and chronic bowel incontinence. After six weeks I had lost 9.6 kilograms in weight and suffered a severe and excruciatingly painful bowel blockage. My physical health had deteriorated to the point of tottering weakness and I was confined to bed for several days. Only at that point was it agreed to change my medication but there was never admission or acknowledgment as to the damage done by the previous drug.

Never the truth, just endless duplicitous propaganda. As part of our commitment to perfect care and the pursuit of excellence we have made a commitment to eliminate suicide for all those in our care; the mentally distressed have no choice, no option, no help other than compliance with an instrumental, medically modelled mental health system that inflicts unacknowledged damage and distress with its only treatment – toxic psychotropic medication. In order to eradicate the blemish of suicide, which they will not tolerate, on its record of accountability, it will incarcerate the defenceless in a holding tank of despair to endure the living hell of mental distress along with the destructive side effects of enforced medication.

The erection of multi-million trophy buildings in which to administer this torment is portrayed as evidence of specialist care. Costly bricks and mortar without the cement of integrity to hold them together. Holding tanks of abuse and neglect stripped of the psychological and occupational expertise and support so necessary for mental recovery. These buildings are monstrous white elephants – monuments to psychiatric abuse.

Following a month of medication somewhat less toxic, I was discharged from the embrace of perfect care. I returned home with no continuity of psychological support, one of many on the long waiting list for an inadequate and under-resourced service. Psychotropic medication continued to cause me chronic bowel problems. Two months later a community psychiatrist's brusque response to my desire for support in tapering off the drug was to bark that I could stop taking it altogether and do as I wished. She referred me to community services and ended the consultation. I had a subsequent visit from a brisk, abrasive community nurse who did not want to listen to my concerns. When I voiced concerns to my GP practice regarding their lack of mental health support and the general overprescribing of anti-depressants the response was to remove me from their list. This to a patient of seventeen years recently discharged from hospital following a suicide attempt. I no longer had a GP.

The many headed Hydra of the system continued to wage war. A letter from the DWP informed me that the Disability Living Allowance (DLA) that I had been awarded for life because of severe and enduring mental illness was to be withdrawn within the month and that if I wished to continue to claim benefit, I would need to apply for a Personal Independence Payment (PIP) assessment within that time.

Once again, I descended into hopeless despair. My second admission – this time to Elderly Services – followed a thirty-six hour wait on a chair in A & E. No ward orientation occurred upon arrival to the ward or thereafter. I had been an inpatient for a month before being given the 'Welcome – Useful Information for Service Users' pack, which contained no information relevant to that particular ward. Patients were not verbally advised about their situation or their rights, or assisted to access advocacy. The overall impression was that such conversations were avoided by ward staff and information wilfully withheld. I was assigned a Named Nurse who was on two weeks leave when I arrived and was the nurse in charge on consistent night duty following his return. Even if Named Nurse and care planning were anything more than a fictitious tick box concept how could he possibly be expected to carry out the role? He was responsible for supervision and medication on night shifts with dangerously inadequate staffing levels. And how can you 'co-produce a care plan' in a self-proclaimed 'specialist mental health service' aspiring to 'perfect care' that has no specialism to offer other than feeding and medication?

Elderly Mental Health Services were a sad and shocking revelation. A corrupt, distorted social model combined with a vulgarised, crude, inhumane, reductive medical /nursing model abandons distressed, traumatised, vulnerable people to a confusing, unexplained environment through which they are expected to find their own way unaided. Misrepresentation of terminology and concepts such as de-skilling and functionality leaves vulnerable elderly patients unsupported in basic care such as organisation of their bed space/room/belongings or dressing themselves.

The ward had an alarming number of admissions, from general hospital, of patients who had been plunged into critical mental distress because of abrupt withdrawal from psychotropic medication prior to surgery. I witnessed patients perceived as difficult, challenging, or attention seeking, ignored and unsupported for long periods while suffering severe bowel incontinence. This appalling disregard for dignity and respect left the afflicted patients lying in their own faeces with soiled communal bathrooms and pervasive faecal odour distressing all patients for several hours and, in one case, overnight.

Another consequence of inhumane interpretation of deskilling and functionality was the spectacle of catatonic pre-ECT and disabled post-ECT patients aban-doned, unencouraged and unsupported at meal time, confronted by plates of food that they could scarcely see let alone cope with. I have a particularly poignant memory of a dazed gentleman, who had just returned from ECT, being handed a knife and fork and abandoned at a table in front of a plate of fish, chips and peas. Half an hour later he was still hopelessly chasing the food round the plate while nursing staff stood around the dining room wall ticking boxes.

Desensitised, demoralised staff regularly resorted to inappropriate humour or disrespectful, bullying behaviour as a form of self-defence and self-preservation. The following are direct, and not unusual, quotes –

"What do you expect? This is the NHS".

"That's stupid. You can't do that".

"Take yer dishes back to the hatch. Yer becomin' de-skilled!"

"You're well able to walk now aren't you! Pity you couldn't find your feet this morning when you nearly broke me back!"

"It was relentless yesterday and we're not having it again today if you have diarrhoea".

"Come back in the dining room. We can't be runnin' after everybody. We're short staffed".

The ward reverberated with utterly inappropriate and nerve-racking levels of noise caused by door banging and shouting – this behaviour from staff, not patients. Genu-ine communication with patients was scarce. People need to be spoken to. Notices – frequently months out-of-date – are no substitute for verbal communication. Mental distress causes confusion, poor concentration and poor memory. A common side effect of psychotropic medication is blurred vision. A third of the population of this city have literacy difficulties. Notices on walls are neither sufficient nor authentic communication – although they may enable the duplicitous ticking of a task done box. Communication between members of staff was equally poor. Sloppy, careless, unprofessional office procedure with no proper diarising or recording resulted in messages not reaching patients and inadequate briefing of staff on handovers.

As was the case in Adult Services, there was no structured programme of activ-ity, recovery or rehabilitation on the ward. Neither was there an occupational therapist or a psychologist. It took five weeks of relentless pressure from myself to source the psychological support that I needed. I eventually achieved the miracle of having a psychologist and a psychiatrist present at my ward round in an MDT (multidisciplinary team!!) room. It took a similar amount of pressure to achieve some semblance of occupational therapy – an activity worker was seconded from another site for two days a week. She was, however, almost immediately with-drawn because of some sort of idiotic managerial dispute. Elderly patients with no physical activity or mental stimulation, and rendered comatose by medication, spent their days slumped in armchairs in front of the TV. Their only access to psychological support was from The Jeremy Kyle Show!

The hospital is situated at the edge of one of the most beautiful public parks in the country. The mental and physical benefits to wellbeing of nature and exercise are indisputable yet the opportunity of getting off the ward for a walk in the park was something that was rarely offered to patients. Inadequate staffing levels and the dearth of OT and activity workers enable an easy dismissive assumption that 'they don't want to do anything'. The ward's only accessible outdoor spaces – two courtyard gardens – were in a state of deplorable neglect containing little more than weeds, dead plants and shrubs and dirty, worn out, rotting seating. One of these gardens is also the site of an annual wasp infestation – the wasps nest in the rafters overhead, and not only inhabit the garden, but access the ward through windows and ventilators. This is an annually recurring problem but nothing has been done to properly address it. After weeks of sustained pressure from myself and other patients, a solution was achieved with the installation of plastic hanging wasp traps. This is something that could have been done years ago.

Institutional inertia afflicted and suffocated all ward business. It took several weeks to replace a broken toilet seat and the acquisition of a replacement TV remote control appeared to be beyond the capacity or ability of management. During my ten weeks on the ward the TVs in two separate lounges were reliant on one remote control handset. This caused ongoing confusion, aggravation and bickering among patients. The solution was simple – buy a replacement handset at Argos for a cost of £8.99. Surely a small investment to maintain one of the few 'treatments' available on the ward – TV. Access to the women's lounge – the only quiet, comfortable, pleasant place for women patients to sit is restricted by the same institutional inertia. There is a problem with leakage through the lounge's roof if there is heavy rain. The ward solution to this is to lock the area off. This has been an issue for a long time and workmen have attended on several occasions but the leakage persists. Heavy rain is a regular occurrence. Ignoring the problem will not make it go away but it will continue to deprive women patients of a comfortable refuge.

Mealtimes were reminiscent of wartime rationing with consistent shortages; juice – vinegar – salt – marmalade – fruit – serviettes – paper cups – cutlery – especially spoons – always a radical shortage of spoons. There was a day when the only fruit on offer was a collection of rotting oranges and four cooking apples. Shortages were always blamed on somebody else – They hadn't placed a proper order – They hadn't loaded the trolley properly – They had lost the spoons. Who are they? Could it possibly be them?

Shortly before leaving the ward I witnessed an attempt to discharge an elderly patient four days prior to the date she had previously agreed and felt would be safe. She was informed by her psychiatrist that he was discharging her immediately as her bed was needed and there were those in greater need than herself. Shocked, distressed and upset she explained that she could not leave alone as she would not feel safe and was depending upon the support of her son on the already agreed date. The psychiatrist and nurse attending then told her that she would have to go to a hotel until the weekend. She left the meeting in a distressed, emotional state. Her weeks of recovery were totally undermined by what can only be described as insensitive, heavy handed bullying. Her distress was further compounded by the appearance of a member of staff sent to deliver plastic bags to speed her packing and departure. It took several hours of resistance, urgent appeals to the ward manager and, very probably, the fortuitous presence on the ward that day of a CQC inspector, to reinstate her original discharge date. Hardly surprising that the door to readmission rapidly revolves. If patients are prematurely discharged while feeling unsafe and against their judgement and wishes, relapse is hardly surprising.

My negative experience of treatment with psychotropic medication continued. My body is a sixty year evidence base for the damage caused by such drugs. I now refuse to take any that have damaged me in the past. This leaves psychiatry and its medical/pharma model with very few options in my treatment. On this occasion the first drug prescribed had, within two weeks, caused considerable and significant damage to my eyes and sight. Withdrawal from the drug did not reverse this damage. (Three months later, as I write this account, I am due to visit an eye specialist to investigate whether the damage is permanent.)

Following a two week moratorium on medication, psychiatry came up with a drug of last resort which would – hopefully – do me no further harm. I had been drug free for over two weeks and was already benefiting from the psychological support that was at last in place. I had also, perversely, been energised by sheer anger against damaging psychiatric treatment and the negative ward environment. It was therefore with great reluctance, trepidation and some distress that I was obliged to comply with yet more medication. The immediate effect of the new drug was a worsening of depression. There followed tinnitus, visual disturbance, fine tremor, migraine and nausea. These side effects lessened with time but I continue to experience tremor, tinnitus, intermittent headaches and raised blood pressure.

I survived. I have recovered. I am home again. This, in my opinion, is due to the passing of time and good, ongoing psychological support. I can evidence and add to my record the negative aspects of yet another psychotropic drug. I am currently caught in the psychiatric trap of compliance with medication that is damaging to take but potentially dangerous to discontinue. I have neither conviction nor proof of its efficacy and no faith in a profession that offers me little else. I have already stipulated that I wish to be supported in its discontinuation after some months.

I am fortunate that lifelong exposure to psychiatry has not damaged my mental capacity or ability to fight back. I am blessed with supportive family and friends. My experience of and activism around the mental health system has armed me with the insight and knowledge to confront bad practice and insist on adequate care. So many service users have no such advantage and are abused and destroyed by the system; by the war.

Mental health services, driven and enabled by the perverse incentives of a malign accountability system, have lost sight of the community they were created to serve. Inept, dysfunctional business modelling and commodification of both patients and staff has resulted in services managed by spreadsheet and bereft of humanity. An environment damaging and abusive to both staff and patients has been created. This damage is writ large on wards where under-staffed, under-resourced, disrespected, demoralised and desensitised staff deliver a crude, vulgarised, often abusive and disrespectful, medical model of care. It is a miracle that some small number of nurses and nursing assistants still succeed in maintaining integrity and humanity in their practice.

Occupational therapy's place in services has been abused, marginalised and eroded and psychological services are likewise disrespected and under-resourced. Psychiatry is enabled to continue relatively unchallenged despite so much evidence demolishing the medically modelled myths on which current services and government policies are based. Leadership and management is increasingly remote, indifferent, poor and, in some instances, downright disrespectful and abusive. Ward managers are not supported or empowered to improve quality. They are on constant firefighting duty to plug holes on dangerously understaffed wards.

How should we view the shocking and disastrous inability of a health system to communicate with either staff, service users or carers in an equal, respectful way? It is so deep rooted in delusion and denial that it will not see the irony and cruelty of espousing models such as 'recovery, co-production and peer support, which are founded on core principles of respect, equality, authentic relationships, honesty, support and hope, while practising in a manner opposite to all of these principles.

Service users are in the hands of a fear filled, self-referring health system, incestuously inward looking and dysfunctional, with a malign, bio-medical view of mental illness. It is most afraid of what it most needs – new blood, creative freedom, thought, imagination, risk taking and a workforce with the courage and freedom to think, challenge and deliver real, courageous, meaningful care. Psychology is a major part of what it most needs and fears.

Wherever our own journey into clinical psychology begins, Mary's story and others like it, provides the starting point of our shared responsibilities in the psychological wellbeing of individuals and society. Undergraduate psychology is often the place where we begin to properly consider a career as a psychologist. We get exposed to an inviting world of innovation, understanding, and increased psychosocial awareness of the issues that affect wellbeing. We might get involved in University Societies and groups that seem to fit with our values of social justice and connection with the world and people around us. At universities we have greater opportunity to find our voices and ways to connect our personal experiences with our goals for our professional life. We are now selecting our learning opportunities, connecting with new groups and perhaps meeting a broader range of people than at any other point in our lives.

This can be a space where the social consciousness of our childhood starts to play a big part in shaping who we become as adults. As we enter university life, we can become particularly aware of the privileges we are afforded, and the inequalities in the structures we are part of. By virtue of being in academia, we are presented with opportunities that the vast majority of people do not have. Those of us who want a future in which we work to build communities, often have powerful memories from our childhood. Perhaps we witnessed deprivation first hand, or contributed to a good cause even though we were too young to understand what we were doing; maybe we gave our pocket money to a disaster fund, or our lunch to a homeless person. Whatever it is, these stories become integral to our sense of self.

Thinking space

How does your current work interact with your personal values?
What gives you the belief that clinical psychology is a profession congruent with your values?

University can be a platform for addressing injustices and showing an awareness of and concern for the factors that maintain them. For example, the 'Help the Homeless Society' of Liverpool University began in 2013 as a small group of students who were dissatisfied with the plight of rough sleepers in Liverpool, and wanted to do something to help change it. Since then the Society has grown and now aims to support those who have been displaced internationally, as well as locally. The Society aims to provide a platform for people to create a positive change towards social justice. Through volunteering opportunities, educational discussion and meeting other compassionate people with a similar aim, its members hope to create an environment where members feel able to support those within society who have been displaced.

Support may be very practical, such as delivering weekly breakfasts and donations to asylum seekers in temporary accommodation, holding fundraisers to support community projects, or hosting a 'family fun day' to welcome local vulnerable families to the University to enjoy being part of activities (including crafts, clothes stalls, food and drama classes/performances). These attempts to connect with our communities also enable us to 'be the change we want to see'; they are ways to show support to those made to feel vulnerable by the government, to show that they are supported by the local community.

Apart from helping others, socially conscious work and connecting with the issues in the local community can foster our own sense of agency. Using methods of co-inquiry and speaking to all relevant members of the community, we become better able to understand the practicalities of what needs to change. What can at first seem like an impossibility can become more manageable when you start at a smaller scale, involving all key stakeholders in the decisions.

Recognising the injustices in the world can, and perhaps should, lead us to the conclusion that we have to take action in order to affect change. If we want the world to be a better place, we cannot just work at an individual level; so much of our struggles are due to the social policies that affect wellbeing. The question is how do we best act to affect change. Many clinical psychologists turn to activism as a potential way forward as it can feel a way to visibly enact the values that brought us into this profession. Broadly speaking we might consider there to be three forms of activism:

Direct Action – This is where we stretch the limits of the law in order to draw attention to an important social issue. We might stage sit-ins, block roads, engage in other forms of civil disobedience.

Active Resistance – These are public displays of disaffection. Examples might include protest marches, writing an open letter, and/or engaging in peaceful and visible acts of demonstration.

Systems Change – This is perhaps the safest way to affect positive change. Here we see people in positions of relative power take action to bring more fairness into existing systems. Examples might include changing referral processes to make services more accessible, taking on inclusivity roles in organisations, or creating new 'outreach' provisions.

The world needs all the different forms of activism if we are to make a sustained difference. We may adopt different approaches in different parts of our lives, **but whichever position we hold we will still be criticised for not doing enough.** At these times, it is important to remember that whatever we do, and however we do it, we are working to make the world a better place and it is important to remember that "[w]e are all healers of the world . . . . It's not about healing the world by making a huge difference. It's about healing the world that touches you, that's around you" (Remen, 2018). We will also receive criticism from the alternative standpoint where we are accused of 'virtue' signalling. Well, Tara Flynn has some sage words on this one: "Fuck this noise. Frankly, not seeing enough goodness or kindness is depressing the hell out of me. Signal your virtues more. Sing 'em. Make a TV movie about them and Roma Downey can be in it and yer woman Laura Ingalls and DO NOT BE AFRAID OF BEING KIND" (Flynn, 2018, p. 56).

However you show your values, be proud of your actions, stay true to who you are, and above all, be honest with yourself and others about why you are taking a stance.

In focus: beautiful trouble

The more visible and openly resistant to the status quo we become, the more risks we take. The 'Beautiful Trouble' website provides guidance and resources on managing some of these challenges – https://beautiful trouble.org.

Some sample words of wisdom include:

"Because direct action is a physical act, it often speaks louder and deeper than anything you might say or write. Ideally, you should choose your target and design your action so that the action itself tells the story".

"Needlessly endangering the safety of you or the people around you hurts the movement. Don't sacrifice care of self or others for the sake of being 'hardcore'".

"We need to build a culture where we're all invited to step up. This means stepping up in ways that make space for others to step up – where others feel invited to step up and take initiative, too".

After we complete our undergraduate degree and move into clinical psychology, it is important to find a course that fits for us. All courses are slightly different, with their own individual philosophies and practices. If we're lucky, we get onto a clinical psychology programme that facilitates our personal and professional growth. With the right opportunities for reflection and training, this can be a nourishing experience. However, it also comes with some challenges; we might be forced to compromise our values and our view on the profession can become more opaque. Even the process of applying for training, striving to find a 'fit' with a clinical programme and feeling constantly evaluated can take its toll on the idealism and motivation required to persevere to enter the profession.

Reflective spaces bring with them some challenging questions such as 'do I really want to be a clinical psychologist?' and 'is this really what I signed up for?' Training can be very demanding, and at times isolating. Sometimes it can feel as if we have to leave our actual, authentic self aside in order to fully invest time and energy into the model of what we are acculturated to believe constitutes a 'good trainee'. Stubbornness and perhaps a touch of narcissism may sound negative, but they can be useful too! We all need to develop and maintain a sense of self within 'The Course', though it often feels hard won and is always a work in progress. We must remember to regularly check in on our inner dialogues, our own stories and experiences, and practise self-care.

Research can be an important part of this process as we partly use as a process of self-discovery, or exploration of some of the existential questions we are wrestling with. Previous experience and new experiences on training can draw our attention to groups and individuals who fall outside the remit of services despite requiring significant support. This can be a driver for using research to affect change. Research can help shift narratives away from viewing people as 'hard to reach', to instead better understand how people seek support when they are let down by formal services and think about ways in which current models of therapy and service provision may marginalise some people and communities. There can be some parallel experiences here when as a trainee, we are feeling like an outsider. A useful read here might be Winnicott's – "Delinquency as a sign of hope" (Winnicott, 1992). A text that can reassure us that the unfamiliarity and "otherness" experienced at times as a trainee is perhaps no bad thing. It is important to remember however that trainee clinical psychologists in the UK context still have a huge amount of social capital, even when it feels like our profession is jarring with our preferred ways of being.

Clinical psychology is awash with perspectives on ethics, boundaries, disclosure, professional behaviour and other written and unwritten rules that can serve to make us question whether we are 'good enough'. It can feel as though we are being given the message that there is one right way to do things. In fact there are as many ways to engage with the challenges of our profession as there are experiences underpinning our reasons for coming into this profession. Even though these foundations are broad and individual, there are also often similarities. Many of us feel at some point or another that we do not belong here. We can feel alone, scared, uncertain whether we have a purpose or fit in enough. These internal voices are useful; they make us question ourselves in order to keep true to our values. If we can find the courage to share our internal struggles, we can be our most authentic self. This will inevitably make us better clinicians and enhance our profession by opening up space for others to be true to themselves; "Because true belonging only happens when we present our authentic, imperfect selves to the world, our sense of belonging can never be greater than our level of self-acceptance" (Brown, 2015). In an attempt to model this, Ben shares some of his story, and how he came to develop the values of authenticity, compassion, and justice, which he tries to uphold in his professional as well as his personal life.

Ben's story

I grew up in extreme poverty, regularly going without adequate food and clothing. My dad had problems with alcohol and drugs, and we frequently went without as a result. I distinctly remember the feeling of shame in school when I had to explain away the holes in my shoes, or why I didn't have lunch again. I only went on trips if they were paid for by the school, and couldn't ever get involved with any extra-curricular stuff that involved money.

The stress and tension at home eventually turned into physical and emotional abuse. My dad frequently attacked me, knocking me unconscious with whatever was handy. Punishing me for minor misdemeanours with a belt, a slipper or a fist. I don't know what my mum did to drown out the noise, but she never came to my defence. Afterwards, I'd lay still in my room, and my dad would inevitably return in tears, asking for forgiveness. As an 8-year-old, I hated him. I hated having to forgive him. I also hated having to watch every move, having to keep a watch for any change in his tone of voice or mood.

My siblings were born, and things got progressively worse. The struggle for money wasn't just confined to the middle or end of the month, there was never enough, all the time. I'm pretty sure my mum skipped meals so we could eat. The violence that marked my early years spread to affect us all. Any perceived disobedience was heavily punished.

The walls in our house were thin. We could all hear it.

I first tried to kill myself when I was 9. Nothing in the years that followed made me think that was a bad idea, and I tried three more times before I was 16.

As I entered adolescence, my parents rediscovered the church. A fundamentalist, evangelical church in the middle of a council estate. The church reassured my parents that everything in their life was wrong because of the devil, because of man's inherent evil nature, because of immigrants, because of the greed of the scroungers down the street. Most of all, it allowed my dad to be the victim – he was in a low wage job because he was white and straight "the most oppressed group", and as long as they attended church, paid their tithe every month and worshipped god, they would be rewarded.

I found all of this galling. It seemed too unjust. Immoral. We had no money for food, yet we were expected to pay money to this church that preached nothing but hate. Hate against any minority; non-whites, Muslims, gay people, etc. I started to get bullied by other kids in the church because my clothes and shoes were handed down, cheap and full of holes. I have never felt more shame in my life than those first few years of being a teenager. I felt like I had a huge neon sign above my head highlighting every flaw. My family's poverty was my personal shame.

I really wanted to go to the slightly posh, better school down the road, but my dad wouldn't let me study for the entrance exams. He told me if I needed to study then I was stupid and that studying was cheating. When I failed my exams, he was there to tell me I was a failure. In school, I was virtually silent. Coasted through every class. Did just enough to not make any waves. I went through every day absolutely starving, I would only eat at dinner time Monday to Friday. I never had a breakfast, I rarely had a lunch. I remember feeling these sharp burning pains in my abdomen and thinking it was growing pains – actually I was just hungry.

One night when I was 15, I came home and went to my room. My dad quickly followed, burst through my bedroom door and immediately punched me in the face repeatedly. He continued landing punches – my face, my back, my head, my chest – until I was unconscious on the floor. They had read my emails to the Samaritans on the computer, and knew I was gay.

My nose was broken, my ribs cracked. My face was one big bruise, stretching from my nose round my eyes and down my cheeks. I could feel the back of my head like a painful, matted mass of hair and dried blood. So, I left, ran away. Hid at a friend's house. Hid from his parents. Still ashamed.

I went into school on the Monday and that's when the shit hit the fan. My dad turned up at school and said that we had had a fight. The head of year met with me and tried to convince me to go home. Looked at my face and told me to go home. They dealt with things like this all the time – this was a rough school that took in kids from some of the worst estates in the area – I was merely a blip on their radar.

I refused to go home, and after a lot of to-ing and fro-ing, I was given an emergency foster placement. The difference waking up to a cooked breakfast, to a lift to school, to money for lunch, is something I cannot adequately describe without breaking into tears. The look of horror and pain on my carer's face when I flinched when they moved in my peripheral vision is ingrained on my mind.

I was petrified that our family was going to be broken up, my urge to protect my mum and dad and siblings was so powerful. I refused to talk to the police. I refused to talk to anyone at school. I refused to talk to the local "lads" who wanted to sort my dad out. I stopped talking to my friends, and eventually drifted out of school altogether.

———

The years following this were far from pain free, and my life after 'escape' included a lot of pain, a lot of mess. But I did survive. I went to university, a life-time goal of mine, and was so overjoyed to be in this oddly decadent, resource filled existence I couldn't quite believe it. I've never been able to reconcile the life I came from, and the life I am in now. It feels like a story I read, or a film I saw.

I struggle with depression and anxiety, and I feel a sense of loss and grief most strongly around times of the year or events that are family oriented. Christmas is hard. I've had negative experiences of antidepressants, public mental health services have never been any help to me, and I quickly gave up trying to seek help from my GP. Personal therapy has been a godsend, but obviously this is expensive. I wish I had the money to invest in more of this.

I worked hard, and accumulated a lot of debt in the process, but eventually got to the point of postgraduate training in psychology. The transition from the service user side of things to the professional side of things has been a real steep learning curve. The middle-class sensibilities of the profession seem to be both a blessing and a curse. I'm surrounded by a lot of privilege, which at times is a really difficult thing to be around. I have aspired to lead this imaginary lifestyle since I was a child, the pain of being without taught me what I wanted in my future life- but now that I'm 'in it' I feel like an alien. There are daily reminders that I don't belong. I don't play the game, I don't know how to network, I don't always say or do the 'right' things- there seems to be an unspoken set of rules which I've never been privy to.

My experiences put me firmly within the 'wounded healer' trope – I feel that they can be an invaluable resource, as long as I'm open to reflection and maintaining a sense of self awareness about the impact they have on my perceptions of the 'system' and mental health difficulties. I've encountered many professionals and systems in my life that have told me 'no', and I encounter this in my professional practice all the time, when people in distress are left out of decision making regarding their own care and 'othered' by utilitarian bureaucracy. The Kafkaesque system we have in place where people need to prove their distress is of sufficient magnitude in order to receive a meagre offering of support is horrifying to many people, but to me it's no surprise. The difficulty I'm working through is trying to make sense and meaning out of this 'dual identity'. I struggle to relate

*to other professionals working in the system in the same way I struggle to recon-
cile my existence now with the one I grew up in. There seems to be a language, an
unspoken set of rules that I haven't been briefed on. Battling this sense of otherness is an important part of my own work on myself.*

*What can I offer in this system as a therapist? I can offer empathy and under-
standing to a person who has experienced trauma or adversity. The psychological
models we learn through clinical training are important, and massively useful to
conceptualise a person's distress, but also important is the felt sense of sitting in a
room with someone who validates how crap it can be to feel alone, to feel permanently fatigued or stressed, to be sleepless and thinking about future or past worries. The very real shame that comes from having your card declined when you
have a house full of people to feed, or having to survive on the coppers lying in the
bottom of a drawer. Understanding the long-term effects that stress has on your
body and mind is something that can be intellectualised and put in a textbook, but
having lived it – there is no way to adequately describe that feeling. Offering true
empathy, not pity, is vital.*

Ben faced challenges in not only accessing psychological therapies, but also in
being understood within current services structures. There are a lot of limitations
in the form and availability of therapeutic support people can receive. There are
many barriers a person may need to overcome, at a point in their lives when their
capacity to overcome barriers is limited. For many, it is systems and structures
that are the problem, not an internal problem that needs 'fixing' with therapy.

Clinical psychology training has always held therapy skills at its core. For
some people, direct, one to one therapy can be very effective and can lead to a
much-improved quality of life, but we are also becoming increasingly aware of
the limitations of direct therapy. A hypothetical, but rooted in experience, training
example we would like to share is of working with a young male who had recently
been involved in a fight that had left him with a traumatic brain injury. He was
experiencing high emotional distress as a result, and was having difficulties sleeping at night. A direct therapy intervention of highlighting the psycho-education of
good sleep hygiene was suggested in supervision as a means to help his distress.
The man was sleeping on a mattress on the floor of a living room, in a shared
house, where he was crashing with friends. He had no money to buy a bed, and
nowhere to put it if he did buy one. The measured outcomes showed little evidence that therapy had improved this man's level of distress. As a trainee clinical
psychologist, it can sometimes be difficult to know what alternative interventions
there are to offer; or, if we had an alternative intervention in mind, we can struggle
with not having the power to put the intervention into place in services which
often have set ways of working. Indeed, a common narrative we have heard from
supervisors is that the person "just isn't ready for therapy". Once the person has
a more stable home, with better sleeping conditions, has sorted out their benefits
– maybe then they will be ready for therapy; that is when we as clinical psychologists can see them. However, what about the people who are not able to get to that

stage of 'readiness'? What about the people for whom there is no social support, or who are part of a social care system that cannot support their needs due to under funding and under-resourced services? It feels like more and more people are falling into that 'gap'.

> ## Thinking space
>
> How do you find ways to be open about your experiences, transparent about your values, and compassionate towards yourself and your struggles?

As we start looking for solutions rooted more in community approaches, we come across professional divides that need bridging and 'turf wars' that require diplomacy. The interactions between clinical psychology and community psychology come to the fore and cynicism becomes apparent with questions about why clinical psychologists might want to 'do community psychology'. We can all learn from each other, and share the experience that we cannot face turning one more person away because "they are not ready for therapy". We would like to be a part of a solution that looks at social reasons for not being able to access therapy and collectively enables people either to be ready for therapy, or have such a level of systemic support that they do not even need individual therapy.

Perhaps some of these inter-disciplinary challenges are rooted in how clinical psychology has developed as a profession. A critical lens might draw one to conclude that it is a profession built on:

- **Appropriation:**
  The process whereby a dominant culture takes ownership of elements of another culture.

- **Secularisation:**
  Taking the spiritual components out of an experience or system of beliefs.

- **Marginalisation/exclusion:**
  Silencing the voices of minority individuals and groups.

- **Discomfort with power:**
  Failing to acknowledge the power one has, or trying to minimise it instead of using it positively.

- **'Faux critical psychology':**
  Criticising other perspectives or paradigms, without acknowledging the weakness in one's own position, or passive aggressively criticising a position without actually taking the risks associated with challenging the problem.

Clinical psychology may 'sell itself' as a profession built on warm reflection and a strong social conscience, but there are many who do not experience us in that way. For some, we are experienced as self-serving, unwilling to make a stand, and reluctant to risk our comfortable positions and associated pay packets. Read some of the arguments in social media, some of the activist groups' assertion that we need to take a stand, and perhaps most importantly, read into the silences when our profession fails to take a stand.

In focus: the case of Mindfulness within clinical psychology

Take a critical lens on the application of Mindfulness for example. The practice has strong religious origins; meditative practice is part of most religions. Here there are tangible links to Buddhism. Yet a lot of money has been made in detaching Mindfulness from its religious roots, stripping it of these connotations, and applying it in therapy settings in a secularised form.

One of those applications is in settings where workload and stress levels are high. Instead of dealing with the context driving this stress, we see staff being offered Mindfulness in the workplace. The implicit message is that the solution lies with the way the individual engages with their work environment. This serves to detract from the fact that it is the work environment which needs changing.

Clinical psychologists are aware of this and we often criticise 'toxic environments' – yet we continue to promote and deliver mindfulness sessions in these contexts.

In overcoming the difficulties with our profession, when applied to community contexts, the skills are not just in what we do, but how we do it; the spirit of working together to overcome barriers. It is of course challenging to work with the uncertainty that comes with being outside the safety and security of an established organisation (although there are ways to balance this), but there is greater freedom to be creative, to meaningfully include those with lived experience and escape the barriers imposed by organisational hierarchy. This does not even need to take place within an organisational structure. Communities have their roles and rules, but also a fluidity often lacking in formal structures.

One example of psychology being part of its community is *Café Psychologique*. The project was originally piloted at the Greenbelt Arts festival before a regular Café was set up in Leeds by Chris Powell in 2011. It has since become somewhat of an international movement with several Café Psychologiques sprouting up across the UK, followed by one each in Prague and Sydney. Each Café has its own unique identity heavily influenced by the local context. The Café's core ethos is to provide a space for people to talk about life from a psychological perspective. Importantly, the Café is a place to engage in open conversations rather than listen to a lecture or seminar by a professional. It was inspired by the *Café Scientifique* philosophy, which sought to take ideas out from universities, clinics, and other professional settings to make them accessible to people in everyday life. The Cafés take place monthly in community settings with a different topic explored every month.

Four of the guiding principles of the Café are:

1   Anybody can speak (this is a conversation, not a lecture).
2   All points of view are valid (respect other people's views, even if different to your own).
3   Statements work better than questions (to promote open conversations).
4   You set the agenda (the conversation goes where it flows, even if off topic).

Each Café adopts its own approach to choosing topics and applying the principles of the project. The Liverpool Café is heavily influenced by the city's tradition of social activism. While not a therapeutic setting, the Café does seek to reduce the barriers and other issues people experience when seeking support. There is no attendance fee and all are welcome to attend. To foster equal conversation, no labels or professional titles are used. Individuals are encouraged to speak from their own human experience rather than professional knowledge. There is no obligation to speak or attend more than once, instead attendees choose how they prefer to make use of the Café. To promote equal ownership, there is an open invitation to attendees to come together every few months to choose the topics for subsequent Cafés. Individual attendees take responsibility for a particular month's topic, including how to introduce the topic. Depending on personal experience or interests, attendees may spark off the conversation themselves, find another facilitator, or employ an alternative creative approach to explore the topic (such as poetry or music). Topics have included: "How to reduce divisions in society?" "The role of story-telling in our lives", "Loneliness", and "Rejection".

The mix of creativity and lack of hierarchal systems can lead to quick starts to projects such as the Liverpool Café. The lack of resources inherent in many community projects can actually foster resourcefulness (and boldness). Subsequently, as individuals see the value of the project it can build momentum, maintaining the energy of those involved.

Thinking space: building bridges with those who hold different values to us

"Civilisation is the process in which one gradually increases the number of people included in the term 'we' or 'us' and at the same time decreases those labelled as 'you' or 'them' until that category has no-one left in it".
(Howard Winters, 1994; as cited in Devarakonda, 2012, p. 9)

> It can be easy to 'preach to the converted' or hold close to those with similar views as us, but if we are to build strong communities, we need to see ourselves as also connected to those who hold very different values to us. How can we do this more as individuals and as a profession?

The arts offer a great medium for connecting communities. Castaway is a Yorkshire and Humber member-led theatre charity. For over a decade it has been empowering individuals with disabilities to grow and develop through a wide range of artistic endeavours. Integral to its success is its linking with the community including regular performances at local arts and cultural venues. The impact has been widespread including a positive change in people's perception of those with learning disabilities. Music, theatre, poetry, dance, and other art forms can speak to our souls and the hearts of our communities in ways traditional psychology cannot.

If we are to truly become a profession that influences our communities' wellbeing with integrity then we need to grow with our communities and be led by the people who need us as their allies. This can be difficult at times because our social power brings egotism with it, and our personal insecurities stop us seeing our potential to influence. We also care too much and have the potential to become a group of 'pathologically empathic' individuals, laboured by the weight of caring, to the point of compassion fatigue. The social power that comes with our position, means we are commonly thrust to the fore through conference presentations, journal papers and invitations to write book chapters! This can be enticing as we start to see that people care about what we think and value the way we express feelings we have had for a long time. As we drift towards saying yes to these invitations, we can also experience a sense of incongruence in feeling that we are actually powerless to affect change in a system that is overwhelming. However, we must gain motivation from knowing that however oppressed we feel by a system, the people who access our services feel even more disempowered by it. Consequently, we MUST use our platform to make space for people who are not afforded the same opportunities. We must stand with our communities, and wherever possible use our position to enhance the position of another. Systems are only as strong as the junctions at which they interlock.

Note

1 Read, Harrop, Geekie, and Renton (2018)

References

Brown, B. (2015). *Daring greatly: How the courage to be vulnerable transforms the way we live, love, parent, and lead.* London: Penguin.

Devarakonda, C. (2012). *Diversity and inclusion in early childhood: An introduction.* Thousand Oaks, CA: Sage.

Flynn, T. (2018). *Rage-in: Trolls and tribulations of modern life*. Ireland: Mercier Press.

Read, J., Harrop, C., Geekie, J., & Renton, J. (2018). An audit of ECT in England 2011–2015: Usage, demographics, and adherence to guidelines and legislation. *Psychology and Psychotherapy: Theory, Research and Practice, 91*(3), 263–277.

Remen, R. N. (2018). The difference between fixing and healing. *On Being Podcast updated 22nd November 2018, originally aired 11th August 2005*. Retrieved from https://onbeing.org/programs/rachel-naomi-remen-the-difference-between-fixing-and-healing-nov2018/

Winnicott, D. W. (1992 [1956]). Delinquency as a sign of hope. In *Collected papers: Paediatrics through psychoanalysis*. London: Karnac Books.

Chapter 17

The personal weight of political practice

A conversation between trainees

*Farahnaaz Dauhoo, Lauren Canvin,
Rosemary Kingston, Stella Mo and Sophie Stark*

In this chapter, we share our conversation about navigating our political selves, as five trainee clinical psychologists, mid-journey into our training. We reflect on the lightness and emotional burden of these experiences and how they reflect the conversations we have in our wider systems. Our dialogue can be perceived as a microcosm of how we navigate differences in our clinical work, and resonates with the conflict between our personal and professional selves. We invite you to consider what it means to carry political weight; weight to who; why do we practise; how do we navigate; and how do we sustain ourselves? In this chapter we do not present any ready-packaged conclusions for the reader to take away, but instead leave the conversation open – inviting the reader to take these conversations further within their practice.

The personal weight of political practice: a conversation between trainees

Sophie: I come into this conversation from a position of being someone who is confused and often uncomfortable when political conversations arise, because I feel out of my depth. This has changed since starting training; I've been able to reflect on my own position and become more vocal about it, and I've been exposed to different opinions which have shaped me. I now enjoy getting others excited about what I'm now excited about. I don't have knowledge or understanding of everything that's in the world, but that's okay for now, if I can only focus on the things that I am passionate about.

Lauren: I bring with me into this conversation, a concern for social justice and liberation issues; thinking about marginalisation and unvoiced experiences, or less voiced experiences, from power structures that might be perpetuating that situation.

Sophie: Whether it's at work or in other contexts, taking a stance can generate conflict in all areas, can't it? How do you work with the weight of that?

Lauren: That's why I love Vikki Reynolds – she tells you how to be okay about dealing with conflict (Reynolds, 2011). Her work is incredible: her idea of burnout being when you are working against your ethics; burnout being spiritual pain. Letting the pain teach you something rather than running away from it is important to me. Being able to take criticism. To welcome criticism and treating your peers as allies rather than enemies.

Rosie: With what you were saying about seeing your team as allies rather than opponents, I really admire that. When it comes to communicating, I don't think it should always be about persuading, in terms of changing the position of the person you are speaking to. I don't know if it should be about being so arrogant as to think that "I must persuade you, I can't respect your opinion being different from mine", but more that if you are really convinced of something, then it helps to open up the conversation to other people. If you are not in an echo chamber and there are others who don't have the same values or views, it can only enrich your position to be exposed to those voices, and invite them to the conversation rather than being alienating and making it "us" and "them".

Sophie: The opening up of the conversation: maybe that's what we are doing now too. Perhaps this is a reflection on how we can work within a difficult system; by opening the conversation to others.

Lauren: And the platforming of different views rather than choosing one to represent. But some conversations between people who don't belong to the group being spoken about, or who are more privileged than the people in that group, can be very dehumanising. For example, all these arguments on TV about whether or not non-binary identities exist, and it's like . . . you are *literally* arguing about whether or not people exist.

Stella: But does everyone who questions whether non-binary exists mean to interpret that these people don't exist? I think we are not curious anymore about people who we perceive as belonging to an opposing group to us. There can be a lack of curious listening which can make us defensive.

Rosie: I wonder whether conversations between people with opposing views could be had more like a therapeutic conversation, where both people approach the conversation with curiosity . . .? It brings to mind the idea from our systemic teaching, approaching with the notion that everyone is trying to do their best with the resources they see as available to them.

Lauren: But I don't know if I need to approach someone who thinks that my sexuality is an abomination with curiosity. Sure, there could be great reasons why they think that, I understand religion, upbringing, they have maybe also had some trauma themselves, but I don't think I always have to engage with that.

Rosie: I don't think anyone has to do anything.

Stella: I think it's an interesting question. I don't think you *have to* engage with people who don't respect you, but why not?

Sophie: Why should I? [laughs]

Stella: There was this really interesting podcast where this woman was sick of men coming up to her, wolf-whistling, making derogatory comments (This American Life, 2016). And so, she went up to them, and interviewed them. Some of them were very rigid with their views and refused to change, but at the same time, they had a good conversation. And it was respectful. They were able to respect each other's differences. She had the chance to be heard by the very person who would slap her on the backside. I think maybe it's not about necessarily talking to people who don't respect you for their sake, but for your sake. If you can make someone who is on the opposing side at least respect you and hear you, why not?

Lauren: I'm just thinking of the emotional burden one has to go through to have these conversations and be heard. I just don't think it's fair because if you have a certain identity, you have to do that all the time, to everyone.

Stella: You don't have to. I'm not saying you have to, and I'm not saying it's fair, but I don't think it's helpful for anyone to *not* talk. You will just carry that anger with you because you're the only one not being heard. You will never be able to make the change that makes a change.

Lauren: Luckily, there's people who do it for themselves, and do it for everybody, and there's people who can't because it's too hard.

Sophie: I think that brings it back to the burden carrying. There's the burden of staying silent, and there's the burden of speaking out. If you think about being an activist or doing nothing, both have equal weights, someone could argue that they are both equally emotional, to suppress as well as to voice.

Rosie: I don't know what I feel about the term "activism", but if you're thinking about trying to act for a change, I wonder if you can think of different ways of approaching that task, some of which may be emotionally burdensome, and some might be smaller, and more tolerable. Rather than an adversarial exchange, you could sit down with someone and ask them some curious questions, and have a good conversation. I've never been to a march or protest but I consider myself quite politically engaged, and I enact that value through having difficult conversations with my peers, or purposefully approaching people who I think may think differently from me.

Stella: It's not like a debate, where people go in to deliver and defend their messages, and it's not conversational at all. You can't make a change if you don't acknowledge the other person's views.

Rosie: Everyone has an easy rebuttal for the things that they feel confident with, that they know will trip up most people that challenge them.

Stella: Then they've already thought about what your rebuttal is, and they've got a rebuttal for that, everyone is acting on rehearsal.

Rosie: Is the aim of the debate to win? Or to learn? If your aim "I want to learn things", or "I want to come away from this discussion changed in some way" – either through new knowledge or a strengthening of your position, you can't lose.

Sophie: That's how I kind of view relationships, even if you've had a terrible relationship, you still come away having learnt something. If you take that into the political sphere, even the biggest dickheads will teach you something, even if it is, "this is how I never want to be in my life!"

Rosie: Is politics about relationships then?

Sophie: Politics would be a better place if it was more focused on relationships.

Rosie: Perhaps politics has deliberately become not about relationships. It reminds me of how political debates are set up, with people sitting physically far away or across from each other. It becomes about "sides" rather than "people".

Lauren: I know what you mean about debates and conversation and getting lessons out of it, but I guess it's different when the outcome of that debate or that conversation directly affects your rights and your quality of life, and whether or not you live the life that is true to your identity or not. When there's that much emotion in it . . .

Rosie: Such as debates about gay marriage legislation?

Lauren: Yeah, like gay marriage, or being able to have your gender legally understood.

Rosie: Is there a way of still having conversations about things that affect someone legally, or that are highly emotional?

Lauren: It feels like from a liberation point of view, it would be listening to the marginalised, listen to their pain, they know it better than you do, you don't have that identity.

Stella: The "oppressing" people probably feel marginalised too. For example, I do not support views on criminalising abortion, but people who do, may feel that supporting abortion violates their religious views, and feel oppressed by that. They may feel like it's life and death if abortions happen, or if laws change, people will burn in hell. It may be a completely different view to someone who is pro-choice, but what's shared is that emotion of struggle and fear. That is something I think people can start with: finding what's similar rather than what's different. Maintaining the difference is only going to keep the extremities, the opposing sides, the dichotomies.

Farah: This conversation makes me think about times in which I have been the only person from a BME background in a team. I have tried to introduce ideas of culture and diversity into conversations, but it's not very easy. It seems to be easily glossed over. I think there is a fear. Both from myself, to bring up these topics, but also from the teams to listen and engage with them. There is something about this space, discussing with fellow trainees, away from placement, that feels different. It allows us to have these conversations, which can be very difficult at times.

Lauren: There are a lot of power structures we are navigating as trainees, which seem to be further emphasized when other areas of difference are at play.

Stella: I think the fear comes from those with more power as well. As an ethnic minority, I have had experiences where it has been difficult trying to open up conversations about racism in the clinical environment. It's made me wonder if the fear of being labelled as someone who is racist or prejudicial in some way can be really silencing and closes down conversation. People can't be honest if they're so afraid of being ridiculed, shamed and mislabeled. And I think that's a shame.

Lauren: It reminds me of what we spoke about in our diversity lectures. That tentativeness you might take when trying to talk about issues of difference and identity with people. But that kind of tentativeness is discriminatory as well, because it means that just because somebody is different from you for whatever reason, they get a different experience of you because you're being tentative.

Rosie: You can see how people might feel tentative because of a fear of hurting someone or being labelled in a particular way. Whether you are more tentative, or less tentative and don't overthink your response, both come with a risk.

Sophie: It's reminding me again of the NHS being a political sphere, and how what plays out in the clinic or society can play out more broadly, or even microcosmically, in your interactions with clients. What happens in the therapy room can mirror what happens in the MDT.

Rosie: I connect with that. I don't think many people would say that they want to be judgmental in the therapy room, but it's pretty easy to be judgmental outside of it. I feel that in the therapy room, people are aspiring to be the most humane they can be. And I think that's probably quite exhausting. I can't help but wonder: wouldn't it be wonderful if you could carry that with you beyond the therapy room?

Stella: When it comes to the political atmosphere of teams, you don't necessarily get to choose the attitudes you want to work with. That's when it becomes a lot harder. It's so much easier to be empathetic with a person or a group who, for personal reasons, you identify with, or have strong connections to.

Lauren: I was thinking about the dynamics that can make it more or less difficult for people to speak against an established view. Recently, a lecturer talked about a previous experience where she had found it hard to speak up in an MDT meeting, as a young female trainee, with lots of senior, older male colleagues. Although she felt that what was being said was unethical or wrong, she said that she couldn't find her voice to speak out against it. She reflected on the experience and realised that her feeling unable to speak up was understandable, because of all of the identity structures and systems going on around her.

Stella: I do not think that it was a wasted opportunity where she should have, could have, spoken out. If anything, I think that experience in itself was valuable when she reflected on her identities, and the situation. That may not have happened had she not had that experience.

Lauren: I'm also thinking about the real-life repercussions for people, if they say something that shakes things up too much. For example, if someone's identity is visible, such as race, and it is related to the topic they speak up about, this may put them at risk of being seen as less professional and more biased.

Rosie: That example is interesting, because I think in those situations I would also have naturally been drawn to thinking, "I would have learned something if I had spoken up". But on reflection, given that she remembered the story, held it with her, and retold it to us: something has evidently changed, learning has taken place. So even though something seemingly did not go well in that meeting, the ripple effect caused different, unexpected impacts.

Stella: I once had an experience in a room full of eminent male psychiatrists, which I found very intimidating. I wanted to raise a point about a piece of clinical work and felt unable to voice my opinion. It was frustrating, because my conviction in my views strengthened over time and over subsequent meetings, but I felt silenced by the way I perceived these professionals as having authority. Exploring this in supervision, it became apparent that there were a lot of political reasons that influenced the actions of the other professionals. It was not that they could not see the other options available, but there was a tacit understanding that they were not viable within the restrictions of their own systems. As clinical psychologists in training, it's easy to feel that our involvement will make a difference, particularly when we see others' inaction. However, I think it's important to stay curious about people's motivations and intentions for what they do.

Rosie: It's interesting, the hubris that you allude to and your response to it.

Farah: I've also found that I have loads of internal conversations with myself before I speak out, especially in team meetings. I get really frustrated because by the time I've come up with something clear, the conversation has moved on.

Stella: Also, the cost of feeling humiliated or shamed when speaking out about something meaningful to you is so much higher than when speaking out over something less personally significant.

Sophie: The more important the idea is to you, the more difficult it is to say.

References

Reynolds, V. (2011). Resisting burnout with justice-doing. *International Journal of Narrative Therapy & Community Work*, (4), 27–45.

This American Life. (2016, December 2). *Once More, With Feeling*. [Audio Podcast]. Retrieved from www.thisamericanlife.org/603/once-more-with-feeling

An ending [sic]¹ of sorts...

---

1 Could this not be *the beginning* of something?

Epilogue

"Just stop talking and start to dance"

James Randall

These are the type of words you really ought to listen to. The sort of words that should conclude a clinical psychology book that respects what it means to be human. *Surviving Clinical Psychology* thus positions the profession as reaching out and connecting us not only with the intellect within our heads, but the will and passion within our hearts. A profession that does not just listen, but witnesses and acts. These words represent a moment in which I wholeheartedly realised that I seriously needed to stop talking and start to dance. These were the words of an eight-year-old I once worked with, and boy, did we dance.

What did this young girl teach me? She reminded me that within a world that can be so damaging, relationships matter. She reminded me, that in going beyond our clinic rooms, we can achieve much, much more. She taught me, that to go beyond our encounters and beyond those immediate relationships – we can create something different for people beyond the narrow confines of clinical 'spaces'. And all this, through a moment of taking play really seriously. For me, this encounter was a poignant reminder that no matter our pull towards the societal influences of change:

> we cannot, I think, escape the clinic. . . . It would be a callous society indeed that stood back and offered [individuals] nothing just because nothing much is likely to provide any real 'cure' at the personal level. It is incumbent on us to do what we can, even if we cannot do much.
>
> (Smail, 2005, p. 80)

However, the two cannot be mutually exclusive. To use similar phrasing: within the realms of helping the person, *we cannot, I think, escape the social context.* It is clear that such a sentiment is widely shared within the wider community of clinical psychologists – as attested to throughout *Surviving Clinical Psychology*. Within our individual practice then, "the duty of the witness is to use their access to resources of power, to change the social context in which suffering has occurred" (Reynolds, 2016).

Ultimately, we must become more visible and vocal as a profession. In changing clinical psychology to better suit the needs of our communities, we must also begin to take social action very seriously – to take the personal and professional risks that enable us to move towards a more value-based, ethical practice. In doing so, we must consider the personal, professional and political within our practices and truly *witness* one another's experiences through our shared humanity. In witnessing and reaching out, we must use the power afforded to us through our privilege, to practice in a way that is conducive to creating contexts for meaningful change within people's lives. In interview, for example, David Smail confronts clinical psychologists with the proposition that we must be prepared to stick our necks out:

> A lot of people in clinical psychology are not as powerless as they think . . . Psychologists and people in the helping professions generally can be pretty chicken-hearted when it comes to political issues . . . It's because people who come into this kind of job are on the whole menders and compromisers or believers in being nice to people . . . and I think when you get down to political activities with a small p those aren't the most useful characteristics. You've certainly got to be able to be diplomatic, you've got to be able to see where the lines of influence run, but you've got to be prepared to stick your neck out when it matters.
>
> (Moloney, 2016, p. 12)

Surviving Clinical Psychology highlights the necessity of a both/and approach within our personal and professional development, and the political engagement this permits us. These are the ways in which individuals can play a significant part in changing the psychological terrains. Holding a reflective focusing on the *selves* in practice on one hand, whilst holding the fact that we must also reach-out, connect and seek change through solidary actions, on the other. It is an inescapable truth, that where the personal and professional meet, the political comes to the fore.

> [For] the suspension of self is an unconvincing theatrical trick; a game of power that fuels a disingenuous exchange of misery for 'expertise' that trivialises, devalues and subtly oppresses the person and context. By playing the suspended-self expert role, I deem the therapy room only fit for furthering disconnection to emotions, identity, and communities, lacking relational depth in favour of the intellectualising and problematizing of being human. I wonder what this expectation of suspension tells us about fragility, pain and suffering; is it that pain must be kept at a distance to selfhood; is suffering infectious; must the other protect their personal selves from witnessing and connecting with fragility on a human level? The therapy room can be a scary place, but we've perhaps got it the wrong way around if it is the therapist that finds themselves having to defend against the vulnerability of being seen . . . This endeavour of visibility is . . . a political means to (re)participation in life.
>
> Randall (2018, pp. 23–24)

What can clinical psychology become? The answer to this question can only really materialise through the ways in which you participate with the ideas in this book and actions you take next. Perhaps you'll just stop talking and start to dance?

References

Moloney, P. (2016). An interview with David Smail. *Journal of Critical Psychology, Counselling and Psychotherapy, 16*(1), 3–17.

Randall, J. (2018). The personal politics of becoming a visibly tattooed psychologist: Participating in a chosen social grace of appearance. *Context, 158*, 21–24.

Reynolds, V. (2016, February 14). Activism in therapy: An ethic of witnessing. *The Radical Therapist Podcast, #15*. Retrieved from https://chrishoffmft.podbean.com/e/the-radical-therapist-015-%E2%80%93-activism-in-therapy-an-ethic-of-witnessing-w-vikki-reynolds-phd/

Smail, D. J. (2005). *Power, interest and psychology: Elements of a social materialist understanding of distress*. Ross-on-Wye: PCCS Books.

Resources to enrich the journey

Share your own experiences and resources on #SurvivingClinicalPsychology

Key books

Byron, T. (2014). *The Skeleton cupboard: The making of a clinical psychologist*. London: MacMillan.

Golding, L., & Moss, J. (2019). *How to become a clinical psychologist*. London: Routledge.

Johnstone, L., & Dallos, R. (2013). *Formulation in psychology and psychotherapy: Making sense of people's problems*. London: Routledge.

Perry, S. (2017). *Effective self-care and resilience in clinical practice: Dealing with stress, compassion fatigue and burnout*. London: Jessica Kingsley.

Professional representation

The Pre-Qualification Group represents pre-training and in-training members of the Division of Clinical Psychology (DCP) – representing members' views and pre-qualified practitioners' interests, and influencing policy and broader practices within the profession. The group produces free resources (including the *Alternative Handbook*), delivers workshops, and convene an annual conference. More information can be found at www.bps.org.uk/member-microsites/division-clinical-psychology/dcpgroups

The Minorities in Clinical Training Group represents practitioners who identify as belonging to a minoritised group, offering peer-support and networking with others with similar experiences. The group organises regular networking meetings, convenes an annual conference, and addresses issues relating to marginalisation through consultation and collaborative writing. More information can be found at www.bps.org.uk/member-microsites/division-clinical-psychology/dcpgroups

The Association of Clinical Psychologists (ACP-UK) is a professional representative body that aims to promote psychological perspectives at a national level – promoting the discipline and profession of clinical psychology. More information can be found at https://acpuk.org.uk/

The Division of Clinical Psychology (DCP) is a professional representative body for clinical psychology and is situated within the British Psychological Society, who represents all other applied psychologists (e.g., health psychology, forensic psychology). The DCP's aims are to support the development of clinical psychology as a profession and a body of knowledge. More information can be found at www.bps.org.uk/member-microsites/division-clinical-psychology/

Unite the Union is Britain and Ireland's largest trade union and unlike many other unions, specifically has applied psychologists representing the concerns and employment issues relevant to clinical psychologists. More information can be found at https://unitetheunion.org

Personal resources

In2gr8MentalHealth is a growing community for clinical psychologists and other mental health practitioners who identify as having lived experience of mental health difficulties, offering peer-support networks in person and online. More information can be found at www.in2gr8mentalhealth.com/

Hell Yeah, Self-Care by Meg-John Barker, is a free online resource that offers a range of engaging ideas about self-care in austere and troubling times. More information can be found at https://rewriting-the-rules.com/wp-content/uploads/2017/02/HellYeahSelfCare.pdf

Professional resources

The Alternative Handbook: Postgraduate training courses in Clinical Psychology is an annual survey of current trainee clinical psychologists across the UK, detailing experiences at interview, academic teaching, research areas, support systems, and much more. Available annually from https://shop.bps.org.uk

The Guidelines for the Employment of Assistant Psychologists were produced in collaboration with Unite the Union and published by the British Psychological Society. Further details are discussed in Chapter 3.

Clin Psy Form is an online discussion forum with over 7500 members. Members share their learning, ask questions and explore what it means to work within applied psychology. The forum is infamous for its annual 'Doctorate Application Progress Thread'. More information can be found at https://clinpsy.org.uk/forum/

Psychology and Mental Health: Beyond Nature and Nurture is a free online course delivered by Professor Peter Kinderman and Kate Allsopp through Future Learn. This course can be accessed via www.futurelearn.com/courses/mental-health-and-well-being

Psychology: Let's Get to Clinical is a podcast founded in 2019, which seeks to enrich the journey for anybody working towards a career in

clinical psychology. You can listen via https://podtail.com/en/podcast/
psychology-let-s-get-to-clinical/

Political resources

Psychologists for Social Change is a network of applied psychologists, psychology graduates, academics, therapists and others who are interested in applying psychology to policy and political action (formerly known as Psychologists Against Austerity). More information can be found at www. psychchange.org/

Doing Justice as a Path to Sustainability in Community Work by Vikki Reynolds, is a free online resource that describes an approach that bridges activism and practice through *doing justice* – contributing to a collective sustainability. This can be accessed via www.taosinstitute.net/Websites/ taos/files/Content/5693763/ReynoldsPhDDissertationFeb2210.pdf

Index

Page numbers in italics indicate a figure on the corresponding page. Page numbers followed by b indicate boxes.